Brent

The Descendants of
Hugh Brent

IMMIGRANT TO ISLE OF WIGHT COUNTY, VIRGINIA, 1642

AND SOME ALLIED FAMILIES
CURD, DOGGETT, EDMONDS, FLEET, LAWSON, NUTT
& WALE. Also Lineages of BEHETHLAND, BERNARD
BUNTING, HATHAWAY, NEVIL, NEWTON
SAVAGE & VAUGHAN Families

AND *Notes* FROM SOME *DIARIES* [1793-1909]
OF THE *Piedmont* SECTION OF *Virginia*

By
CHESTER HORTON BRENT

THE TUTTLE PUBLISHING COMPANY, INC.
RUTLAND, VERMONT
1936

CONTENTS

EXPLANATIONS AND ABBREVIATIONS

The plan of tracing descent adopted in this book is the same used by the Rev. Horace Hayden in his "Virginia Genealogies," and will be readily understood by anyone who will examine the illustration that follows. On page 43, the children of Hugh Brent are numbered first by Arabic numerals from 16 to 32, then by Roman numerals from i to xvii. The first child is given thus: "+ 16 i James." The *plus* sign indicates the continuation of his record as the head of a family on page 62; the number 16 is his family number, and the letter i is the number of his order of birth. By turning to page 62, he will be found recorded as the head of a family, his record reading thus, paraphrased: James Brent, 4th generation, son of Hugh 3rd generation, son of Hugh 2nd generation, son of Hugh 1st generation. However, the easiest way to get your line is to look in the index, find your name, or your father's name and number, and turn the pages backward until you find the record of your entire line to the immigrant.

b., born.

d., died.

m., married.

d. u. m., died unmarried.

d. s. p., died *sine prole*, without issue.

d. v. p., died in her or his father's lifetime.

(*w. 1760*), will was probated in 1760.

(*i. 1760*), inventory was recorded 1760.

L. D. W. B., *Lancaster Deed & Will Book*; the first letter of each county designated the county, except Fr. for Frederick; where the county is not named, Lancaster is to be assumed, and where the state is not named, Virginia is to be assumed.

M. B., with the first letter of a county preceding, signified *marriage bond* of that county.

O. P. R., *Overwharton Parish Register*, Stafford County.

Hayden, Hayden's *Virginia Genealogies* (reprint).

Green, *St. Mark's Parish*, Culpeper County, Va.

Nugent, *Cavaliers & Pioneers*, by Mrs. Nell Marion Nugent.

D. Reg., *Douglas's Register* of Goochland County, Va.

TO

MY GRANDFATHER
LANDON NEWTON BRENT (1824-1909)
A GENTLEMAN OF THE *old school*,
AND IN HAPPY MEMORY
OF THE MANY CHILDHOOD SUMMERS
SPENT AT HIS HOME,
Wellington,
IN NELSON COUNTY, VIRGINIA

FOREWORD

WHEN my grandfather Landon Newton Brent, Sr., died in 1909 at "Wellington," in Nelson County, Va., I fell heir to some old diaries, letters, account books and family registers, etc., dating back to 1711. Many of these old papers had come up from Lancaster County, Va. Several years later my attention was called to Mr. Thomas B. Chilton's genealogical history of the Brent Family published in the *Virginia Magazine of History and Biography*.

Knowing the regularity in each generation of the appearance of the given name "HUGH" in my family, and not finding it in Mr. Chilton's work, except in the *Charles Brent* line of Stafford County, I began a personal search to satisfy my curiosity.

At the Virginia Land Office I found that one *Hugh Brent* settled in Isle of Wight County, 1642, on land adjoining Capt. Peirce. Knowing the trend of migration following that date, from the formation of new shires or counties, I found, after much searching, the will of one *Hugh Brent* in Lancaster County, probated 1671; and he named among his children, a son Hough.

After that my work to 1800, was just routine—searching the Will and Deed books, the Order books, Land Causes, and studying the marriage bonds of Lancaster and adjoining counties.

Shortly after 1800, began the Great Migration to the Western Country. The Revolutionary War had been over for twenty years; the new Federal government was fostering the settling of this new country through the issuance of land bounty warrants to soldiers who had won freedom from English taxation. The Indians had been pushed further across the mountains, and those soldiers of the State Militia who had done the pushing, had seen the fertile fields west of the Alleghenies.

Kentucky became a state in 1792; Tennessee in 1796, and Ohio in 1803.

The departure of a family to the new country was a great event which called for much celebration, and many of the neighbors rode on horseback for several days to wish them Godspeed.

As a result of this migration I find descendants of *Hugh Brent*, the immigrant, leaving from Lancaster, Faquier, Frederick, Loudon and Charlotte Counties, Virginia, for Kentucky, Tennessee, Ohio and Illinois, and later for Louisiana, Alabama and Texas.

These settlers did not take along with them clerks who were willing or could do the yeoman service of a Stretchley or a Dale, as the early Lancaster County records attest. Then the ravages of war and fire have destroyed a great deal of what was recorded. As a result I have had to depend almost entirely on family registers kept by a few genealogically minded souls who must have held in their hearts a fond memory for relatives left behind in the mother state of Virginia.

If there is any relationship between the Hugh Brent and the Giles and George Brent lines as published by Mr. Chilton, I have been unable to find it in the records searched. The Charles and Hannah (Innes) Brent line of Stafford County, included in Mr. Chilton's history of the Maryland and Woodstock branches, does not belong there. Mr. Chilton took the children of George Brent of Lancaster County, and transplanted them in Stafford County as the children of a George Brent living there. Then he takes Charles Brent, one of the above children, who was named a minor in his father's will in 1748, and has him a husband and father in 1727. I believe the deed, made in 1710, Hugh Brent(5) to his daughter Mary and son Charles, proves my case conclusively.

The source of this work being entirely factual, very little will be found in it to appease those seekers after glorious ancestors. This latter group (and there are many in all families), will have to be satisfied that they were sprung from hardy stock, or else they would not be among those present; that all of their early ancestors could sign their names, and that none of them had been put in gaol as early as 1740 (that was as late as I paged the Order Books of Lancaster County).

The immigrant Hugh was made constable of Lancaster County in 1665; his progeny held practically every civil office in Lancaster County before the third generation, and of the seven accredited officers of the Revolutionary War, six were his offspring.

No work of this kind, following the many lines into practically every state of the union, and also one province of Canada, and into old Mexico, can be done perfectly. Any errors either of commission or omission will be corrected after the publication of this work upon authentic evidence of the mistake. To those members of the family whose help was most beneficial, I offer my most sincere thanks: Mr. Charles Scott Brent, of Lexington, Ky.; Mr. Thomas N. Wrenn, of New York City; Mrs. Linda F. Braucht, of Des Moines, Iowa; Mrs. Jane C. Brooks, of Smithshire, Ill.; Mrs. Lawrence D. Brent, of Clarendon, Va.; Mr. Bernard Cameron Brent, of Kilmarnock, Va.; Miss Allie Lee Brent, of Gibson Station, Va.; and Mr. Frank D. Fuller, of Memphis, Tenn.

CHESTER HORTON BRENT

512 East Beverly Street
Staunton, Virginia
15 Dec. 1936

THE BRENT FAMILY OF SOMERSET
AND KENT, ENGLAND

IT is recorded in the Red Book of the Knights Fees in the Exchequer that "*Odo* de Brent*, at the time of the Conquest, was Lord of Cossington. The name of Odo's son was not known, but his grandchild was Jeffrey, whose son was Nicholas, whose son was *Sir Robert Brent*, and his son was Robert, who had a son Robert, and his son was Robert. So there were four Roberts successively. The son of the last was John, and his son was Robert, and his son was likewise Robert, which Robert married Margaret and had two sons, viz., John and Robert. The said John who married Pontfoot, died anno 1524, and had two sons, William and Richard, which William had Richard to his son, who married the daughter of Lord Stirton and had Anne who was married to Thomas Lord Paulet by whom he had a daughter who was married to Hobby and died without issue. So that the eldest line ended in the time of Queen Elizabeth. Richard the son of John the brother of William aforsaid had issue, Stephen, Giles and John. Stephen had John to his son, to whom, after the death of Hobby, Cossington descended as next heir; his son also was John who possessed the land 1676. From Giles Brent descended Thomas Brent of Salisbury, but John the brother of Giles, died without issue. The aforsaid Robert, the son of Robert by Margaret in 1487 . . ." (From *De Bow's Review*, 1859).

According to Collinson the name Brent (from an Anglo-Saxon word meaning *to burn*), as applied to certain portions of the coast,

---

*The name of Odo de Brent does not occur in that part of the Domesday Book relating to Somerset, but an Odo surnamed Baucas and his grandson Geffrey, are mentioned as holding lands under the abbots of Glastonbury at an early period. Surnames did not become hereditary in England until late in the eleventh century, and were not common until Henry II, *circa* 1162, introduced the practice of commuting military service for what was called scutage (shield-money). They were not legally recognized until Henry IV (1413-1422), passed his "Statute of Additions."

occurs in the annals of Glastonbury before the time of the Danish invasions (787-1066). It was, he says, to the devastations caused by the Danes that some had traced a fancied origin of the name. (*Va. Mag. of Hist. & Biog.*, Vol. 12, p. 445).

Collinson's account of Cossington, the home of the Brents in Somerset, contains a somewhat extended history of the family from the earliest date, and it is, therefore, quoted in full.

Cossington

In the time of Henry I (1100-1135), this manor was in the possession of Gilbert Marshall, of England, and was by him conveyed to Jordan Ridel, a descendant of which Jordan, of the same name, granted it in 1254 to *Robert de Brent*, to be held of him and his heirs by service of a knight's fee, which service William Ridel, son of this last Jordan, granted over to Sir Baldwin Malet, of Enmore (MS., Palmer).

This *Robert de Brent* was the first that assumed the surname of Brent, from having his habitation at South Brent, in this county, where he was possessed of considerable estates, which continued in his family till the last age. His grandfather was called Sauvinus de Turre, and was by Henry de Blois, Abbott of Glastonbury, constituted porter of that abbey, with certain lands, and other profit of victuals, clothing and money, annexed to that office; all of which profits, together with the office, were again granted by Michael, the then abbott, to this Robert,* and to his heirs, to be by them held in as ample a manner as Robert the Son of Sauvin his father, or Sauvin his grandfather, ever held them, provisionally, that they and their servants should take the same due care of Strangers, sick people, and others, who came thither for God's Sake. This *Robert de Brent* died before 46 Henry III (1262) leaving by Millicent his wife (afterwards married to Raymond Malet) a Son of his own name.

Which *Robert de Brent* 5 Edw. I (1277) attended that King into Gascony, as he did in most of his expeditions into Scotland, being then a Knight. 25 Edw. I (1297) he was a knight of the shire for Somerset at the parliament then held at Westminster. He died about 2 Edw. II (1309),

---

*One of the barons who signed the Magna Charta, 1215.

Isabella his wife, daughter of Simon de Montacute, surviving him. He was the first of the family that used a seal of his arms, viz.: a wivern, as it is now borne, and has generally been used by his descendants. He was the father of another Robert, who was also a knight and a great benefactor to the abbey of Glastonbury. He married Claricia daughter and heir of Sir Adam de la Ford, of Ford, in the parish of Bawdrip, by whom he had the manor of Ford, and other lands in this county, Wilts, Hants, and Essex. He had by her a son of his own name, who succeeded him at Cossington, and also another son called John, who, settling himself at Charing, in Kent, on some lands which were Sir Adam de la Ford's, became the progenitor of a family which continued there with great dignity for many generations, and at last by some heir female had their possessions in the time of Queen Elizabeth transferred to the family of Deering.

Besides these sons, he had two daughters, Havysia, the wife of Hugh de Popham, and Joan, wife of Thomas Deneband. He was buried on the north side of the choir of the abbey church of Glastonbury.

Robert de Brent, son of the last mentioned Robert, married Elizabeth, daughter of William Deniband, and died 25 Edw. III (1357), being then succeeded by *John Brent*, who married Joan, daughter and heir of John le Eyre, of Middlezoy, by whom he had a manor in that parish held of the Lady Stury by the service of half a knight's fee, and several other lands in this neighborhood.

John Brent, of Cossington, son of John, 1 Henry V (1413), was twice married; his first wife was Ida, daughter of Sir John Beauchamp, of Lillisdon, knt., by whom he had issue *Sir Robert Brent*, his successor in the estate of Cossington, and Joan, first married to Thomas Horsey, of Horsey, Esq., and afterwards to Thomas Tretheke, of Tretheke, in the county of Cornwall, Esq. To his second wife he married Joan, the daughter of Sir Robert Latimer, knt., by whom he had a son called John.

Sir Robert Brent, his son by his former wife, and heir to this estate, married Jane, daughter of John Harewell, of Wotton, in the county of Warwick, who survived him and had this manor for her dower, which was, after her death, together with the rest of the estate, entered upon by Joan, his sister and heir by the whole blood, to the exclusion of John, son of John Brent by the second marriage. But this Joan being in a state of insanity, the fines that were levied in her name were not sufficient to bar the heir male, who, after several suits at law, and at length an arbitration by John Hody (afterwards chief justice of the King's Bench) 10 Henry VI (1440), was adjudged the right heir, by virtue of two entails made in the time of Edw. II, and Rich. II (1307; 1377), and soon after this manor was again entailed to this John Brent and the heirs of their body forever.

The eldest son of this John Brent was called Robert, and married Margaret, daughter of Hugh Malet, of Currypool, by whom he had another John, who added to his estate the manors of Goodwin's Bower and West Bagborough, which he purchased of Thomas Godwyn, as also (from his wife Maud, the daughter and co-heir of Sir Walter Pouncefoot) the manor of Compton-Pouncefoot, and Pouncefoot Hill, all which descended to *William Brent*, their eldest son, under age.

Which William had livery of his lands granted him 15 Henry VIII (1524), although he was not then twenty-one years old. He married a daughter of Lord Stourton, by whom he had one son, Richard, who died 23 Eliz. (1581), and was succeeded by Anne, his only daughter and heir, married to Lord Thomas Poulett, son of the Marquis of Winchester, and was mother of Elizabeth, wife of Giles Hoby, Esq., which two ladies sold and squandered away all the patrimony of this ancient family. The manor of Cossington, with Ford, and part of Godwin's Bower, was purchased by *John Brent*, the heir male of the family, viz., son of Stephen, son of John, second son of John Brent and Maud Pouncefoot. Which John, by that marriage, was an officer under William Warham, Archbishop of Canterbury, and afterwards under the treasurer of Calais.

It appears by papers found at Cossington that, upon the dissolution of the religious houses, he was employed by the commissioners to take account of the lands and muniments of such of them as were within this county, particularly of the abbey of Clive, to which he seems to have been steward. This John was twice married; his first wife was a daughter and co-heir of Thomas Godwyn; his second was Mary, granddaughter and sole heir of Thomas Culpeper, of the city of London. He died in 1557, and was buried at Bexley, in the county of Kent.

[14]

Stephen Brent, son of John,* was a lawyer, and lived at Dorchester, in a house that was his mother's in whose right he had several other lands in that county and in Kent, all which were sold by his son John, upon his purchase of this manor of Cossington, an estate in which he seems to have taken great delight. This John died here in 1610, leaving behind him a son of his own name, who was seventy-eight years in possession of this manor, and died A.D., 1692; but though twice married, left no children. His first wife was Winifred, daughter of Sir John Arundel, of Lanheron, in Cornwall, and his second was Mary, daughter of Sir Henry Ludlow, knt. On his death one Hodges, a poor man, then living near Highgate, was by Virdict found to be grandson of Anne, daughter of Stephen, and real heir to the estate, which he sold soon after to Mr. Robert West, of the Inner Temple, who had assisted him in the discovery of his title to this inheritance. Whence the manor of Cossington came to Sir John Gresham, bart., who sold it to Benjamin Allen, Esq., the present possessor.

The living of Cossington is rectorial, in the deanery of Pawlett, and was in 1292 valued at ten marks. The Rev. Charles Hobbs is patron and incumbent.

The church, which is dedicated to St. Mary, is of one pace, with a tower at the west end, containing a clock and five bells.

In the chancel floor is a brass plate, whereon are engraved the effigies of *John Brent, Esq.*, who died Aug. 22, 1524, and Maud, his wife, with an inscription to their memory; and on the north wall another inscription to John, son of John Brent, Esq., who died Jan. 24, 1691, aged 80 years.**

It will be noticed in the foregoing account, that Sir Robert de Brent who married Claricia, daughter and heir of Sir Adam de la Ford, had a second son John, who settled at Charing in Kent, and was the ancestor of a family which continued there for many generations.

The account given of this branch of the family in Hasted's *History of Kent*, is quoted in full below.

---

*Second son of John Brent and Maude Pouncefoot.

**From the *History and Antiquities of the County of Somerset*, by John Collinson, London, 1791, Vol. III, pp. 434-7.

THE HISTORY OF KENT

Charing, 1367.

Wickins is a manor in the Southern part of this parish, adjoining to Westwell, in which part of the lands of it lie. It was originally the patrimony of the family of Brent, and was their most antient seat. *Robert Brent*, the first of this name mentioned in their pedigree, lived in the reign of Edward II, and is styled of Charing, as were his several descendants afterwards, one of whom, William, son of *Hugh Brent*, married Juliana, relict of Thomas Paunsherst, of this parish, by whom he inherited the Manor of Pevington, and other estates near this place. He died *anno* 27 Henry VI, leaving issue a Son *Hugh Brent*, who was of Charing, and had issue four Sons, of whom *William Brent, Esq.*, the eldest, inherited this Manor, and resided at it; and Robert, the second Son of Wilsborough, an ancestor of the *Brents* of that place.

At length his great-grandson *Thomas Brent, Esq.*, succeeding to this Manor, resided at it till the 12th year of Q. Elizabeth (1570), when becoming heir to Wilsborough, by the devise of his kinsman, *Robert Brent*, of that place, who died without issue, he removed thither, where he died likewise without issue in 1612, and was buried there. By his last will he bequeathed his manor or tenement called Wickins Device and Caprons in Charing and Westwell, and all the lands and appurtenances thereto belonging, to his nephew Christopher Dering, of Charing who then occupied them. He was the fifth and youngest son of John Dering of Surrenden-Dering, Esq., by Margaret, sister of the above-mentioned Thomas Brent, and married Mildred, daughter of Francis Swann, of Wye, gent., by whom he had several children, of whom the eldest, John Dering, was of Wickins, gent., as was his eldest son Christopher Dering, gent.

Weever, in his *Funeral Inscriptions*, published in 1631, mentions several members of the Brent Family of Kent. He gives the following inscription from a tomb at Kensington:

> *Orate pro animabus Willemi Brent, arm. & Elizabethe uxoris ejus, filie Rise Madris.*

The tomb is ancient but has no date.

Concerning Charing, he says:

In the year 1590 this church was with fire consumed

[16]

. . . The windows and the gravestones (where-in divers
of the antient and worthy family of Brent were memoria-
lized) at this time were defaced, yet on the outside of the
Bellfrey do remain carved in stone the badge of Edward
IV (1461-1483), and a wiver (wyvern), being the arms of
Hugh Brent, Esquire, who in the reign of Edward IV was
the principal founder of that belfry, which before was of
wood. From the time of Henry VI (1399-1413), the family
of Brent, being branched out of the antient stock of
Brent in Somersetshire (of which house Sir Robert de
Brent was a baron of the Parliament in the time of
Edward I (1272-1307), both flourished as the prime name
of this parish until *Thomas Brent, Esquire* (the last male
of the line), did remove to Wilsborough, where he died
issueless. On the South side of the chancel here and
annexed to the church, is a convenient chapel, founded
by *Amy Brent*, widow of *William Brent, Esquire*, who
died in the reign of Richard III (1483-1485) . . . Mr.
Brent Dering of Charing is now the owner of the antient
house of the Brents here, which is stored with badges of
Edward IV in every quarry of glass in the hall windows,
in which house also (as goes by tradition) *John Brent,
Esquire*, feasted King Henry VIII.

From the Harleian Society, Visitation of Kent (lineage) taken
1619-1621 (Vol. 42, pp. 221-223), there is a chart of the Brent
Family of Wilsborough and Charing (Kent), which shows that
Robert Brent had a son Robert, who married Elizabeth, daughter
of William Denebauld, and they had a son John, who had a son
Hugh, styled "of Charing." This Hugh had a son Hugh, who
married Christine, daughter and heir of Henry de Rey, of Cherring,
14 R. 2 (1391). William, son of the above Hugh and Christine,
married Julia, relict of Thomas Paunsherst, and daughter of John
Gobyon of Essex, and his wife Amobilia, who was daughter of
John de Pevynton, and Katherine his wife, and had two sons,
William and Hugh. *Hugh Brent*, of Cherryng, married daughter and
heir of —— Hunt, of Cherryng, Ar., and died 1 R. 3 (1484). This
lineage is carried on to 1600, but nothing more is mentioned that
would connect *Hugh Brent*, immigrant to Virginia, with this
branch of the family. As all lineages are carried from the eldest
male heir, or, if no male heir survives, the eldest female heir, and

as this Kent line is the only one listing a Hugh, it might be possible that the subject of this work was a younger member of this same family.

THE
ROLL OF BATTEL ABBEY*

From Holinshed

The Table containing the following names, was formerly in the *Abbey of Battel, in Sussex* . . . The authority of this celebrated document cannot, however, be much relied upon. "There are," says Sir William Dugdale, "great errors or rather falsifications, in most of the copies of it; by attributing the derivation of many from the *French*, who were not all of such extraction, but merely *English*. For such hath been the subtilty of some monks of old, that finding it acceptable unto most to be reputed descendants to those who were companions with Duke William in his expedition, therefore to gratify them, they inserted their names into that ancient catalogue" (*Burke's Peerage*, 1846, p. 629).

The largest list of names is from Holinshed, many of which are duplicated. The versions of Leland and Duchesne, though much shorter, each contain names not found in either of the other lists. An attempt to vindicate the above data and set forth the correct facts pertaining to it was made by the last duchess of Cleveland in 1889. However, the character of the roll has been misunderstood; it is not a list of individuals but of family surnames, and it seems to have been intended to show which families had "come with William the Conqueror," and to have been compiled about the 14th century (*Ency. Britannica*, 11th edition, p. 534).

Among the list of Holinshed appears the name BRENT.

---

*Battel Abbey: William (the Conqueror) ordered the foundation of a monastery to be laid on the spot where he gained the victory over Harold; from which circumstance it was called BATTEL ABBEY. As it was there he won the crown, he wished the new establishment to enjoy all the privileges of the royal chapel, and having obtained the consent of the metropolitan, and of the bishop of the diocese, declared it in a full assembly of prelated and barons, exempt "from all episcopal rule and exactions." It became in the language of later times *nullus diocesis* (*Encyc. Britannica*).

OTHER BRENT IMMIGRANTS TO VIRGINIA

Below is some data from the Virginia Land Office and various County Records about the Brents not descended from Hugh, the immigrant.

Capt. Gyles Brent imported into Northumberland County *Mrs. Margaret Brent* (his sister), *Mrs. Mary Brent* (his sister), who died 1658, leaving her estate to her sister Margaret, and *Mrs. Mary Brent,* his wife. (Northumberland County Order Book, 1650-52.) The Overwharton Parish Register of Stafford County shows that "Col. Giles Brent of Potomac died Sept. 11th, 1679, and was buried in the Great Churchyard ye next day following." The history of this branch of the family has been printed in the *Virginia Magazine of History & Biography.*

Richard Brent came to Gloucester County 1653, as one of the headrights of George Thompson. Cannot find anything more concerning him.

William Brent came to Northumberland County 1651, as one of the headrights of George Coleclough. No other data concerning him.

John Brent came to Lancaster County 24 Nov. 1653, as one of the headrights of Capt. Henry Fleet. The Parish Register of Christ Church, Middlesex County, shows that "John Brent, son of John Brent and Jane, his wife, was baptized 22 August 1680." No other data concerning them.

Edmund Brent died in Westmoreland County 1659, leaving a widow and one son and one daughter, all of whom had died by 1674, leaving no issue. Giles Brent was a witness to his will.

Charles Brent—"To Mr. Wm. Fitzhugh & Mr. Charles Brent, Undertakers for Potomack Garrison . . . 28,714 Lbs. of tobacco" (Lancaster County Orders, 1680-86) No more data on this Charles.

Robert Brent—attorney for Eliz. Spencer, 13 April 1693. He is dead 1697, and his wife, Ann, is settling up his estate. She is dead by 1717. (Lancaster County Orders.)

George Brent of "Woodstock," Stafford County—will 1700. (See *Va. Magazine of History & Biography.*)

Thomas Brent and his son-in-law John Adams (under 21 years), of Norfolk County, Va. (mentioned in will of Wm. Knott, 1694). No more data on this Thomas Brent.

HUGH BRENT, IMMIGRANT TO ISLE OF WIGHT COUNTY, VIRGINIA, 1642

[1] HUGH BRENT, according to the records searched, is the first member of this family to settle in either Maryland or Virginia. The earliest reference to him is found in the Virginia Land Office Records as coming to Isle of Wight County 20 June 1642, one of the headrights of Francis England, and settling on land "adjoining Capt. (Wm.) Peirce."

> Capt. Wm. Peirce was in 1623, Capt. of Gov. Wyatt's guard and lieutenant governor of James Cittie. He prepared in 1629, in England, *A Relation of the Present State of the Colony of Virginia, by Capt. William Perse, an Ancient Planter of twenty Years standing there.* Capt. Peirce came with Sir Thomas Gates . . . He was appointed to Councill in 1631; Member of the Convention, 1625 . . . His daughter Jane was the third wife of John Rolfe (Nugent, p. 30).

> Capt. Wm. Peirce, Esq., one of the Councill of State, (pattented) 2,000 Acs. on Lawnes Creek, 22 June 1635 (Nugent, p. 29). Lawnes Creek was in that part of Isle of Wight County which in 1645 became *Nansimum* County.

How long HUGH BRENT, immigrant, stayed in that neighborhood is not shown by the Patent Books; but it is certainly proven that he was in the "Chickacoon Country" by 1649. He and some of his neighbors might have gone on an exploration of the Northern Neck, or possibly on a foray against the Indians.

Toby Smith, "*Cl. Cur.* of Nansimum County, 1646," was "*Cl. Cur.*" of Lancaster County 1654; Tobias Horton must have been with them; Epapphroditus Lawson patented land in Isle of Wight

1635, and was in Lancaster by 1649, and died there 1652. Many other immigrants to Isle of Wight (Va.) are found in Northumberland and Lancaster Counties about this same time.

The deposition of Thomas Gaskins, 24 May 1656, states:
. . . seven years ago, he (Gaskins) and others were to take up land in Fleetes Bay . . . they went to Corotoman Creeke, viewed the land and took up same, next going to a Creeke where HUGH BRENT now lives, we giving it the name of Haddowais Creeke . . . Roland Haddaway taking up the land that HUGH BRENT is now seated upon, there being three or four Indian Cabbins upon the sd. land . . . over a Run about the Sd. HUGH BRENT now dwelling house, we coming upon the Land over the Run . . . (Northumberland Records, 1652-58, p. 141).

11 Oct. 1654, Hugh Brent buys land from John and Eleanor (Swann) Sharpe (she married later, Richard Price, and died 1702).

6 Feb. 1655, he is granted administration papers on the estate of Walter ffleming, deceased (L. O. B., 1652-57, p. 252).

In 1656, he is on Capt. Henry Fleete's list of tithables; in 1657-58, he pays two tithes; in 1659, one; 1661-62, two, and in 1664, six tithes (L. O. B., 1655-66, p. 101, 131, 162, 199 and 302).

In 1665, Hugh Brent is appointed constable in Lancaster County (1655-66, p. 340). He is witness to deed, Griffin to Johnson, 7 Nov. 1660 (Rappahannock County).

"Mark Watkins, runaway servant of Hugh Brent" (L. O. B., 1666-80, p. 49). Hugh Brent, administrator of the estate of Lancelot Sockwell, "being his largest creditor" (*Ibid.*, p. 75). Hugh Brent, attorney for Tobias Horton, 15 Feb. 1668; petitions for the estate of Tobias Horton, 6 Jan. 1669 (*Ibid.*, p. 98 and 134).

Eppy Bonnison appoints Hugh Brent his attorney, 25 Jan. 1658 . . . to sell or assign land called *Muscatoe Point*; again in 1662 and 1665.

George Thompson and Cleare, his wife, appoint Hugh Brent their attorney, 26 July 1659 (L. O. B., 1654-1702, p. 197).

Joseph Hunt, of the Citty of Bristol (Eng.), mercht . . . . appoint my trusty and well beloved friend Hugh Brent of Fleetes Bay in County of Lancaster,

[21]

Planter, to be my lawful Atty . . . 28 August 1663 (*Ibid.*, p. 282).

Hugh Brent patented several tracts of land in Lancaster County, Va., viz:

> On 6 Feb. 1654/5, Hugh Brent is granted a certificate of land for five persons transported into the Colony: his own transportation (*sic*) and that of John Noble, Robt. Warner, John Girton and *Mary Ochersone (Acherson?)*. (L. O. B., 1652-1657, p. 171).

> 18 March 1662, he patented 200 Acs. in Lancaster County:— butting So. into Haddawais Creeke, E. upon the Bay, N. into the Woods, W. upon a branch of Haddawais Creeke, including three Indian Cabbins formerly granted to Capt. Henry Fleete 1652, and by him assigned to John Sharpe, and by Sd. Sharpe sold to Hugh Brent (*Va. Land Book* 4, p. 633).

6 May 1664, Hugh Brent patented with Abya Bonyson 200 Acs. in Lancaster County:—

> Lying on Haddawais Creeke and Corotoman Creeke in Fleetes Bay . . . 200 Acs. with Toby Horton in the same district (*Land Book* 4, pp. 627-8).

On 10 July 1663, Hugh Brent patented 100 Acs. on Northside of the Rappahannock River in Fleetes Bay for the transportation of two persons into the Colony, viz: Wm. Lumpton and Thomas Bromstead (*Ibid.*, p. 629).

On 7 Sept. 1657 Wm. Shorte and Wm. Lippeate patented 400 Acs. in Lancaster County, which they assigned to Hugh Brent, who assigned one half to Eppy Bonnison, and same was renewed in their names, 18 March 1662 (*Ibid.*, p. 193).

Hugh Brent was born *circa* 1620 in either Kent or Somerset Counties, England, and died in Lancaster County, Va., between 8 Jan. and 13 March 1671. His port of departure in England was in all probability Bristol (see Joseph Hunt above). The name of his wife does not appear in the records searched, but it is possible that he married Mary Ochersone (Acherson?) whom he imported into the Colony in 1654 (she is not styled "servant"). He certainly was not married long before this date as his children were minors at his death; his eldest daughter married 13 Nov. 1672.

[22]

The fact that he left Mr. Thomas Haines (w. 1678/9), "my cast'r* hatt and one pr. of gloves," and also that two of his grandsons married members of Thomas Haine's family (Hugh, a daughter of James Haines, nephew of the above Thomas, and William, married Margaret as second wife, a daughter of his son James and Frances (Pinckard) Haines, and also because Thomas Haines was one of the overseers of his estate, certainly shows a connection that dates back before their immigration to Virginia.

WILL OF HUGH BRENT, 1671.

In the name of God Amen this eighth day of Jany, 1671: I Hugh Brent of ye P'ish of Christ Church in ye County of Lancaster, being sick of body but in sound and p'fect memory God be praised therefor, do make constitute and ordain this my last Will and Testament in manner and form following Viz:

Imp. I bequeath my soul into ye hands of Almighty God my maker hoping to be saved by ye meritorious death and passion of my only Saviour and Redeemer and my body to be buried in Christian buriall.

It: I give to my eldest daughter *Jean* ye neck of land which was cleared by Mr. Wale and so as far as my bounds goeth down to ye Pocoason by patons ye Indian hollowing point for her life time and no longer.

It: I give to my daughter *Elizabeth* ye neck of land next adjoining to ye aforesaid as farr as Thatchers neck and so as far as ye middle of ye main neck for her life time and no longer.

It: I give to my daughter *Martha* ye neck of land which is called Thatchers neck for her life time and no longer and after the decease of either or all of my daughters ye land to return to my sonn *Hough*.

It: I give to my sonn *Hough* and unto his maile children lawfully begotten my whole dividen of land as far as exprest by paton and so successifely from heir to heir.

It: I give to John Coan, one pair of russett French foll shoes and one pair of gloves.

---

*A castor hat was made from beaver skins; what in the last generation was called a "beaver hat."

It: I give to Mr. Thomas Haines my cast'r hatt and one pr. of gloves.

It: I give to ffortunatus Sydnor one pr of French foll and one pr of wosted stokins and one pr of gloves.

It: I give to my man Howell the first cow calfe that shall fall after he is free.

All my worldly goods I give to my children to be equally divided between them, my debts being pd., making them my sole executors of this my last Will and Testament.

It is my desire yt there shall be shipt on board Capt. Plonders ship three hogsheads of tobb. for ye use of John Haukins living in Greenhine. I do alsoe appoint my loving friends Mr. Thomas Haines and ffortunatus Sydnor to be ye overseers of this my last will and testament as also suddenly after my decease that they the sd Thomas Haines and ffortunatus Sydnor to take an inventory of all my goods.

In witness of this my last will and testament I set my hand and seal revoking all other wills and testaments whatsoever ye day and year first above written.

Teste:

     his
John + Andros
     mark
     his   Hugh Brent (Wax wafer:-H. B.)
John + Thomas
     mark

Probated, March 13, 1671.

                      Test: Edw. Dale, Cl Cur.

Probate of ye last will and testament of Hugh Brent, Gent., dec'd is according to ye tenor of ye Sd. will graunted Hugh Brent, his sonne, Joane, Elizabeth and Martha Brent, his daughters . . . Mr. Thomas Haynes and Fortunatus Sydnor being in respect of ye Sd age of ye Sd children, overseers of ye Sd will . . . 13 March 1671 (L. O. B., 1666-1680, p. 220).

Children:

2   1   Joane or Jane, b. *circa* 1657; d. after 1700; m. (1), 13 Nov. 1672, John Reddock of Lancaster County.

Cannot find his will. He was listed as a member of the Lancaster County militia 1687, "appointed for ffoot Service." Richard Redock was in Isle of Wight County, 1637; John Redicke was in Warwick Riv. County, 1643; John Reddock, headright of Francis Hobbs, 20 Aug. 1650, "on N. side of Rappa. River, along a creeke at the foote of a mountaine"; John Redock, "headright of Richard Normansell, 5 June 1666, Stafford County, on N. W. side of Potomack River on the maine run of Pohicke Creeke." She married (II), after 1688, William Edmonds, widower, viz:

> . . . Wm. Edmonds aforsd & Joane to Hugh Brent land formerly purchased by Hugh Brent, dec'd, & given unto ye Sd Jane Edmonds daughter of ye Sd Hugh Brent, dec'd, by his will for her natural life & noe longer (L. D. B., 1687-1700, p. 168).

Wm. Edmonds in his will, 1697-1700 names his wife Jane. On 9 April 1688, he sells land to John Wale, & his wife is Lewys. She was the relict of Geo. Wale (d. 1671). From the above data, Joane or Jane (BRENT—Reddock) Edmonds left no heirs "of her naturall body."

3 II Elizabeth, b. *circa* 1658 in Lancaster County, Va.; m. 11 Feb. 1679, Thomas Bonnison son of Abya (Abia or Eppy—the same person) whose will was written 21 March 1663, and Honoriah Bonnison. Hugh Brent and Thomas Medastard "overseers of my will." Elizabeth and Thomas Bonnison probably died without heirs or returned to England, as I cannot find further data concerning them.

+ 4 III Martha, b. *circa* 1659; m. 10 Sept. 1673, Tobias Horton, Jr.

+ 5 IV Hugh, b. *circa* 1660; d. 1716; m. *circa* 1675, Katherine ——.

[4] MARTHA[2] BRENT (Hugh[1]), was born in Lancaster County, Va., *circa* 1659, and had died by 1710, viz:

Ordered that ye deeds acknowledged by Tobias Horton & Jane his wife, to Hugh Brent, be admitted to record (L. O. B., 10 May 1710).

[25]

She married 10 Sept. 1673, Tobias Horton, son of Tobias (Sr.) and Elizabeth Taylor, relict of John Taylor (d. 1653) "Ancient Planter." Toby Horton, Sr., came to Isle of Wight County, Va., 28 May 1638, as one of the headrights of Sarah Cloyden, Widdowe (Nugent, p. 89). He was in Lancaster County, 1 Feb. 1653:

. . . betwixt two maine creeks issuing out of Fleetes Bay next to land of John Taylor, dec'd, bounding S. W. upon one of the creeks dividing this from land of Eppy Bonison . . . & bounding N. E. upon the one towards the Indian Towne (Nugent, p. 289).

Tobias Horton (Sr.), 600 acs. in Northumberland County, 18 March 1662. Upon the N. part of Fleetes Bay, about a half mile up Haddawaies Creeke, granted to Thomas Humphries 1 Sept. 1654, and assigned to sd. Horton (Nugent, p. 437).

Tobias Horton (Sr.), 1200 acs. in Lancaster County, 16 June 1662 (By Francis Moryson). Between Tabb Creek and Nanty poyson Creek, issuing out of Fleetes Bay . . . for transportation of 24 persons . . . [among whom was John Coane (Nugent, p. 437).]

Tobias Horton (Sr.), 500 acs. Lancaster County, 29 Nov. 1652. 200 acs. part upon the Southermost side of Fleets Bay, abutting N. upon a creek dividing this and land of Hump. Tabb and Easterly upon the bay. The remainder upon the head of the aforsd. creek. Trans. of 10 persons (Nugent, p. 263).

John Taylor. In the *Swan*, 1610. 'Of Newport News, Yeoman and Ancient Planter,' patent 10 Sept. 1624 . . . 'In Court 28 Nov. 1633 . . . his whole dividint . . . granted him to take it up where hee shall find convenient.' In J C G C, p. 73, is found deposition of a John Taylor, aged 37, date 23 June 1625 (Nugent, p. xxx). Tobyas Horton (Sr.), was probably a 'practitoner of Physicke,' viz: 'Whereas Tobyas Horton hath impleaded Walter ffleming for a debt of 300 pds. of tobacoe in casque being for ye Cure of a soare leg and whereas by oath it appears that ye sd tobacoe is not due till ye sd Cure be accomplished wch being not yet performed ye Court hath annihilated ye sd Acct and judged ye sd bill Cancelled and voyd.' (L. D. B., 1652-1657, p. 171.) Walter Fleming died shortly afterwards, whether from the treatment or the *soare leg*—the records are not

clear. Tobias Horton, Jr., died between 13 June and 12
Aug. 1748.

Children (HORTON):

9 1 George, b. *circa* 1675; d.; his will was written 26 April
1753, and probated 16 June 1753; he married Judith
———, and had —
  1 George (i. 1772).
  2 John.

10 11 John, born *circa* 1680, and died before 20 Aug. 1756;
m. Ellinor ———, who died 1778. They had—
  1 Judith, m. (1) 3 Oct. 1774, William Norris (i. 1792),
and had Geo. Horton, Wm. Richard and Charlotte
Norris; m. (11), John Brent (81).

  2 Sarah(?), m. John Hutchings, and had at least,
Nancy.

[5] HUGH[2] BRENT (Hugh[1]), was born in Lancaster County,
Va., *circa* 1660, and he died there, intestate, between 15 March
1715 (old style) and 14 June 1716, viz:

 Hugh Brent Gent being arrefted to this Court for ye
 Sum of 18524 pounds of tobacco att ye Suit of Robt.
 Carter Esq. and Thomas Carter Gent Church Wardens
 of Christ Church P'sh and he not appearing order is
 therefore granted agt the Sheriffe upon whose peticon
 attachmt is awarded agt ye sd Brent returnable to next
 Court (L. O. B., March 15, 1716, p. 133). . . . The
 Suit *Inter* Robt. Carter Esq. and Thomas Carter, Gent,
 Church Wardens of Christ Church Parish is dismt the
 deft *mortus Est.* (L. O. B., 14 June 1716, p. 147).

From the above notes it would appear that Hugh Brent was
short in his accounts. However, such was not the case. The records
show that on 9 May 1711, he was to receive the tithables "Between
Coll Carters mill and Mr. Jacksons mill run," and also from his
will, that he was sick for some time before his death, viz: the gifts
to the people who attended him, and then the suit he brought
against Jno Cooke, 11 May 1715, viz:

 The Suit Inter Hugh Brent Gent and Jno Cooke is Continued ye plt attoe: being sick.

Descendants of Hugh Brent

I have not been able to find the surname of Hugh Brent's wife. She is not named in any of his transactions except as shown in the following:

> This indenture made this 20th day of July in the year of our Lord 1682 between Hugh Brent and Katherine his wife, Planter, of the County of Lancaster on the one part, witnesseth that the sd Hugh Brent and Katherine his wife for and in consideration of a man servant and Six pounds Sterling in hand, the receipt thereof they do hereby acknowledge and of every part and parsell thereof doe hereby remitt and discharge to the sd John Norris, his heirs, and assigns, all that therein parsell of Land lying in the County of Lancaster, scituated and being on the S. side of the sd Indian Creeke on a point . . . Corotoman Point . . . bounded in the land of Tobyas Horton containing 100 A., mentioned in a paton bearing date of 8th of May 1680, first pattented by Hugh Brent and Tobias Horton . . . (L. O. B., 6, p. 75).

In 1709, Hugh Brent and Katherine Brent are witnesses to the will of Capt. John Swann. No family connexion is mentioned. Hugh Bent and Geo. Brent, sons of the above, were appraisers of the estate of John Swan, Gent., 8 Nov. 1721, and on 14 March 1721:

> Ordered that Sarah Swan pay Hugh Brent for having attended one day, as witness for her.

Among the items listed in the inventory of Hugh Brent, dec'd taken 25 Oct. 1716 is this:

> *To 1 psell of Woman's old Cloathes @ 2£s.,*

which undoubtedly shows that his wife preceded him to the grave.

Hugh Brent was an active man among the citizens of Lancaster County as the following notes from the Order Books show. Besides appearing in numerous suits, sometimes as plaintiff and at other times as defendant, he seems to have been both a member of His Majesty's Court of Justices and High Sheriffe at one and the same time.

He was appointed constable for Lancaster County in 1691. On 12 May 1703, he is appointed Surveyor:

> Ordered that Mr. Hugh Brent be Surveyor of the highway from Capt. Swans to ye Road and thence from

Mr. Jacksons mill to Coll Carters mill . . . 13 Sept. 1705: Mr. Hugh Brent Surveyor of ye Highway from the old mill to Coll Carters Mill and from his own houfe up ye necke to ye maine Roade.

Hugh Brent was appointed one of His Majesty's Justices for Lancaster County 10 May 1710:

> Mr. Hugh Brent being likewise desired by the Court to take ye oath of a Juftice answered he refufed it for he thought him selfe not fitt to be a Judge of ye Law that did not know ye Law.

He must have read up on the law during the next two months, for on 12 July 1710,

> Att this Court ye Oathes appointed by Act of Parliamt of ye oathes of Allegiance and Supremacy is admitted to Mr. Hugh Brent, one of his Majts Juftices for ye sd County together with ye oath of abjuration and Teft and ye oath of a Juftice.

Hugh Brent was sheriff of Lancaster County 10 April 1712, viz:

> Att this Court it is ordered that Mr. Richard Chichester Mr. Rowland Lawson and Mr. Hugh Brent be Recommended to the Honourable Governor as persons fitt and able to have and Execute the office of Sheriffe of this County . . .

> 11 Dec. 1712: The County of Lancaster Being indebted in the Sum of 20185 pounds of Tobacoe Doe order that a Levie of 19½ pounds of tobaccoe be Collected by Hugh Brent Gent Sheriffe of this County of and from Every Tithable person in this County and that he pay the same to ye several Creditors here under written . . .

> 13 May 1713: Att this Court the Othes appointed by act of Afsembly instead of the oathes of alegiance and Supremacy ye Oath of Abjuration and Oath of a Sheriffe was admitted to Hugh Brent Gent and the Teft by him subscribed.

Hugh Brent seems to have held these two positions concurrently or intermittently. He is "present" as Justice from 9 August 1710 to 12 Oct. 1715. He is "present" as Sheriffe from 13 Jan. 1713/4 to June 1714, and up to the time of his death, as the Lancaster County order books show on 14 June 1716:

[29]

Descendants of Hugh Brent

Hugh Brent Gent late Sheriffe of the sd County . . . the deft *mortus Est.* (is dead).

Hugh Brent was a member of the Lancaster County militia, "Foot Service," in 1687, viz:

May it please your Excellency:

In obedience to your Excellency's order directed to this Court (1687) for the returning an Account of all Such persons that are able to Bear Arms both for Horse and Foot Service in the County (Lancaster), We have duely Examined the list of the Free holders and house keepers inhabiting in ye sd county and wee doe find upon ye due inquiry that many of them are very Poore Desperable Persons. We have Returned Yo'r Excellency the full Number Express't by y'r order as ffolleth: (fifty-two persons are appointed for "Horse Service," a few of whose progeny will appear later in this work are listed below):—
John Chin, Thomas Martin, James Haynes, Rob. Pollard, Richard Merryman, Jno. Chilton, George Wale;
Some of the Persons appointed for "ffoot Service":
Robt. Mitchell, Jno. Swann, Wm. Mitchell, John Sharp, John Flowers, Christopher Kirk, Thos. Carter, Will King, Jno. Redork, T'bias Horton, HUGH BRENT, Charles Kirby, Jno. Coane Jnr.

Since Hugh Brent died intestate, the following deeds and orders show some, and I believe all of his children who attained their majority.

Hugh Brent to son Hugh Brent Jr., 1704-1706
(D. B., 9, p. 140—Lancaster County)

Know all men by these presents, that I *Hugh Brent* of the County of Lancaster, do owe and stand justly bound unto *Hugh Brent Junior* of the sd County, him his heirs Exors Admns or assigns in the just and full sum of two hundr pounds Sterling money of England sd wch payment will truely be made and done I bind myself my heirs Exors admns etc by these presents as witness my hand and sealed with my seale dated the 12th of Feby Ano Dom 1704.

The condition of the above bounden *Hugh Brent* is such that if ye above *Hugh Brent Junior* shall and will enjoy a certain tract or parcel of land given to him by the above bounden Brent and bounded as followeth, (viz) beginning on ye Indian Creeke on Tobias Horton's line and running from ye said Creeke up along the said Horton's line to a marked pine and running easterly from there along a line of marked trees to a marked corner pine standing near ye head of Pockonces Cove and running from ye said pine down ye said Cove to ye Indian Creeke and soe running up the severall courses of ye maine Creeke to ye first place it began. Which tract or parcel of land with all houses fences and with all profits emoluments whatever thereunto belonging to or thereunto appertaining excepting ye orchard and ground it stands on and Carrway to and from ye said orchard to be forty yards below or above ye Carrway that now is which said orchard and Carrway ye above bounden Brent doth reserve to himself out of this tract or parcell of land and nothing else whatsoever and further the said *Brent Junior* shall fully absolutely clearly peaceably and quietly enjoy ye said tract or parcell of land excepting before excepted during his life and in case ye said *Brent Junior* shall marry and he should happen to dye before his said wife that then his wife after his death during her widowhood shall accordingly enjoy the said tract or parcel of land and noe longer than she remain a widow and not to make any manner of waste of any timber but for the use of the plantation and further the above bounden Brent doth oblige himself his heirs etc not to disturb him ye sd *Brent Junior* during his life nor his wife in case of his death during her widowhood now if ye aforsd *Brent Junior* and his wife in case of marriage shall and will according to this condition peacefully have hold and occupy ye sd land without ye lest lettsure or trouble of him ye sd Brent or by or through any means or provement of his or his heirs whatsoever that then this obligation to be void and of noe effect or else to stand remain and be in full force power and virtue and this bond never to be out of date notwithstanding any law or usage to ye contrary and witness my hand and seale the day and date above

Signed sealed and   Hugh Brent (Seal)
delivered in ye presence of
  W. Tyler
  John Flower   Recorded the 9th day of July 1706 at ye Instance and request of James Haines/smith/ Jas Taylor, Cl. Cur.

Descendants of Hugh Brent

Hugh Brent to daughter Mary Brent, and son Charles Brent, 1710 (Lancaster D. B. 9, p. 357)

Know all men by these presents that I *Hugh Brent* of ye P'sh of Christ Church in ye County of Lancaster afors'd Gent. for and in consideration of the naturall Love and Affection which I have and beare unto *Mary Brent*, my daughter, Have given and granted and by these presents doe for myself my heirs Exors and Admns give and grant unto the aforsd *Mary Brent* one certan mulattoe slave named and commonly known by the name of Jack and one certain negroe slave named and commonly known by the name of Mingoe, To have and to hold the aford negroes and mulattoe slaves unto the aforsd *Mary Brent* and the heirs of her Body Lawfully begotten, and if she dyes without such Issue that ye aforsd negroe and mulatoe slaves shall be and . . . unto my son *Charles Brent* and his heirs forever.

In witness whereof I have hereunto sett my hand and Seale this 12th day of Sept. Anno Dom 1710.

Wit: { John Turberville   Hugh Brent (Seal)
     { Wm. Dare

Recorded 11 Oct. 1710

William Brent and *George Brent* being cited to this court to Satisfye the Court whether they would join in administracion wth their Elder brother on their fathers Estate who died intestate And they refuſing Administracion upon the Estate of *Hugh Brent* Gent decd . . . it is granted unto *Hugh Brent* he making Oathe in Open Court That ye sd *Hugh Brent* Gent departed this life without making any will so farr as he knows or believes, And on his Motion and giving Security for his juſt and faithfull Administracion of the Said deceaseds Estate Certificate is granted him for Obtaining Letters of Administracion in due form (Lancaster Orders, 1713-1716, p. 153, 10 October 1716).

Hugh Brent son and heir of *Hugh Brent*, Gent., dec'd to *William Brent*, second son of the said *Hugh Brent*, Gent., dec'd (D. B. 11, p. 138, Lancaster County, Va.)

This Indenture made the 8th of June Anno Dom 1719 Between *Hugh Brent* son and heir of *Hugh Brent* late of the County of Lancaster and P'sh of Christ Church, Gent.,

Dec'd, of the one part and *William Brent* 2nd son of the sd *Hugh Brent* Gent., and bro. of *Hugh Brent* party to these presents of the other part.

Witnesseth—that the sd *Hugh Brent* for the love and natural affection he bears unto his sd brother *William Brent* and for divers other good causes and considerations him thereunto moving hath given granted aliened Enfeofed and confirmed and by these presents doth give grant alien Enfeoff and Confirm unto the said *William Brent* all that messuage or tenement tract piece or parcel of land now in possession and occupation of the said *William Brent* Containing one hundred acres of Land Scituated lying and being in the Parish of Christ Church and County of Lancaster and is the same land that the sd *Hugh Brent* Gent bought of Mr. Robt. Gibsone as by his deed of sale bearing date the Seventh day of August *anno* 1714 relation thereunto being had may more fully and at large appear AND all and singular the rights profits Emolus and appurtenances with all edifices orchards pastures fences woods underwoods timber and lumber mayne waters and water Courses and all other advantages in any way belonging to the sd hundred acres of Land and premises or any part or parcell thereof TO HAVE AND TO HOLD the sd one hundred Acres of Land hereby granted and Enfeoffed with all other the premises with their and every of their appurtenances unto the sd *William Brent* and male heirs of his body lawfully begotten forever and for want of Such heir the sd Land to return to the sd *Hugh Brent* or his heirs and the sd *Hugh Brent* for him . . . Death Covenant and promise loaned with the sd *William Brent* that the sd *William Brent* and his heirs as aforsd shall peacably and quietly have hold occupy and possess the sd Land and all and singular the premises hereby given and granted from the claim of him the sd *Hugh Brent* or any persons by from or under him IN WITNESS whereof the sd *Hugh Brent* hath hereunto set his hand and seal the day and year above written.

The word for ever interlined   Hugh Brent (seal)
before signed
Signed sealed and delivered in presence of
Thom⁸ Lee
Nichos. Martin
Memorandum—that this day to witt the seventh day of Sept Anno 1719 the wtin named Hugh Brent delivered to

the within William Brent peaceable possession of the lands and tenements within mentioned by delivery of the latch of the door of the Chief mansion house and also of turf and twig upon part of the premises in the name and token of livery and seizine of the whole land comprised in this deed of Gift in presence of all the subscribers.

Thom^s Lee, Nicho^s. Martin.

At a Court held for Lancaster County the 14th day of Oct Anno Dom 1719 this deed with the Livery and Seizen thereon endorsed was acknowledged by Hugh Brent to William Brent and at his motion ordered to be recorded and is recorded this 25th day of Oct. 1719.

Wm. Dale, Cl. Cur.

INVENTORY OF HUGH BRENT 1716

Lancaster County, October 25th, 1716. In obedience to an order of the Court of ye sd County held the 10th day of October, wee whose names are here under subscribed have valued the following particulars presented to us as ye estate of Mr. Hugh Brent (de'cd) as followeth (viz)—

Imp:	£	s	d
To one negro man named Tom, at	35		
To one Do. named Dick, at	33		
To 1 Do. man named Plod, at	33		
To 1 negro woman named Moll, at	28		
To 1 Do. woman named Jane, at	28		
To 1 negro boy named Sampson, at	13		
To 1 negro guirle named Betty, at	10		
To 6 rushshia Leather Chares, at 8s	2	08	
To 1 dutch ouill table and counterpin	1	10	
To 1 oack ouill Table, at	1	05	
To 1 Cabinett of Drawers, at		15	
To 1 Large Looking glass, at	2	10	
To 1 Mapp, at		06	
To 1 bed and furniture in ye new house, at	8	16	06
To 66£s of puter, at	3	06	
To 34£s of old Do., at	1	06	11

In ye old house

	£	s	d
To 1 iron bound Chest, at		12	
To 1 Large Chest, at		10	
To 1 Do., at		12	
To 1 old trunck, at		05	
To 1 box, at		03	06
To 2 Small Do., one 2s. and ye other 1s		03	
To 1 Large Bible, at		11	
To 1 Small Trunck Leather torn and Lid off, at			09
To 1 box wch. glass came in			06
To 1 old Large Table, at		10	

[34]

To 5 new Cotton blankets at 4s	1		
To 4 old Do., at 3s		12	
To 30½ yds of Cotton at 13s	1	13	00½
To 12 yds. of Sagity at 2 and 6s	1	10	
To 13 yds. of Canleloons, at		08	08
To 4 yds. of narrow Lining, at		04	
To 1½ yds of plaines at 1s		01	06
To 24 yds of hardins at 10s	1		08¾
To 15 yds. of Do., at 10		12	06
To 23 Ells of Do. wless, at 2s, 6d	2	17	06
To 18¾ of Irish Lining (linen), at 1 and 6	1	08	01½
To 18½ of Dutch Check at 2 and 1	1	17	01½
To 18 yds of broad Cotton Check		19	06
To 13¾ of narrow Check, at 11		12	07¾
To 20 yds. of fustian dimity, at 14p	1	03	04
To 07 yds. of flaning, at 13p		07	07
To 2 yds. of Druget, at 2s		04	
To 9 yds. of Coarse Cearsy, at 2		18	
To 8 pr. of playn shoes at 3 and 8	1	09	04
To 1 laddow, at		03	
To 1 psell of Woman's old Cloathes, at	2		
To 1 pocket book almost all written			06
To 1 old Chest, at		05	
To 4½ £s of Drop Shott, at 2p			09
To 21¼ £s of powder, at 15p		02	09¼
To 18½ £s of nails at 4p		06	02
To 1 manty and petty Coat of Callico	1	05	
To a psell of small truck and 5 small boxes	1	19	08
To 1 small table cloth 4 napkins hucker back, at		06	
To 1 table cloth and 7 napkins old damask, at		10	
To 1 table cloth, 6 napkins of Cotton, at		12	
To 2½ yds. of Virginia Cotton, at ½p		05	
To 1 raisor, at		02	06
To 3 pr. of new Coarse Shetes at	1	15	
To 2 pr. of old Do		16	
To 1 Small Looking glass, at		03	06
To 1 box Iron and heaters, at		02	06
To 1 wollen wheale, at		07	06
To 1 Cresent Saw file and rest at		06	
To 1 handsaw and 1 Joyn Saw, at		04	06
To 1 Iron Chaine		11	08
To 1 feather bed boulsters and pillow con'tn. 66£s, at 10s	2	15	
To 1 rugg, 1 blanket, 1 pr. of sheats 1 bedstead, and cord, Curtains and rualients(?)	2		08
To 1 Small feather bed boulster and two pillows, at	2	10	
To 1 rugg, blankett, 1 pr. of sheats, 1 pr. of curtains, bedstead cord and hide	2	05	08
To 1 small feather bed and boulster weighing 44£s	2		04
To 1 pr. of Small Cotton Sheate, one old rugg, 1 blankett	1	06	08
To 1 trunell bed stead Cord and Hide		07	
To 1 old bed, rug and a blanket, one boulster bed sted Cord and Hide	2	10	
To 2 Elboe Chairs, one at 6 and ye other at 4	2	10	
To 5 hide Chaires, at		04	
To 1 potrack; 1 fier shouett; 1 pr. of tongues		08	06

Item	£	s	d
To 1 old tin lantern; 1 pr. of fier tongues, and 1 pr. of nipers, at		05	
To 1 pr. of old brass Scales and weights...................		05	
To 1 warming pan, at....................................		06	
To 1 puter gate'n pot at...............................		07	
To 11 Wooden bowls great and small, at 3s...............		02	09
To a psell of Coarse Earthen ware, at....................		05	
To a psell of fine Earthen ware, at.....................		03	
To a psell of Carplend and Joyners tools.................		12	
To 2 meale Lines? at 21d; 1 Cloth breshe, at.............		02	09
To 1 puter pocket bottle, at...........................		01	
To 3 pr. of wool cards, at.............................		03	
To 46£s of old Iron, at 1d............................		03	10
To 2 small books and psell of old peaces.................		05	06
To 40£s of good brass, at 14d..........................	06	06	08
To 20£s of old brass something useful, at 10..............		16	08
To 1 old belmettle skilet, at...........................		03	06
To 11 old tin pans, at.................................		04	06
To 1 grid Iron; 2 pr. of Sheap Shears, 1 Cuting Knife, 1 box Iron and 2 heaters; Ladle Candle Stick, 1 dore hinges, 1 pr. of marking Irons, 1 flesh torch.........................		11	
To a parsell of Sederware..............................		12	06
To 1 pr. of Small Stilyards, at..........................		03	
To 8 narrow hoese at 1 d.; 2 broad Do. at 15d..........		15	
To 3 narrow axes; 4 worn weading hoes and 1 old hilling hoe		04	
To 1 old spades at 18d. and 5 knives and forks............		04	03
To 1 Duz. of hard mettle spoons, at....................		02	
To 1 pr. of old Stilyards and poize, at...................		02	06
To 160£s of pot Iron, at...............................	02	06	08
To 1 Spit at 4 and 6; to 1 frying 4 and 6; 1 driping pan and brass Spoon 4 and 6; 3 old frying pans at 4; 1 homony pestle at 2 and 8..	01		
To 50£s of wool, at 7d......'........................	01	09	02
To 2 Duzn. and 9 black mohair Coat buttons, at...........		01	10
To 18£s of Cotton in ye Stonie, at 3d...................		04	06
To 770 galls of Syder—Casque at ¾d. gall...............	02	08	01½
To 1 old Grubing hoe, at...............................		01	03
To 1 Steare of 6 yrs old, at............................	02	15	
To 3 Steares of 4 yrs. old, at..........................	06		
To 13 Cows, at...	26		
To 3 hyfers of 2 yrs. old, at...........................	03		
To 4 young Steares of 3 yrs. old, at.....................	05		
To 2 bulls of 5 yrs. old...............................	03		
To 3 yearlings, at.....................................	01	10	
To 3 Calves, at..		18	
To 17 Sheape at 6 and 6...............................	05	10	06
To 1 new Cannew, at...................................		16	06
To 1 worn Cannew, at..................................		11	
To 1 old Large Split Cannew, at........................		12	
To 1 Large mare and Small Colt, at.....................	05		
To 1 yong horse, at....................................	04		
To 1 Sorry old mare and Small Colt.....................	03		
To 1 Saddle; housing Saddle Cloth and old Cerb bridle......		12	06
To 1 Servant Woman, at................................	01	10	
To 1 lot of wedges, at.................................		05	
To 1 Stone Jugg at....................................		02	06

To a psell of old tubs; 3 sifting trays; 1 old Chare.........	19	
To 1 Sider Still at..	09	
To 1 pottle bottles and niatt, at..........................		06
To 1 Chest and Lock, at...................................	09	
To 1 Do. without lock.....................................	08	
To 6£s of old Iron at 1d..................................		06
To 2 meale bags, at.......................................	04	06
To 1 Cooper's adz, at.....................................	01	06
To 1 tennant Saw...	05	
To 4 pillow cases of Cotton, at...........................	09	
To 1 old fish gigg, at....................................	03	
To 4 hard mettle Spoons...................................		08
To 10 Duzn. of pipes, at..................................	02	
To 1 yd. of Cearty, at....................................	03	03
To 3,000 London:10 (?) nails, at..........................	15	

Suma... 353   17   08¾

Robert Gibson
Epa: Lawson
fforts: Sydnor
Geo. Flower

At a Court held for Lancaster County the 9th day of
Jan'y Anno Dom 1716 this Inventory was Exhibited upon
oath by Hugh Brent Admn., and is ordered to be recorded and is recorded.

Wm. Dale, Clk Cur.

Children:

+ 11   I   Hugh, b. ——; d. Lancaster County, Va., 1750; m.
(I), 1706, Ellinor Haines, dau. of James Haines (w.
1711/2) and Elizabeth Haines; m. (II), 30 Sept. 1726,
Elizabeth Morris, dau. of William Morris and ——
Wale, dau. of George Wale.

+ 12   II   William, b. ——; d. Lancaster County, Va., 1740;
m. (I), *cir.* 1708, Sarah Fleet, dau. of Capt. Henry[2]
Fleet (Henry[1]), a family long prominent in both
Maryland and Virginia before 1700. Sarah (Fleet)
Brent, d. before 1717; m. (II), 7 Jan. 1723/4, Margaret
Haynes; m. (III), 9 Aug. 1734, Letitia Wale.

+ 13   III   George, b. ——; d. Lancaster County, Va., 1748;
m. *circa* 1715, Judith Pursell.

+ 14   IV   Charles, b. ——; d. 13 Jan. 1756, in Stafford County,
Va.; m. *cir.* 1725, Hannah Innis of Richmond County,
Va. She d. 1762.

[37]

+ 15   v   Mary, b. ——; d. ——; m. 10 Aug. 1724, James Carter, widower, son of Capt. Thomas Carter and his wife Catherine Dale, daughter of Edward Dale and his wife Diana.

[11] HUGH[3] BRENT (Hugh[2], Hugh[1]), was born in Lancaster County, Va., *circa* 1680, and died there; his will was written 26 Oct. 1748, and probated 11 May 1750. He married (i), 1706, Ellinor Haines, daughter of James and Elizabeth (Coane?) Haines (see deed below). He married (ii) ,30 Sept. 1726, Elizabeth Morris, daughter of William Morris and —— Wale, daughter of George Wale, a large landowner in both Maryland and Virginia, and his wife Mary Jones, daughter of Robert Jones and his wife Martha Llewellyn, daughter of Daniel Llewellyn, Burgess of Charles Cittie County, 1642-1644 (Boddie).

Hugh Brent, being the eldest son, inherited all of his father's estate and was a man of prominence in Lancaster County. His attachment to his next younger brother, William, is as striking as is his total neglect of his other two brothers, George and Charles, when his deeds of gift are studied. In the long drawn out suit of Schoefield vs. Brent, it would appear that William Brent had named a son "Hugh"; however, no son by this name appears in his will.

Hugh Brent is mentioned frequently as a grand juryman 1717-1725. He paid 6 tithes, 1717, 7 in 1718, and 8 in 1719. He appraised the estates of George Wale, George Flowers, Jacob Carroll, Mark Atkins (who was a "runaway servant" of his father's), Catherine Lawson, John Swan, Lee Flower, Samuel Holloway, and others; he was trustee of the estate of Eppa Lawson, all before 1726.

On 12 April 1727 (Old Style), he was made a Justice of the Peace, and also took the Oath of Justice for Lancaster County, which position he held unto his death in 1750.

Bond from Hugh Brent, Gent., and Thomas Edwards to His Majesty's Justices (L. O. B., 1721-1729, p. 257).

Hugh Brent was a Vestryman of Christ Church Parish, and also church warden:

Hugh Brent, Gent., is appointed to take a list of tithes in the middle precinct of Christ Church Parish (*Ibid.*, 8

[38]

May 1728, p. 269) . . . Hugh Brent, Gent., church warden of Christ Church Parish, plaintiff, and Elias Edmonds, Jr., defendant (12 June 1734).

Hugh Brent was Sheriff of Lancaster County:

Hugh Brent, Gent., produced a commission from the Governor appointing him Sheriffe of this County . . . and he took Oathe (L. O. B., 1729-1740, p. 112). Hugh Brent, Gent., took the Oath of Oyer and Terminer, 9 Feb. 1736 (*Ibid.*, p. 159). The Sheriff of a county was regarded as the *judge* of the County Courts, as they now exist; he was an officer in the Church of England, and the laws of the Church were the laws of the land.

Hugh Brent, the immigrant, and his son Hugh, from the records as found in the counties searched, were most indifferent as to the other early settlers by the name of Brent. The only recorded data which I have found that shows any connexion between this family and any other of the same name is this:

In ye Suite in Chancery depending in this Court between Jno Mahallam Extr of ye last will and testament of ANN BRENT dec'd, complainant and HUGH BRENT defendant for money (?) of certain Henry Offley, in the hands of the sd deft. Upon hearing the whole matter the Court do declare That the sd HUGH BRENT do pay unto the sd Jno Mahallam the Sum of one pound eleven Shillings and Six pence being what ye Sd Defend is indebted unto the sd Henry Offley (L. O. B., 1717-1721, p. 196—8 May 1717).

Ann Brent is named in the Northumberland records as relict of Rober Brent, viz—

Account of Ann Brent relict of Robert Brent vs. William Wood (N. C. O., p. 87—1699). She sues Alexander Swan prior to this, in 1697, when she is admrx. of Robert Brent's estate.

Benjamin Wale, in his will, written 26 March 1709, names wife, Ann, and "wife's son John Mahallam," among others. Why she is "named" *Ann Brent* if she had married Benj. Wale before 1709, is hard to understand. Early settlers in the colonies changed their names easily, and the changes were not always recorded in the Order Books, but probably were in the Church Parish Registers. As the Lancaster Parish Registers appear to be lost, there is no

[39]

way to check this data. I cannot find anything in the Lancaster records to show a relationship between the above Robert and his wife Ann Brent, and Hugh Brent.

Elizabeth Brent, the second wife of Hugh, died; her will was written 24 Nov. 1762, and probated 19 July 1770.

Elizabeth Haynes gives to daughter *Eleanor Brent* and husband *Hugh Brent*, and their son *Morrice Brent*, slaves, 9 April 1713 (L. D. B. 9, p. 485). Instead of Elizabeth Haynes being a "Coane," she might have been a "Morris," before her marriage to James Haynes.

James Brent, planter, sells to Thomas James, 235 Acs. of land, 13 July 1744. This is the same tract of land "which in 1669 was granted by patent to John Coane, and afterwards fell into the possession of James Haynes who by his last will and testament bearing Date the first Day of January 1711/2 . . . gave and bequeathed the sd Land unto his granson Haynes Brent son of Hugh Brent Gent. . . . and the sd Haynes Brent dying without issue, the same descended to his brother, James Brent one of the parties to these presents . . ." (L. D. B. 14, p. 24).

> Know all men by these presents, that I Hugh Brent of the Parish of Christ Church in Lancaster County and Colony of Virginia for and in consideration of the Naturall Good Will and Affection I have and do bear unto my Sons and Daughters hereafter mentioned, Have given and by these presents give unto my Sd Children as followeth, To my Son *William Brent* my negro man named Tom, To my Son *Hugh Brent* my negro woman named Dinah with her increase, to my Son *John Brent* my Negro Woman Fillis and her increase, to my Daughter *Katherine Brent* my Negro Girle Lucy and her increase, to my Daughter *Elizabeth Brent* my Negro Girle Judy and her increase, And also give my Negro Woman Sue and her future Increase to be divided between my said Daughters. The aforsd Negroes to be delivered to my Sd children immediately after my decease, And in case of the death of either of my Sons his Brother or Brothers before named to enjoy his part, and in case of the death of either of my Daughters the Survivor to enjoy the whole Estate herein given to such Daughter. IN WITNESS whereof I

have hereunto set my hand and Seale this Thirteenth
day of September 1726.

Sealed and Delivered   Hugh Brent (seal)

in presence of ⎰ Thos. Edwards
               ⎱ William Brent
               ⎱ Alex. McPherson

At a Court held for Lancaster County on Wednesday
the Fourteenth day of Sept. 1726 This Deed of Gift was
this day in open Court Acknowledged by Hugh Brent to
be his Act and Deed and by the Court admitted to record
and is recorded.

Test T. Edwards Cl Cur

Hugh Brent was making a "peace offering" to the children by
his first wife, preparatory to his second marriage, which took place
seventeen days later.

Hugh Brent gives land to his son James Brent and wife Catherine, 8 Nov. 1738 (L. D. B. 13, p. 145).

The will of Hugh Brent, which follows, separates the children
of the "whole blood" in a manner that leaves no doubt as to the
issue by his two wives.

The Will of Hugh Brent of Christ Church Parish, 1748-50
(L. D. B. 14, p. 280)

In the name of God, Amen. I Hugh Brent, of the
Parish of Christ Church in the County of Lancaster,
gent., being very weak in Body but in my perfect sense
and Memory, praised be God, do make and ordain this
my last Will and Testament in manner and form follow-
in and first and principally I give and resign my soul to
God that gave it me trusting in the merits of my blessed
Redeemer Jesus Christ for a Joyful Resurrection, and
as for what worldly Estate it has pleased Almighty God
to bestow on me I give and dispose thereof in the following
Manner—

Item—I give to my son *James Brent* my looking Glass in
my Great Room and also a large Chest that was his
grandfather's.

Item—I give to my son *Maurice Brent* my violin.

Item—I give to my son *William Brent* my piece or parcel

[41]

or panll of land purchased from Tobias Horton dec'd, as also my negro girle Lucy to him and his heirs forever.

Item—I give unto my granddaughter *Mary Brent* daughter of my deceased son *William Brent*, two ewes in full for her part of my Estate, having provided sufficiently for her Father heretofore.

Item—I give to my son *Hugh Brent* my young Negro man Stephen.

Item—My will is that my Loving Wife *Elizabeth Brent* have and enjoy one tenth part of my negroes not in this my Will heretofore bequeathed during her natural life and that after her decease the said portion of Negroes with their increase be equally divided between my nine children, *Ellinor, Nicholas, Maurice, Richard, George, Mary, William, Haynes* and *Anne.*

Item—I give the remainder of my Negroes to my afors'd children, Ellinor, Nicholas, Maurice, Richard, George, Mary, William, Haynes and Anne equally to be divided, and my will is that my said Children's Negroes work on my wife's third of my Land for their maintenance and support until they severally come to age or marry.

Item—I give the Remainder of my personal Estate to my said wife and *her Nine Children* equally to be divided, and my will and meaning is that in case either of my aforsaid children Ellinor, Nicholas, Maurice, Richard, George, Mary, William, Haynes and Anne die before they come to age or marry that his or her Negroes and personal Estate be divided amongst the brothers and sister of the whole blood, and not otherwise.

Item—I give to my good friend Robert Edwards son of Mr. Thos. Edwards, one of my best sows and pigges.

Item—I do nominate and appoint my afor'd wife and my sons Nicholas and Maurice whole and sole Executors of this my last Will and Testament and I do revoke all other Wills by me heretofore made. Lastly, I do desire my friends Mr. Thos. Edwards and Mr. Thos. Pinckard to be my Trustees to advise and direct my afor'd Executors as also my children in their management of their Estates. In Testimony whereof and this in writing contains my true last will and Testament, I have hereunto set my hand and affixed my seal this 26th Day of October Anno Dom. 1748.

Hugh Brent (Seal)

Negroes and personal interlined in the bequest of the residue of my personal Estate interlined before signing. Sealed and Delivered and Published and Declared by Mr. Hugh Brent before named to be his last Will and Testament in presence of
T. Edwards
John Horton
George Horton
Willoughby Allerton
Richard Edwards

At a Court held for Lancaster County the 11th day of May 1750 this will was proven in open Court by the oath of Thos. Edwards, gent., a witness thereto, and ordered to be recorded.

Test—Thos. Edwards, Gent., clerk.

At a Court held for Lancaster County on the 13th day of July, 1750, this will was further proven in open Court by the oath of George Horton and ordered to be Certified.

Test—Thos. Edwards, Gent., Clerk.

Children 1st marriage:

+ 16   I   James, b. *cir.* 1706 in Christ Church Parish, Lancaster County; d. 1750; m. 26 July 1727, Catherine (Newton) Martin.

   17   II   Haynes, d. v. p.

   18   III   Morrice, d. v. p.

+ 19   IV   William, b. *cir.* 1710; d. 1738 in Northumberland County, intestate; m. *cir.* 1733, Elizabeth Lee.

+ 20   V   Hugh, b. ——; d. 1750/1; m. Catherine Martin.

   21   VI   John, d. v. p.

+ 22   VII   Katherine, b. ——; d. ——; m. 19 Aug. 1734, Merryman Payne, son of Wm. and Judith Payne, and grandson of Wm. Payne and his wife Susanna Merryman.

   23   VIII Elizabeth.

Children 2nd marriage:

   24   IX   Ellinor, m. before 1748, probably Capt. John Heath of Northumberland County (named in her father's will "Ellinor Heath").

[43]

25 x Nicholas, probably d. s. p.

26 xi Maurice, b. *cir.* 1732; d. 1782, in Richmond County; m. (i) Lucy Flower (46), 16 July 1764; m. (ii) Sinah ——, who m. later —— Lewis.
1 Hugh.

+ 27 xii Richard, b. *cir.* 1734; d. 1771; m. Anne ——; she died before 1782.

28 xiii George.

+ 29 xiv Mary, b. *circa* 1738; m. Col. John Gibson, who is living in Faquier County, 1787 (*Va. Mag.*, Vol. 23, p. 326).

+ 30 xv William, b. *circa* 1740; d. 1806; m. 20 May 1779, Ellinor Stott, widow.

+ 31 xvi Haynes, b. *circa* 1742, in Lancaster County, and died 1801 in Princess Ann County, Va.; m. 1 Feb. 1776, Tamer Gamewell, in Princess Ann County. She was probably relict of Lawrence Gamewell (w. 1774).

32 xvii Ann, mentioned in will of her brother Haynes as "Nancy" in 1801; probably died unmarried.

[12] WILLIAM³ BRENT (Hugh², Hugh¹), was born in Lancaster County, Va., *circa* 1685, and died 1740, July-Aug. He married (i), Sarah Fleet,* daughter of Capt. Henry Fleet (w. 1733), and his wife Elizabeth, daughter of Jane Wildey of Northumberland County; m. (ii), 7 Jan. 1723/4, Margaret Haynes, daughter of James Haynes (d. 1726, in Princess Ann County, Va.) and Frances Pinckard, dau. of Capt. John Pinckard, who was Burgess for Lancaster County, 1688; m. (iii), 9 Aug. 1734, Letitia Wale,** daughter of John and Alice Wale. She was born 17 Aug. 1711 and died 26 April 1776. She married second, William Griggs, *circa* 1744. John Wale married 1705, Alice Wright, relict of Samuel Wright (Lancaster O. B., 13 March 1705).

Att this Court Mr. Thomas Crompton, Mercht., Records Mr. Wm Brent his attorney (L. O. B., 14 March 1715, p. 124).

*See Fleete Family.
**See Wale Family.

Ordered that Wm Brent be Surveyor of ye highway in this County in ye room and precinct of Henry Fleet, Junior, and that he clear and amend ye roads according to Law (L. O. B., 13 Aug. 1718, p. 246).

On motion of Hugh Brent, Wm. Brent is sworn under sheriff (L. O. B., 14 Aug. 1734, p. 115).

The following deeds made by William Brent, together with his will proves, as well as separates his children by his three wives.

I *William Brent* of Christ Church Parish Lancaster County for the love and affection I have for my two children born of the body of *Sarah Brent* dec'd, To say *Elizabeth Brent* and *Major Richard Brent*, I give and bequeath to my two sd children four negroes as followeth: I give unto my daughter *Elizabeth Brent* one negro woman called Kate and all her future increase and one negro boy called Sam, to her and her heirs forever lawfully begotten of her body, the sd *Elizabeth Brent* to receive and enjoy ye aforsd negroes at ye age of eighteen years or day of marriage. I give to my son *Major Richard Brent* one negro girl called Beck and all her increase and one negro boy called Dick, to him and his heirs forever lawfully begotten of his body and if it should so happen, which God forbid, that ye sd *Elizabeth Brent* should dye before she attain to ye age of eighteen years or day of marriage, that ye aforsd negroes Kattie and Sam and increase to fall to my son *Major Richard Brent* and his heirs, and if it should so happen, wch God forbid, that ye sd. *Major Richard Brent* should dye before he comes to the age of twenty years or day of marriage that ye aforsd negroes to fall to my daughter *Elizabeth Brent* and her heirs.

My desire is that my son *Major Richard Brent* shall enjoy ye aforsd negroes Beck and Dick and all their increase when he arrives to ye age of twenty-one or day of marriage, as witness my hand and Seale this 12th day of March Anno Dom 1717.

William Brent (seal)

Signed Sealed
and delivered in
presence of
Thos. Thompson
Henry Fleet, Jr.

Recorded 12th March 1717.
(L. D. B. 11, p. 89)

[45]

Letitia Brent appeared in Court Oct. 10th, 1740 to ask that her unborn child share in her late husband's estate. Her claim was denied. The unborn child evidently turned out to be twins (John and Lettice).

Memorandum of a deed of gift from *Letitia Brent* to her three children:

I give to my son *John Brent* one Negro girl named Fanny and my best feather bed and furniture and one cow and calf. I give to my daughter *Lettice* one Negro boy named Harry and my next best feather bed and furniture and one cow and calf. I give to my son *James Brent* my gold ring reserving my life interest in the sd ring. Witness my hand this 26th day of Feb. 1744.

Lettice Brent

Wit: Bransford Flower
     George Wale
     John Wale

(L. D. B. 14, p. 53)

Will of WILLIAM BRENT, 1740, Lancaster County

In the Name of God Amen, I *William Brent* of the parish of Christ Church and County of Lancaster being very sick and weak in Body, but of perfect mind and memory thanks be to God for it, Calling unto Mind the Mortality of my Body, and knowing that it is appointed for all Men once to die, do make and Ordain this my last Will and Testament in manner and form following.

Imprs: I Give and Recommend my Soul into the hands of God that gave it, and my Body to the Earth, to be buried in a decent manner according to the discretion of my Exors. hereafter named, not doubting but at the Genl. Resurrection I shall receive the same again by ye mighty power of God, and as touching such Worldly Estate wherewith it hath pleased the Almighty God to bless me in this Life, I give, devise and dispose of the same in manner and form following—

Item: I give and bequeath unto my Son *Wm.* all my Lands and Tenements, to him and his Male heirs, and in case of his decease without such Issue, I Give and Bequeath all my Said Lands and Tenements unto my Son *James* and the Male heirs of his Body, and in case of his decease without such Issue, then I Give and

[46]

Bequeath all my Said Lands and Tenements unto my next Lawful male heir.

Item: It is my Will and desire that my Loving Wife *Letitia* do live on the said plantation during her Widowhood.

Item: It is my will and desire that my two daugh^{rs}, *Sarah* and *Frances* do dwell upon the said plantation or anywhere Else according to the discretion of my Exors. hereafter named.

Item: It is my Will and Pleasure that my Son *Wm.* do observe and follow the Orders and directions of Mr. James Haynes one of my Exors until he arrive at the age of twenty one years or day of marriage according to ye discretion of my Exors hereafter named.

Item: It is my desire that my Children may be debarred from the Liberty of Choosing Guardians, and to be under the Immediate care of my Exors hereafter named until they arrive to the age of twenty one years or day of Marriage provided it be with the consent of my Exors.

Item: Whereas I have lent unto my Daughter *Elizabeth Hinton* a horse and Sundry Cattle and Sheep, It is my Will and desire, and I do give and bequeath unto my said Daugh^{r}. *Eliz^{a}.* the afforsaid Horse Cattle and Sheep, and their Increase, to be in right of all or any Claim or Claims, She hath or may have, to any part of my Estate.

Item: I Give and bequeath unto my Son *William* my Gun, Pistols, holsters and Sword, and also a case of Bottles to him and his heirs.

Item: I lend unto my Loving Wife a Negro fellow named Jack during her Widdowhood, and in case of her decease then to be equally divided amongst my children to Witt, *Sarah, Frances, William* and *James.*

Item: I give unto my Friend Robert Biscoe the sum of Four hundred pounds of Tobacco or forty shillings.

Item: All the rest of my Estate of what nature or kind soever I Give to be equally divided between my Wife and Children, to Witt. *Sarah, Frances, William* and *James*, and in case of Either said Children's Decease in their nonage, or without Issue, It is my desire that the said Child or Children's part or parts may be Equally divided amongst my Surviving Child or Children as afforsaid, my Daughter *Eliz^{a}. Hinton* only Excepted.

[47]

Item: It is my Will and desire that my Estate be not appraised.

Item: I do nominate and appoint my Loving Broth^r. *Mr. Hugh Brent*, Mr. James Haynes, Capt. Wm. Steptoe, and my Cozen *Mr. James Brent* to be my sole and only Exors to this my Last Will and Testament. IN WITNESS whereof I have hereunto Set my hand and Seal this Second day of July 1740.

William Brent (seal)

SIGNED SEALED AND DELIVERED
IN PRESENCE OF

Isaac Currell
Jane Heard
Robt. Biscoe

At a Court held for Lancaster County on the 8th day of August 1740 This will was proved in open Court by the oaths of Isaac Currell Jane heard and Robert Biscoe witnesses thereto and admitted to record and is Recorded.

Test   T. Edwards Cl Cur

Children, first marriage:

33 I Major Richard, d. v. p.

+ 34 II Elizabeth, b. *cir.* 1715; d. after 1785; m. (I), *cir.* 1735, Samuel Hinton (w. 1771) of Lancaster County, Va.; m. probably (II), 30 Dec. 1774, Thomas Hunton (L. M. B.).

Children, second marriage:

35 III Sarah, d. before 17 Dec. 1762.

36 IV Frances, b. *cir.* 1727; m. 10 Nov. 1747, Wm. Carter (L. M. B.).

+ 37 V William, b. *cir.* 1726; m. (I) 11 May 1753, Judith King, wid.; m. (II), in Sussex County, 19 April 1779, Mary Parham, wid.

Children, third marriage:

+ 38 VI James, b. *cir.* 1736, in Lancaster County; d. *cir.* 1815, at "Wellington," Nelson County, Va.; m. 4

Oct. 1768, Sarah Cammell, relict of Jas. Cammell,
Jr., and dau. of William Doggett (w. 1772) and
Johanna (Wale) Doggett. Johanna Wale was dau. of
John and Alice (——-Wright) Wale.

39 VII   Lettice, b. posthumously, 1741, one of twins.

40 VIII John, b. posthumously, 1741, twin of above.

[13] GEORGE³ BRENT (Hugh², Hugh¹), was born in Lancaster
County, Va., *cir.* 1690, and died: his will was written 6 July 1748,
probated 12 Aug. 1748. He was of age in 1716, when he was
ordered to participate in the settlement of his dec'd father's
estate with his brothers, Hugh, the eldest, and William, the second
son. There was a *George Brent* apprenticed to Rodham Kenner of
Westmoreland County before 1700. He married Judith, daughter
of Tobias* and Mary Pursell, by March, 1715, viz:

Ordered that ye Honorable Robert Carter, Esq one of
the Exors of the Laft Will and Testamt: of Tobias Pursell
dec'd be made acquainted that he is desired by this Court
to appear at ye next Court With Mary Pursell the other
Exor who is ordered to be cited to ye sd next Court to
ansfer ye complaint of *George Brent* and Judith his wife
relating to their part of ye sd Tobias Pursells Estate
(*Lancaster Order Book*, 14 March, 1715, p. 123).

George Brent, Planter, bought land in Lancaster County, 1715:

This Indenture made the eight day of Sept. Anno Dom
1720 Between David Flukor of Northumberland County,
Taylor, of the one part and *George Brent*, Planter, of Lancaster County of the other Part WITNESSETH That the
Sd. David Flukor for and in consideration of one Negro
woman named Dinah and two thousand five hundred
pounds of merchantable Tobacco and three casques clear
of all charges to him in hand paid by the aforsd *George
Brent* the receipt thereof he the sd David Flukor doth
hereby acknowledge and thereof and of every part and
parsel thereof doth fully acquit exonerate and Discharge
the aforsd *George Brent* his heirs . . . by these presents
hath given aliened bargained enfeoffed . . . all that
plantation . . . in the P'sh of Church in the County of

*Tho: Pursell, aged 26 yeares, aboard the *Constance*, Clement Campion, Mr
(master), bound to Virginia, 24 Octobris 1635 (Hotten, p. 136).

Lancaster aforsd containing one hundred and fifty acres of Land and is the same . . . that was sold by William King of the county of Lancaster and since Deceased To a certain David Flukor . . . father to him the sd David Flukor party to these presents who was eldest son and heir at law . . . in the Year of our Lord 1692.

David Flukor (seal)

Wit: Geo. Wale
     Hugh Brent
     William Coan

At a Court held for Lancaster County ye 14th day of Septm. Anno Dom 1720 this deed with Livery and Seizin thereon Endorsed was acknowledged by David Flukor unto *George Brent* and at his motion ordered to be recorded and is recorded this 17th day of Septem.

Wm. Dale Cl Cur.

George Brent, Planter, buys land from the Pasquott Indians, 12 Nov. 1720. Hugh Brent is one of the witnesses.

George Brent Att this court made application to be allowed for a certifict. for taking up a runaway Negroe named Red belonging to Mr. Thomas Glasscock in Richmond County above ten miles from his masters houfe and has made oath that he never recd any satisfaction for ye same (Lancaster Orders, 27 July 1715, p. 104).

George Brent appointed Constable 13 May 1730 (Lancaster County Orders, 1729-40, p. 13).

George Brent and James Pollard were appointed Tobaccoe viewers in the upper district of Lancaster County, 10 Nov. 1725 (*Ibid.*, p. 384).

Will of GEORGE BRENT of Lancaster County
(W. B. 10, p. 206)

In the name of God Amen, I, *George Brent* of the Parish of Christ Church in the County of Lancaster and Colony of Virginia, being very sick and weak in body, but of perfect mind and memory, thanks be to God, therefore, calling to mind the uncertainty when death will happen to me and knowing that it is appointed for all men once to die and for the better settlement of my worldly affairs do make and appoint this my last will and testament.

Imprimis, I give and bequeath my soul to almighty God who first gave it me, my body to the earth to be Buried in a Christian decent manner at the discretion of my Ext. herein and hereafter mentioned, in hopes of a joyfull meeting and reuniting again by the mighty power of God at the great and general resurrection to life eternal and that I shall be found in Christ, the only Redeemer of mankind, and through his precious merits and mediation receive a general pardon of all my sinfull crimes and a happy admission into his Heavenly Kingdom, and as for what worldly estate it hath pleased God to bless me with, all I give (after my debts and funeral expenses are first paid) in manner and form following:

Item: I give and bequeath all my land and appurtenances to my son, *George Brent*, and to the male heirs of his body lawfully begotten and for want of such heirs to my son, *Charles Brent*, and his heirs forever.

Item: I give and bequeath to my son, *Charles Brent*, sixty pounds Curr: money to be paid him in cash, to be paid him by his two brothers and three sisters or raised out of the estate given them to be paid him to enable him to buy land with.

Item: It is my will that my son Charles, and my daughter *Lucy Brent* have a home here upon my plantation and in my houses till they arrive to age and likewise liberty to work their people till that time.

Item: I give and bequeath to my sons, *George Brent* and *Charles Brent* and my daughter, *Lucy Brent*, each of them half dozen plates, three dishes, three Basons, one bed and furniture with a dozen spoons and one iron pot to be first set apart out of the best of my estate before any division be made.

Item: I give and bequeath to my son *Thomas Brent*, one sixth part of my negroes and their increase, to him and his heirs forever.

Item: I give and bequeath to my son, *George Brent*, and his heirs forever, one sixth part of my negroes and their increase.

Item: I give and bequeath to my son *Charles Brent*,

[51]

and his heirs forever, one sixth part of my negroes and their increase.

Item: I give and bequeath to my daughter, *Amy Hains* and her heirs forever, one sixth part of my negroes and their increase.

Item: I give and bequeath to my daughter *Lucy Brent* and her heirs, forever, one sixth part of my negroes and their increase.

Item: I give to my daughter *Judyth King* the use and profit of one sixth part of my negroes during her natural life and the property of the said negroes and their increase; I give to my three grandchildren, viz: *Wm. King, John King* and *Mary King*, the children of my daughter *Judyth King*, to them and their heirs forever, to be possessed by them at the death of their mother by an equal division.

Item: I give and bequeath to my son, *George Brent*, my Gun Holsters and pistols.

Item: I give and bequeath to my son *Thomas Brent* and my son *George Brent* and their heirs my still Etc.

Item: I give to my two daughters *Judith King* and *Lucy Brent*, thirty-five shillings Curr money to buy them rings.

Item: I give and bequeath all my wearing cloths to be equally divided between my two sons, Thomas and George.

Item: I give and bequeath all my household goods and stock of what kind soever to be equally divided amongst my six children, viz: *Thomas Brent, George Brent, Charles Brent, Judith King, Amy Haynes*, and *Lucy Brent*, only my son *Thomas Brent* is to allow out of his part of stock, two cows and calves to the rest of his brothers and sisters, he having already received them and also forty-five shillings current money on account of a mare received already.

Item: I give and bequeath to my daughter, *Lucy Brent*, one silver spoon. I do hereby by these presents appoint and nominate my two sons, *Thomas Brent* and *George Brent* and my friend Anth° Kirk to be my Exors. of this my last will and testament disanulling and revoking all other wills and ratifying and confirming this to be my last will. In witness whereof, I have affixed my hand and seale this 6th day of July 1748:

George Brent (Seal)

Signed and published and sealed in presence of us:
John + Hubbard
John Norris
Dale Carter   at a Court held for Lancaster County on the 12th day of Aug. 1748.

This will was proved in open Court by the oaths of Dale Carter, gen't, John Hubbard and John Norris, witnesses, thereto, and admitted to record and is recorded.

Test   Thomas Edwards, Jr.
C. L. C.

Children:

+ 41   I   Thomas, b. 1724; d. "in 58th year," 13 Oct. 1781; m. 19 Nov. 1741, Anne Yerby, daughter of Thomas (w. 1756) and Hannah (Doggett) Yerby (w. 1761), who were married 22 Feb. 1717/8.

+ 42   II   George, b. ——; d. ——, 1778; m. *circa* 1750, Margaret, daughter of Elizabeth Simmons (w. 1774). She died 1784.

43   III   Charles, "youngest son"; d. s. p. 1772.

44   IV   Amy, b. ——; d. ——; m. (I) *circa* 1745, James Haynes, Jr., son of James and Sarah (——) Haynes, and he died 1748; m. (II) 23 July 1750, Harry Carrell.

Children (HAYNES):

1 Elizabeth Weathers, m. 26 Dec. 1762, Capt. Thomas Snail.

2 Judith, m. 19 May 1768, Henry Towles.

+ 45   V   Judith, b. ——; d. ——; m. (I) *circa* 1748, John King, who died 1752; m. (II) 2 May 1753, William Brent (37).

46   VI   Lucy, b. ——; d. ——; m. 21 Aug. 1758, George Flower, son of George and Elizabeth (——) Flower; m. (II) 16 July 1764, Maurice Brent (18).

[53]

Children (FLOWER):

1 George.
2 John.
3 Betty, m. before 1774, Robt. Roebuck, and had at least Lucy, who m. 24 Oct. 1794, Jas. Connoly.
4 Ann, m. 27 Dec. 1783, Henry Chilton.

[14] CHARLES[3] BRENT (Hugh[2], Hugh[1]), was born in Lancaster County, Va., *circa* 1695, probably the youngest son. He is named in the deed with his sister Mary as receiving slaves from his father in 1710 [see notes under Hugh(5)]. As he was not mentioned in the court order issued to his two older brothers, he must have gone to Richmond or Stafford County before his father's death. He married *circa* 1725, Hannah Innis, daughter of James Innis of Richmond County. James Innis died in Richmond County, 1710.

Charles Brent died in Overwharton Parish, Stafford County, Va. 13 Jan. 1756. Hannah (Innis) Brent died 4 Feb. to 13 April 1762, in Stafford County.

The following Grant of land to Charles Brent is recorded:

The Rt. Honble: Thos. Lord Fairfax of Leeds in the County of Kent Baron of Cameron in Scotland Wm Page of Milgate in ye Parish of Bearstead in ye said County of Kent Esqr. Devisee in trust and Sole Exec. of ye last Will and Testament of Ye Honble Catherine Lady Fairfax Dec'd proprs of ye Northern Neck of Virga to all whom this present writeing shall come greeting

Know Ye that for diverse good causes and considerations of Ye Compo: for our use paid unto our Agent and Attorney and for Ye Annual Rent hereafter reserved, Wee have Given Granted and Confirmed and by these presents for us our heirs and assignes Do Give Grant and Confirm —unto *Mr. Charles Brent*—of King George County One Certain Tract or parcell of Land Containing 506 acres Situated lying and being in the Counties of Stafford and King George and bounded as followeth viz: Beginning at a post of Wm. Hackneys in a Poyson fieild between three white oaks, thence along Hackneys line S. 85° E. 214 po: to a White Oak thence N. 70° E. 73 po: to a White Oak in a Valley between three Angular trees; thence S. 14° E. 82 po: to a red Oak in Michael Douments line, thence along Doument's line N. 10° E. 260 po: to a post in Douments line on ye west Side of a branch between three Angular trees, thence along ye line of Literal S. 69° W. 103 po: to a white Oak in a Valley between three Angular trees, thence along Berry's line N. 64° W. 358 po: to a post on ye West side of a small branch of Elk run between Six inward marked trees, Thence S. 10° E. 336 po: to a Post in Finis line Thence S. 32-12° E. 26 po: to the first station Together with all Rights Members and Appurtenances Thereunto belonging Royal Mines excepted and a full third part of all Lead, Copper, Tin, Coals, Iron Mines and Iron ore that shall be found thereon To Have and to Hold the said five hundred and six acres of Land and Together with all Rights Profits and benefits to ye Same belonging or in any wise appertaining Except before Excepted to him ye said *Chas. Brent* his heirs and assigns forever, he ye said *Charles Brent* his heirs and assignes therefore Yielding and paying to us our heirs and assignes or to ye certain Attorney or Attorneys Agent or Agents of us ye Sd proprs of ye said Northern Neck Yearly and every Year on ye Feast of Saint Michael ye Archangel ye fee Rent of one Shilling Sterling money for every fifty acres of Land hereby granted and so proportionately for a greater or less quantity provided that if ye said *Charles Brent* his heirs or Assignes shall not pay ye before reserved Annual rent, so that ye sum or any part thereof shall be behind or unpaid by ye space of two whole years after ye same shall Become due if lawfully demanded that then it shall and may be lawful for us our heirs or Assignes, Proprs as aforesaid Our or Their Certain Attorney or Attorneys Agent or Agents into ye above granted premises to reenter and hold ye same so as if this Grant had never passed.

Given at our Office in Lancaster County within our said Proprietary under our Seal Witness our Agent and Attorney fully Authorized thereto Dated ye third day of December in ye second Year of ye reign of our Sovereign Lord George ye Second, of Great Britain France Ireland King Defender of the Faith and Anno Dom 1728 (*Book "A,"* p. 164, Va. Land Office).

Descendants of Hugh Brent

Will of Charles Brent, 1756

In the name of God Amen, I, *Charles Brent,* Gent. in the parish of Overwharton in the County of Stafford, being mindful of the frailty and uncertainty of human nature and that it is appointed for all men once to die, but considering the uncertainty of the time thereof, being of sound mind, memory and judgment do therefore make this my last will and testament in manner and form following, that is to say First and principally I commit my Soul to Almighty God, my body to the Earth there to be decently buried according to the discretion of My Executors undernamed.

All my debts lawfully contracted I desire may first be honestly paid and then what worldly estate it hath pleased God to bless me with, I dispose of as follows.

Imprimis. I give bequeath to my loving son *Charles Brent* two negroes named Ned and Beck and their future increase, and one equal part of all my household goods and stock to him and his heirs forever.

Item. I give and bequeath to my loving son *Hugh Brent* two negroes named Harry and Will and one equal part of all my household goods and stock to him and his heirs forever.

Item. I will and bequeath to my loving sons *William* and *George Brent* six negroes named Sam, Ben, Jenny, Dinah, Lucy and Grace and the future increase to be divided between them when they come to age, with one equal part of all my household goods and stock each of them and their heirs forever.

Item. I will and bequeath to my loving daughter *Catherine Wren*, three negroes named Mall, Sarah and Hannah and their future increase and one equal part of all my household goods and stock including what she hath already received to be part of the same to her and her heirs forever.

Item. I give and bequeath to my loving daughter *Mary Brent* two negroes, named George and Winny and their increase and one equal part of all my household goods and stock to her and her heirs forever.

Item. I give and bequeath to my daughter *Ann Brent* two negroes named James and Phillis and their future increase and one equal part of all my household goods and stock to her and her heirs forever.

Item. I lend to my dear and loving wife, *Hannah Brent*, six negroes named Tom, Forrester, Dick, Betty, Judah, and Sonnah during her life or widowhood and then to be divided between my four children *Hugh Brent, William Brent, George Brent, Ann Brent* except any of *Charles Brent's* or *Mary Brent's* negroes should die before my wife's death or the division then what negroes are wanting to them if it shall so happen shall be made up to them out of those I lent my wife, and the remainder only shall be divided between the above mentioned persons. I also give unto my said loving wife one equal part of my household goods and stock.

Item. I desire that all my horses or mares I have given to any of my children before this day may be reckoned as part of their Est. and not appraised as part of mine. Also that the crop of corn and tobacco now growing may not be appraised and that my wife and family may have the benefit of it.

It is my will and desire that all my children shall be paid of their fortunes when they arrive to the age of twenty one, or at their marriage if it is previous to that said age.

Item. If either of my children shall die before age or marriage as aforesaid, my will is that their respective share or shares shall be equally divided among the survivors of them. Lastly I nominate my said dear and loving wife Hannah Brent and appoint her Exectr. of this my last will and testament, and guardian if she remain a widow, and I also appoint my two sons *Charles Brent* and *Hugh Brent* to be joined with her when they shall come of age. But should it please God that my said wife should die before my said sons shall come to age, or if she shall marry before that time, I nominate my friend and neighbor Mr. Peter Daniel Exer. and guardian to my children in her stead, confiding in his friendship to advise and assist her—and them to the best of his power, and I hereby revoke and disanull all former wills by me made, and declare this writing contained in this and the foregoing page only to be my last will and testament. In Witness

[57]

whereof I have hereunto set my hand and affixed my seal this 26th day of Aug. in the year of our Lord 1755.

Charles Brent (Seal)

In the presence of
John Anderson, Clemt Cheveral, Mary Cheveral
Sarah Daniel, Mary Carter.

At a court held for Stafford County 13th. April 1756, the within last will and testament of *Charles Brent* dec'd was presented into court by *Hannah Brent* Exer. therein named who made oath thereto according to law and the will was proved by the oaths of two of the witnesses of the will, and a Certificate was granted to the widow for obtaining a probate thereof in due form.

The Will of HANNAH BRENT, 1762

In the name of God Amen, I, *Hannah Brent* of the County of Stafford and Parish of Overwharton being sick and weak of body but in perfect sound memory, do therefore make this my last will and testament in manner and form following this is to say. First and principally I commit my Soul to Almighty God my blessed Creator my body to the Earth, there to be decently buried according to the directions of my Ex'r., hereinafter named. All my debts lawfully contracted I desire may be lawfully and justly paid and then what worldly estate it has pleased God to bless me with I dispose of as follows.

Imprimis. I give and bequeath to my loving son *Charles Brent* four bushels of wheat.

Item. I give and bequeath to my loving son *Hugh Brent* one sorrel mare named Fly.

Item. I give to my loving son *George Brent* one English colt, out of the Sorrel Mare.

Item. I give to my loving daughter *Ann Brent* one bay horse colt.

Item. I give to my loving daughter *Catherine Wren* five shillings current money.

Item. I give to my daughter *Mary Lewis* five shillings current money.

Item. All the rest of my estate I give to my loving sons

William Brent and *George Brent* to be equally divided between them.

Lastly I nominate and appoint my loving son *Hugh Brent* Ex'r of this my last Will and testament.

In Witness Whereof I have hereunto set my hand and affixed my Seal this 4th day of Feby in the year of our Lord 1762.

Hannah Brent. Seal.

Witnesses: Peter Daniel, Sarah Daniel.

The above will was probated at a Court held in Stafford County on April 13th, 1762.

Children, from Overwharton Parish Register, Stafford Co.:

47	I	Innis, b. 24 July 1727; probably d. s. p. as he is not mentioned in either his father's or mother's will, nor do I find any other mention of him.
48	II	Catherine, b. 13 Jan. 1729; d. ——; m. 27 March 1753, James Wren of Fairfax County.
49	III	Mary, b. 25 May 1732; d. ——; m. 24 Aug. 1756, Zacharias Lewis of Prince William County.
+ 50	IV	Charles, b. 11 June 1735; d. 11 April 1822, in Frederick County, Va.; m. 1761, Anna Gunnell. She was b. 16 Feb. 1744; d. by June 1826—her will was written 2 June 1824: probated 6 June 1826, in Frederick County, Va.
51	V	Ann, b. 5 Dec. 1737; d. ——; m. Hugh Atwell, of Loudon County, Va.
+ 52	VI	Hugh, b. 3 Nov. 1739; d. *cir.* 1813, near Paris, Ky.; m. 19 Oct. 1764, Elizabeth Baxter. She was born 17 Oct. 1746.
+ 53	VII	William, b. 14 May 1742; d. 1800, in Faquier County; m. *circa* 1765 Hannah Neale of Fairfax County, dau. of Christopher Neale.
54	VIII	George, b. 7 June 1744; d. ——; m. —— Wilson.
55	IX	James, b. *circa* 1746; d. 6 Sept. 1754.

[15] MARY[3] BRENT (Hugh[2], Hugh[1]), was born in Lancaster County, Va. When the Christ Church Parish Register is found, if ever, the many hundreds of dates will be forthcoming! I did not

[59]

ry to search the records for the Carter obituaries, as I would have had too many deductions to work out. In Miller's *History of the Carter Family*, she is listed as a "spinster" when she married James Carter, widower, 10 Aug. 1724. This marriage was made in Lancaster County, but fortunately they soon moved to Stafford where the watchful eye of Mr. Moncure checked on the births and deaths and marriages most diligently—the whites and blacks with equal patience.

"James Carter, an honest good man, died Oct. 24th, 1743." He was the 8th son of Capt. Thomas Carter and his wife Catherine Dale, dau. of Edward and his wife Diana Dale, and was born at "Barford" Lancaster County, Va., on Xmas Day 1684, "it being a Thursday, at 2 in ye Morn^g." James Carter m. (1), 3 Oct. 1715, Hannah Neale, who d. 9 Oct. 1722. Mr. Miller, in his history states that James Carter was one of the largest landowners in Stafford County.

Mary (Brent) Carter outlived her husband. She was one of witnesses to her brother Charles Brent's will 1756, and Charles Brent is one of Exors. to James Carter's will.

Will of JAMES CARTER, Stafford County, Va.

IN the Name of God amen I James Carter of Overwharton Parish in the County of Stafford being Sick and weak of body but of sound mind and perfect memory thanks to Almighty God, and calling to remembrance the frailty and uncertainty of human life have made this my last will and Testamt in manner following. I —— Give and committ my Soul into the hands of my Mercifull Creator, hoping for remission of my Sins through the Merits of my blessed redeemer Jesus Christ; My body I leave to be buried at the discretion of my Ex.rs and trustee hereafter Named. Imp.s (after my Just debts are honestly paid) I give and bequeath to my sons JOHN and GEORGE all that tract of Land on the North side of Acquia Creek where I now Live to be Equally divided between them only that my Eldest son JOHN should have the half on which my dwelling house now Stands to them and their Heirs forever; but if either or both of them should die without heirs of their body then I give and bequeath the reversion of all or either of their Shares to my son HUGH and the Heirs of his body forever and in case of default of Such Heirs to be Equally divided among all my Surviving Sons.

Item I give to my Sons JAMES and WILLIAM my Lands in Fairfax County after William Brewster has gott his complement which I sold him out of it to be Equally divided between my said Sons to them and their Heirs forever but if either of them Should die without Heirs I bequeath the reversion of their Part or parts thereof to my son GEORGE and his Heirs forever and in case of Default of Such Heirs to be Equally divided among my Surviving Sons. Item I give and bequeath two Negroes Mingo and Sharlott with her Increase to my son HUGH and the heirs of his body. Item I give to my son CHARLES and his Heirs two Negroes Sue and Winney and their Increase. Item I give to my Daughter ANN and her Heirs two Negroes great Dick and Hannah with her Increase. Item I give to my Daughter CATHERINE and her Heirs two Negroes Robin and Dinah with her Increase. Item what negroes I die possessed of not yet willed or bequeathed I leave to my Dear and Loving WIFE MARY during her widowhood only and after her marrying again or decease to be Equally divided among my Surviving Children. Item my Personal Estate I leave to be Equally divided among my wife and children or the Survivors of them. Lastly I nominate and appoint my Dear and Loving WIFE MARY and CHARLES BRENT Executors of this my last will and Testament and my son JOHN to be joined with them as soon as he comes of Age. And I appoint the REVER.D MR. JOHN MONCURE a guardian to my children and as a trustee to See this will Executed. Hereby revoking and disannulling all former wills by me made and declaring this only to be my last will and Testam.t.

IN WITNESS whereof I have hereunto Set my hand and Seal this 23d day of October 1743.

James Carter

Signed Sealed and published before us.   Seal
  Thomas Eves
  Wm. Knight
  Jean + Turner
    (her mark)

At a Court held for Stafford County March the 13th 1743 The within last will and Testament of James Carter decd was presented in Court by MARY CARTER and CHAS. BRENT two of the Exrs. therein Named who made Oath thereto according to law and being further proved by the witnesses thereto is admitted to record and these having complied with what is usual in Such cases certificate is granted them for obtaining a probat thereof in due form.

Test. H. Tyler, Cl. Cur.

(Stafford County, Va., Wills, 1729-1748, p. 391)

Children, from Overwharton Parish Register (CARTER):

56   I   John, b. 7 May 1727; d. ——; m. prob. Mary Butler, 4 Feb. 1745 (O. P. Reg.).

57   II   James, b. 31 March 1729.

58   III   William, b. 11 Jan. 1731.

59   IV   George, b. 25 March 1733.

60   V   Catherine, b. 1 April 1735; d. ——; m. 27 Nov. 1755, Wm. Davis(?) (O. P. R.).

61   VI   Hugh, b. 8 Nov. 1740.

62   VII   Charles, b. 10 Oct. 1743.

63   VIII   Ann, b. ——; d. ——; m. 28 Nov. 1745, Joseph Butler (O. P. R.).

[16] JAMES[4] BRENT (Hugh[3], Hugh[2], Hugh[1]), was born *circa* 1706, in Lancaster County, Va., the son of Hugh Brent and his first wife, Ellinor Haines. He died 1750, his will being probated on the same day as his father's; married 26 July, 1727, Catherine Martin, relict of Thomas Martin, and daughter of Capt. Thomas Newton, and his wife Elizabeth Storke. She died 1761, in Lancaster County, Va.

Capt. Thomas Newton, in his will written 28 Aug. 1727, probated 31 Jan., 1727 (old style), gives to daughter *Katherine Brent* "negroes in her possession."

Hugh (11) Brent, gives to his son James Brent and wife Catherine, land, 8 Nov. 1738. (See other data under Hugh[3] Brent.)

[62]

James Brent, in his will written 19 April, and probated 11 May 1750 names wife Katherine, and mentions children, but does not name them.

James Brent appointed surveyor of the highways from Mr. (Wm.) Paynes to Mr. Burgess's Mill in St. Mary's Church Parish, 14 June 1732. He took the oath as under sheriff, 10 Dec. 1735.

Children, from Catherine Brent's will:

+ 64   I   Hugh, b. *circa* 1728; d. 7 Feb. 1778; m. (I), 6 Sept., 1750, Susannah Payne, dau. of George Payne and Frances Edmonds; m. (II), 26 Oct. 1761, Esther Shearman, dau. of Martin Shearman and Esther Chinn; m. (III), 30 Jan., 1766, Judith Kenner, relict of Brererton Kenner, and dau. of Capt. Willoughby Newton and his wife Sarah Eskridge. She d. 22 Jan., 1785.

+ 65   II   Sarah, b. *circa* 1730; d. 1778; m. 4 May 1747, Anthony Kirk. He d. Jan. 1764.

+ 66   III   Eleanor, b. *circa* 1732; d. ——; m. 5 Nov. 1750, Capt. William Stamps, with consent of Charles Chowning to Stamps' marriage.

+ 67   IV   Lucy, b. *circa* 1734, in Lancaster County; d. Mercer County, Ky.; m. 7 April, 1758, John Curd of Goochland County.

+ 68   V   John, b. *circa* 1739; d. 1781; m. *circa* 1760, Margaret Caldwell in Charlotte County, Va.

   69   VI   Willoughby, d. s. p.

   70   VII   Stockley, d. s. p. 1765.

   71   VIII   Beheathland ("my pet," in her mother's will).

EXCURSUS—BEHETHLAND

1 *Capt. Robert Behethland* came to Virginia with Capt. John Smith. His wife's name is unknown. He had among other children—

2 Mary, who married Capt. Thomas Bernard, of Warwick County, Va. and had—

3 Behethland Bernard (1635-1720), who married (I) Capt. Francis Dade, 1652; m. (II) Major Andrew Gilson of Stafford County, and had—

4 Behethland Gilson, who married Nehemiah Storke, and had—

5 Elizabeth Storke, who married Capt. Thomas Newton, and had—

6 Willoughby Newton (1702-1767), who married Sarah Eskridge (1707-1753), and also a daughter—

6 Catherine Newton, who married (I) Thomas Martin; m. (II) James Brent (16) (*W & M Quarterly*, 2nd Series, pp. 61 and 176).

EXCURSUS—NEWTON

1 *John Newton* died in Westmoreland County, Va. between 1695–1697. He married Rose, daughter of Dr. Thomas Gerrard (w. 1672), and had—

2 John, "eldest son," all lands at Carlton and Camilsforth in Yorkshire, England, and the house in Hull which was my fathers . . . also land bought of Joseph Laycock . . . to sd. son John and his four children; to Joseph and his four children; Benjamin and his daughter; Gerrard and his wife Rebecca; Elizabeth Newton; THOMAS—

3 Thomas Newton, above, married Elizabeth Storke, and died 1727 . . . his will names wife Elizabeth, son WILLOUGHBY, "land in Richmond County, near Totusky . . . 350 acres" . . . Elizabeth Waulhope . . . daughter KATHERINE BRENT, "negroes in her possession" . . . son Rev. Walter Jones and Behethland, his wife . . . grandson, Newton Keene.

4 Willoughby Newton, died in Westmoreland County, Va. 1766-1767. He married Sarah Eskridge (1707-1753), and names in his will, son John, and daughters JUDITH BRENT, Katherine, Lettice, Martha, Sarah, Elizabeth and Mary Newton. (Judith Newton m. (I) Brereton Kenner; m. (II) Capt. Hugh Brent–64).

[64]

[19] WILLIAM⁴ BRENT (Hugh³, Hugh², Hugh¹), was born *circa* 1710 in Lancaster County, Va., and died intestate in Northumberland County, Va., *circa* 1738. He married *circa* 1733, Elizabeth Lee, relict of Charles Lee, and daughter of Thomas Pinckard (w. 1740). Elizabeth died 1770 in Northumberland County. She names in her will daughters Elizabeth Lee and Jane Swan. Hugh Brent(11) in his will names granddaughter Mary, son of his deceased son William.

Children:
+ 72   I   Mary, m. Eppa Lawson before 1765.
   72-a II   Jane Swan, m. 27 Oct. 1781, William Nutt.

[20] HUGH⁴ BRENT (Hugh³, Hugh², Hugh¹), was born *circa* 1712 in Lancaster County, Va., and died—his will was written 14 June 1750, and probated 8 March 1750/1. He married *circa* 1745 Catherine Martin, daughter of Thomas and Catherine (Newton) Martin. She married the second time, 14 June 1751, Edward Carter and had issue by both marriages.

Will of Hugh Brent, 1750/1

In the name of God Amen I *Hugh Brent* of St. Marys White Chappell Parish in the County of Lancaster being sick and weak in body but of sound and perfect sense and memory do make and ordain this my last Will and Testament in manner and form as followeth: First I commit my body to the Earth from whence it came to be decently buried and my Soul into the hands of Almighty God who gave it, hoping to find forgiveness for all my sins. And for what worldly Estate it hath pleased God to endowe me with, I give and Bequeathe in manner and form as followeth.

Item. I give unto my deare and loving wife my large looking glass.

Item. I give unto my loving wife *Catherine Brent* four negroes during her natural life yt is James, Black Betty, old Dinah and Pocher, and I also give my negro man Incom and my negro wench Judith to my said wife During

[65]

her widowhood and the said negro Judith immediately after my wifes marriage to return to my daughter *Elizabeth Brent* with her increase.

Item. I give unto my said daughter before mentioned one negro girl named Hannah and one negro Boy named Dick to her and her heirs.

Item. I give unto my daughter *Catherine Brent* one negro boy named Harry and one negro girl named Sarah and one wench named Frankie, to her and her heirs.

Item. I give unto my daughter *Sarah Brent* one negro named Stephen and one negro girl named Dinah to her and her heirs.

I give unto my Daughter *Judith Brent* one negro man named Jack and one negro girl named Nan to her and her heirs.

Item. I leave my wife my deske and what chairs I have in my house at this time and her choice of the oval Tables. All the rest of my estate I leave to be equally Divided between my wife and children.

Item. I leave my wife and my cozzen *Hugh Brent* whole and sole Execor's of this my last Will and Testament as witness my hand this 14th day of June 1750.

Hugh Brent   Seal

Meryman Payne
Thos. Sharpe

At a Court held for Lancaster County on the 6th day of March 1750/1 This Will was proved in open Court by the oath of Merryman Payne Gent. and ordered to be recorded.

Children:

73	I	Elizabeth, m. 22 March 1762, William Pollard.
74	II	Catherine, m. 20 March 1762, Charles Rogers.
+ 75	III	Sarah, m. 16 Oct. 1764, Thomas Chinn, Jr.
+ 76	IV	Judith, m. 17 June 1765, John Bailey.

[22] KATHERINE[4] BRENT (Hugh[3], Hugh[2], Hugh[1]), was born in Lancaster County, Va., *circa* 1715, and died ——. She married 19 Aug. 1734, Merryman Payne, son of William Payne and Judith (Mitchell?). Merryman Payne died July 1773.

[66]

William Payne, above, was the son of another William who married Susannah Merryman, the daughter of Richard Merryman (w. 1696). Richard Merryman, in his will . . . "my worldly affairs I give to my beloved son and daughter William and Susannah Payne . . . my now dwelling plantation . . . Irbington . . . I give to my granson William Payne, Junior, being scituated on the Northside of the Rappahannock . . . also land Northside to my grandson Richard Payne . . . if said two should die without issue, to William and Susannah Payne . . ."

William, the father of Merryman Payne, in his will, names children Merryman, William, Susannah and Judith; also daughter-in-law Katherine, the wife of Mr. Bannerman; loving brother Mr. Robert Mitchell, loving friend Charles Burgess, honored mother Susannah Ladnar (*alias dictus* Merryman), the widow of ,William Payne who died between 1696 and 1700; she married Hugh Ladnar (II) who, in his will 1708, names a daughter Elizabeth, a minor . . . if she should die without issue, his estate to go to the children his wife had by her former marriage . . . William Payne "my son-in-law" (step-son).

Judith Payne (w. 1758), names children Merryman, William, Judith (m. 10 Oct. 1735, George Ball); grand-daughter Judith Ball, daughter-in-law Catherine Payne.

Merryman Payne was vestryman of the Parish of St. Mary's White Chapel 1740. He was attorney for William Payne of London, mariner, and his wife, Olivia Wilmot (Hayden).

Children, from Merryman Payne's will (PAYNE):

77 I Merryman, d. s. p. 1780.

78 II John, left issue, at least Catherine.

79 III Nicholas.

80 IV Daniel (w. 1774, written at Norfolk, Va.; he was probably a mariner with his uncle William. He leaves all of his estate to his brother, Nicholas).

[27] Lieut. RICHARD⁴ BRENT (Hugh³, Hugh², Hugh¹), was born in Lancaster County, Va., *circa* 1734. He died there 1771, or after (his will was written 16 May 1771; cannot find the pro-

bate). He married Anne ——. He was an officer in the State Navy, viz:

It is ordered that John Brent is the only heir of Richard Brent, dec'd, who died in the Navy Service of the State (Lancaster Orders, 1786-1789, p. 18).

Children, from his will:

81 I John, d. s. p. 1811. He married (I), 1 May 1791, Judith Norris, relict of William Norris, and daughter of John and Eleanor Horton (w. 1776-8). He married (II), 8 June 1796, Anne Degge, daughter of Isaac Degge. John Brent leaves all of his estate to his friend Spencer George—"all interest I have in the estate of Isaac Degge, dec'd, which I have in right of my late beloved wife Anne Brent . . . also to him the interest I have in my uncle's [Morris Brent (26)] estate in Richmond County . . ." Judith (Horton) Norris was the granddaughter of Tobias Horton and Martha Brent.

82 II Elizabeth.

83 III (daughter), m. Burgess Longwith, probably a son of Burgess Longwith of Westmoreland County, whose will was written 1751.

[29] MARY⁴ BRENT (Hugh³, Hugh², Hugh¹), was born *circa* 1738 in Lancaster County, Va., and died in Faquier County, Va. She married *circa* 1765, Col. John Gibson [See Mary Waddy Brent (131)]. He died 1788-91.

Children (probably others) (GIBSON):

I Ann Grayson, m. 41 Aug. 1787, Col. Joseph Blackwell of Faquier County, Va. She was his first wife, and died *circa* 1800.
Issue (BLACKWELL)—

1 Susan Gibson, b. 1789; m. 1805, George Pannill.

2 Ann Grayson, b. 1791; m. 20 March 1821, William Hughes, and had, George Hughes of Charlottesville, Va., and Samuel Blackwell Hughes of Richmond, Va.

3 William Taylor, b. 1793; d. in Adams County, Ill.

4 ——, d. in infancy.

5 ——, d. in infancy.

II   Thomas, m. 1782, Charlotte Beale of Faquier County, and left heirs (*Va. Mag.*, XXVIII).

III   John, m. Ann Eustace, 1783 in Faquier County.

IV   Jonathan Catlett, m. a Miss Mallory, and left heirs.

V   Susanna Grayson, m. 26 Nov. 1795, Wm. Berry Taylor and settled in Kentucky.

VI   Mary, m. 7 Dec. 1797, William Mallory and left heirs.

[30] WILLIAM[4] BRENT (Hugh[3], Hugh[2], Hugh[1]), was born in Lancaster County, Va., *circa* 1740, by his father's second wife, Elizabeth Morris, and was the second William in this family. He died 1806: his will was written 3 Jan. 1798, and probated 15 Dec. 1806. He married 20 May 1779, Ellinor (Brumley) Stott, relict of a son of William Stott (w. 1781), and daughter of Samuel and Elizabeth Brumley. Ellinor (Brumley) Brent died: her will was written 18 Oct. 1819, and probated 21 Feb. 1820.

Samuel Brumley deeds slaves to his granddaughter Esther Brumley, "daughter of my son William Brumley," 15 Feb. 1764. William Brumley, in his will, leaves his estate to Sarah McCarty, daughter of Col. Thaddeus McCarty, dec'd and at her death, to his nephew Hugh Brent, son of William and Eleanor Brent.

Ellinor (Brumley-Stott) Brent, had by her first marriage, Eliz. Stott, who married Benjamin Doggett, and probably Samuel Brumley Stott and Wm. Stott, as the last two were named in the will of Wm. Stott as his grandchildren. In her will, Ellinor Brent names daughters Elizabeth Doggett, Eleanor Mitchell and her daughter Fanny Mitchell, and Elizabeth Shearman—"also it is my wish that Mary Judith Stott, Frances E. B. Mitchell, Fanny M. Mitchell, and Addaline Brent (182) have one dress each out of my estate (*Lancaster County Will Book*, 28, p. 203).

The division of the slaves of the estate of William Brent, dec'd, names "James Mitchell who m. Eleanor Brumley Brent, James

D. Brent who intermarried with Fanny Brent, James Brent, Thomas Shearman who intermarried with Elizabeth Mitchell, formerly Elizabeth Brent" (*Est. Book* 1839, p. 302).

Samuel Bromley, son of Daniell Bromley, was born 7 Sept. 1681, recorded at the request of Mrs. Anne Browne wife of Nathaniel Browne, and is recorded 17 Jan. 1690 L. D. B., 1687-1700, p. 37).

Children:

84   I   Hugh, married before 1805, and had—

      1 William Brumley Brent, d. in Texas in the army, Fall of 1837.

      2 Albert Hugh Brent.

85   II   Eleanor, b. *circa* 1783; m. 15 Dec. 1809, James Mitchell, and had at least (Mitchell)—
      1 Frances E. B., m. 20 Dec. 1830, Wm. H. Stott.

86   III   Elizabeth, b. 4 Dec. 1785; d. after 1859; m. (I) 7 Dec. 1808, Henry Mitchell, and had at least (Mitchell)—

      1 Frances M., m. 26 Dec. 1826, Wm. P. Booth.
She married (II) 17 Dec. 1817, Thomas Shearman, and had (Shearman)—

      2 Joseph M. B. Shearman.
      3 Susan P., m. 26 Feb. 1837, Benj. G. George.

87   IV   Frances, b. 30 Nov. 1787; d. 20 June 1848; m. 13 Feb. 1809, James Doggett Brent (96) [line carried from (96)].

88   V   James, b. *cir.* 1789; d. before 1821; m. 24 March 1814, Ann S. Brent (202).

[31] HAYNES[4] BRENT (Hugh[3], Hugh[2], Hugh[1]), was born in Lancaster County, *circa* 1740, and died 1801 in Princess Anne County, Va. He married 1 Feb. 1776, Tamer Gamewell, probably relict of Lawrence Gamewell (w. 1774). Haynes Brent went to Princess Anne County with his cousin Erasmus Haynes and is listed in the first census by John Thorowgood as living in Little Creek precinct (1783), and has six white souls and four black

souls. In 1785 he has eight white souls, one dwelling and two other buildings—so his family is increasing. He is in all probability the progenitor of the Brent family living in the city of Norfolk and that vicinity.

Will of HAYNES BRENT

In the name of God, Amen. I, Haynes Brent of the County of Princess Anne being of sound and disposing mind (blessed be God) do make and publish this as my last Will and Testament in manner and form following Viz: *Imprimis*. I give and devise to my daughter Elizabeth Theleball and her heirs, my House and Lott in the Borough of Norfolk which I bought of John S. Calvert, and also my two Negroe wenches Aliff and Alu. Item—I give to my Son in Law Richmond Theleball all my wearing apparel. Item—I give and bequeath to my sister *Nancy Brent* the sum of Eighty pounds, two Beds and furniture and two Cows and Calves and also the use and enjoyment, during her natural life of my Negro Boy Harry and my Negro Girl Molly, and after her death, I give the said negroes Harry and Molly to my Grand daughter Elizabeth Doghead Theleball and her heirs. Item—I give and devise to my said Grand daughter Elizabeth D. Theleball and her heirs all the remaining part of my Estate of every kind whatever. Item—It is my desire that my Negro wench Peg after she becomes unfit for service, shall be maintained out of the property left to my Grand daughter. Item—I desire that all the property I have herein given to my said grand daughter Elizabeth D. Theleball shall be kept by Thomas Lawson, my Executor hereafter named, in his hands till my said Grand daughter arrives to the age of twenty-one Years or marries, whichever may first happen. Lastly, I do hereby nominate, constitute and appoint Thomas Lawson Executor to this my last Will and Testament, In Testimony whereof I have hereunto set my hand and affixed my Seal this 20th day of December 1800.

Haynes Brent (seal)

Sign'd Sealed and acknowledged
In presence of us—
John Read, Anthony Lawson
Charles Hargrow

[71]

Children, from his will (there were probably others):

89   1   Elizabeth, b. ——; d. ——; m. —— Richmond Theleball, and had (THELEBALL)—
       1 Elizabeth Doghead Theleball.

[34] ELIZABETH⁴ BRENT (William³, Hugh², Hugh¹), was born in Lancaster County, Va., *cir.* 1715; d. after 1785; m. (I) *cir.* 1735, Samuel Hinton whose will is probated 1771 in Lancaster County; m. (II) 30 Dec. 1774, Thomas Hunton (L. M. B.). She was daughter of William Brent's marriage with Sarah Fleet; Samuel Hinton received the larger part of Henry Fleet's estate (w. 1735), this Henry Fleet dying unmarried.

Children, from his will (HINTON):

     I   Richard, received "one shilling sterling" in his father's will; b. ——; d. ——; div. of estate ordered 1780; m. ——.

       Children, from his est. div.:
       1 William.

       2 Sarah.

       3 Elizabeth.

       4 Mary.

       5 Judith.

       6 Ann.

       7 Richard.*

       8 Robert.

     II   William, b. ——; d. ——; will written 2 March, 1790; probated 17 Jan. 1791—"all land to be held intact until son Richard Brent Hinton arrives at age of 21 years, and then to be divided among all of my children." M. ——, Ann ——, who outlived him.

       Children, from his est. div.:
       1 Richard Brent Hinton.

---

*Thomas Hinton, son of Richard Hinton, is legatee of Reuben Cochran of Barren County, Ky., 1814.

2 Sally, m. 24 Sept. 1811, Richard Towell (L. M. B.).

3 Betsy, m. 29 April 1811, John James (L. M. B.).

4 Susannah, m. 13 Dec. 1802, John F. Ingram (L. M. B.).

III Henry, "land in Dinwiddie County," b. ——; d. ——; m. 23 June 1766, Anna Fleet (L. M. B.).

IV Spencer.

V Samuel.

VI Fleet, b. *cir.* 1745; d. ——; inventory of his estate made in 1789; m. 17 Nov. 1768, Catherine Pope (L. M. B.).

[37] WILLIAM⁴ BRENT (William³, Hugh², Hugh¹), was born in Lancaster County, Va., *circa* 1726, and died (cannot find his will or Inven.). He married (1) 11 May 1753, Judith King, wid. in Lancaster County; m. (II) 19 April 1779, Mary Parham, wid., in Sussex County, Va. In the census of 1782, he is listed as having "5 whites and 7 blacks" in Sussex County. In the 1785 listing of Lancaster County, where the real estate is shown he is listed as having "no white souls, 1 dwelling and two other buildings." Judith King was the widow of John King, and daughter of George and Judith (Pursel) Brent. Mary Parham was probably the widow of William Parham, and daughter of John Kelley of Sussex County.

William Brent, Sr., and Judith, his wife, sell to Thomas Pollard, land "formerly known by the name of 'Percillers,' " March 1764.

Charles Brent(43), in his will 1772, mentions *Margaret Brent*, daughter of sister *Judith Brent*.

William Brent of Sussex County, sold to son *Jeduthen Brent*, negro Harry, "now run away," 30 March 1781: 16 Sept. 1785 (*Lancaster Deed Book* 21, p. 53). *William Brent* of Sussex County, "for love and affection for my son *Jeduthen Brent* of Lancaster County," gives negro slaves, Kate, Beck, Sarah, Lucy, Rachael and Tom: 11 Dec. 1783—18 Dec. 1783, wit. Thos. Gaskins, Wm. Brown and Robt. J. Heath (L. D. B. 21, p. 24).

[73]

Children, 1st marriage:

90   I   William.

91   II   Jeduthen*, b. ——; d. ——; m. 15 Sept. 1779, Molly Brent (111), daughter of George and Margaret (Simmons) Brent.

92   III   Margaret.

[38] JAMES[4] BRENT (William[3], Hugh[2], Hugh[1]), born *cir.* 1736, in Lancaster County, Va.; d. 1815, at "Wellington," Nelson County, Va.; m. 4 Oct. 1768, in Lancaster County, Sarah Cammell, relict of James Cammell Jr., and dau. of William and Johanna (Wale) Doggett. In the div. of estate of James Cammell Sr., 1767, "Ann Cammell, orphan of James Cammell Jr.—her part delivered to Sarah Cammell, her guardian." William Doggett, in his will 1764, names Sarah Doggett as one of his "five youngest daughters." On the flyleaf of an old account book brought up from Lancaster County which came into my possession at the death of my grandfather, I found the name *Sarah Brent* written in many places, and having heard from my father's sisters that her family name was Doggett, I searched through all of the Doggett wills before I was finally convinced that I had the right Sarah. She d. by Feb. 1821, leaving her estate to her second son Kendall Carroll Brent.

From the diary of James Brent—"In May 1777 I move to Augusta County. In Aug. 1779, I move upon Back Creek . . . I had all of my people that year. In 1787 I move from Back Creek, in April, it being Good Friday, and come upon Daniel Devaill's place . . . 1788-89-90-91-92-93-94, on the same place" (his account book states that he was on Isiah Ingham's land, and certifies to the rent etc., and fencing and crops he had improved on the place). He moved on Rockfish 19 Oct. 1796. On Dec. 8th, 1796, he moved on Hat Creek, and "I called my place 'Wellington'". This land was conveyed by Thomas Randolph to Porterfield Trent, and by him to John Dobson, and by him to his son Richard Dobson (D. B. "H," Amherst County, p. 159).

---

*Cannot find his will. In the census of 1783, Lancaster County, Va., he is listed as having "four white and 6 black souls"; in the 1785 census of the same county, he has "five white souls, 1 dwelling and 3 other buildings."

Children from his diary:

93   I   Landon Haines, b. Monday, 11 P.M., 9 Sept. 1769; d. 31 Nov. 1857, at "Wellington," a bachelor.

94   II   Kendall Carroll, b. Tuesday, about middle of the day, 7 Feb. 1771; d. s. p., his will written 6 April 1842; probated 27 June 1842; m. 30 Oct. 1808, Polly W. Burton, dau. of James Burton and Mary (White) Burton of St. Thomas Parish, Orange County. James Burton m. Mary White, dau. of Jeremiah White, 19 Jan. 1779. Polly Brent d. Nov. 1814.

+ 95   III   Sarah, b. Sunday night, 9 or 10 o'clock, 14 Feb. 1773; d. 29 Feb. 1848, and is buried at Tinkling Spring Church, Augusta County, in the old cemetery. M. cir. 1795, William Dold of Augusta County. He was b. 1771; d. 3 July 1856, and is buried by his wife.

+ 96   IV   James Doggett, b. Tuesday night about 9 or 10 o'clock, 1 Nov. 1774; d. 7 Sept. 1849; m. 13 Feb. 1809, Frances Brent, dau. of William and Eleanor (Brumley) Brent (30).

97   V   Hugh, b. Monday evening, 23 Dec. 1776; d. 6 Sept. 1778.

98   VI   Kitturn Huson, b. Sunday night, 18 March 1781; d. before 1816.

99   VII   William Sydney, b. Tuesday evening, 21 Aug. 1783; left for Mississippi Terr. 15 April 1810; last letter I can find from him is dated Aug. 12th, 1814.

100   VIII   Allse Kirk, b. Tuesday night after midnight, 16 Sept. 1785; d. s. p. 12 May 1802.

[41] THOMAS[4] BRENT (George[3], Hugh[2], Hugh[1]), was born 1724 in Lancaster County, Va., and died "on Saturday morning, 13 Oct. 1781." He married 19 Nov. 1741, Anne Yerby, daughter of Thomas Yerby (w. 1756) and Hannah Doggett (w. 1761), who were married 22 Feb. 1717. Hannah Doggett was daughter of Benjamin[2] and his first wife, and granddaughter of Benjamin[1] Doggett "Minister."

Children, from his Bible:

+101   I   William, b. 22 Oct. 1743; d. in Scott County, Ky.,

[75]

1829; m. Elizabeth —— in Lancaster County, Va., ——.

+102   II   George, b. 4 Nov. 1745, in Lancaster County, Va.; d. (his will was written 15 Sept. 1785, probated 14 Nov. 1785) in Loudon County, Va.; m. 1 Dec. 1772, Johanna Wale, dau. of George and Sarah (——) Wale, of Lancaster County, Va. She married (II), —— Lewis, and died 1827, in Loudon County, Va.

103   III   Judith, b. 10 Nov. 1747, in Lancaster County, Va.; d. ——; m. *circa* 1767 (Joseph?) Sullivant of Lancaster County; he died before 1783, the taking of the first census, in which Judith Sullivant is listed as having "Seven white souls and two black."

Issue, from L. M. B. (last four not proven)—

1 Peggy, "dau. of Judith Sullivant," m. 14 March 1792, William Haydon.

2 Catherine, m. 19 Sept. 1796, Wm. Cundiff.

3 Nancy, m. 24 Jan. 1797, Wm. M. Robinson.

4 Sabra, m. 30 June 1803, Wm. Dodson.

5 Sally, m. 24 Aug. 1787, Isaac Craine.

+104   IV   Thomas, b. 17 April 1750, in Lancaster County, Va.; d. 10 May 1832 in Scott County, Ky.; m. (I), in Lancaster County, Va., 20 Oct. 1774, Judith King, wid., with the consent of James Pollard. The bond describes him as "Thomas Brent, Jr."; m. (II) in Lancaster County, Va., 18 Feb. 1779, Lucy Brent (108); m. (III) Sarah ——, b. 28 Aug. 1765; d. 7 Sept. 1821, in Georgetown, Ky.

+105   V   Vincent, b. 6 May 1753; d., will written 27 April 1799; probated 16 Sept. 1799; m. (I) ——; m. (II), 24 June 1786, Margaret Steptoe Lawson.

106   VI   Ann, b. 23 Feb. 1760; d. ——; m. —— Kent.

Children (KENT):

1 Judith.

2 Jane.

[42] GEORGE[4] BRENT (George[3], Hugh[2], Hugh[1]), was born in Lancaster County, Va., and died 1778 in the same county. His personal estate was appraised at £1,993. He married *circa* 1750,

[76]

Margaret Simmons, daughter of Elizabeth Simmons (w. 1774). She died 1784.

Children:

107   I   Judith, m. —— Hubbard before 1778.

108   II   Lucy, m. 18 Feb. 1779, Thomas Brent(103).

109   III   Molly, m. 15 Sept. 1779, Jeduthen Brent(91).

+110   IV   George, b. 7 July 1766; d. 11 Nov. 1814; m. 18 Feb. 1792, Sarah Edmonds, daughter of Col. Elias Edmonds, of Lancaster County, Va.

+111   V   Charles, b. 1768; d. 27 Dec. 1814; m. Dec. 1791, Catherine Kirk, daughter of James(144) and Lucy (Carter) Kirk.

112   VI   Margaret, m. 1 Oct. 1787, Richard Riveer.

113   VII   Sarah Ann, m. 20 May 1784, George Kirk.

[45] JUDITH[4] BRENT (George[3], Hugh[2], Hugh[1]), was born in Lancaster County, Va., *circa* 1725. She married (1) *circa* 1748, John King, the youngest son of William King (w. 1716), and his wife Lettice. He was a minor when his father made his will. John King died between 2 March and 19 June, 1752, stating in his will that his wife as Exor. was "to bring up his children in a Christian manner Provided she behave in a Christian manner." She "proved" her Christianity by marrying her cousin William Brent(37) 2 May 1753. Judith Brent died before 1779, as this William married Mary Parham widow, that year, in Sussex County, Va.

Children (KING; for William Brent issue, see 37, his line):

I   William.

II   John.

III   Mary,* m. (1) Coleman Doggett (w. 1782); m. (II), 2 Nov. 1782, John McTyre.

---

*Coleman Doggett stipulated in his will that his wife was to have certain Negroes "in case she does not fly to the Law for a greater proportion of my Negroes" —*she flew*, as the Est. Div. was "agreeable to will of Coleman Doggett," when above dowers were settled (L. W. B. 22, p. 326).

Est. Division of JOHN KING 17 Feb. 1758—Coleman Doggett in right of his wife, MARY.

[77]

Children, first marriage (DOGGETT):

1 John.

2 William (received his dower 1792).

3 Dennis, m. 18 July 1803, Nancy D. Webb, Moses George, Sec. (L. M. B.). (Received his estate 1795.)

4 Mary (not named in estate division).

5 Prescilla (received her share of her father's estate, with Dennis, 1 Jan. 1795).

[50] CHARLES⁴ BRENT (Charles³, Hugh², Hugh¹), was born in Overwharton Parish, Stafford County, Va., 11 June 1735, and died in Frederick County, Va., 11 April 1822. He married 1761, Anna Gunnell, daughter of Henry and Catherine Gunnell of Prince William County, Va. Anna Gunnell was born 16 Feb. 1744, and died, her will was written 2 June 1824, and probated 6 June 1826, in Frederick County, Va. Charles Brent, or his son Charles, was a member of the House of Delegates 1810-11 (Morton). His will is not recorded in Frederick County.

Children:*

114 I Lieut. Robert, b. ——; d. ——; m., probably, Elizabeth T. Palmer, 24 May 1820, in Faquier County. He is named as Exor. in his mother's will, and acts as such in the suit, Brent vs. Gunnell, as the records show in the Superior Court at Fredericksburg, Va., 1830. He was appointed a lieutenant of militia 51st. Inf. Reg., 16th Brigade and 3rd Div., Va. Militia, 13 Jan. 1814.

115 II George, m. 10 Dec. 1812, Susan Anderson (Fr. M. B.).

*The first six children are named in Anna Brent's will. The other seven are as printed in *The Lookout* of Chattanooga, Tenn., Feb. 1917. The first six children were included in this printed data, and not being able to establish the source *of the other seven*, I am using the data as printed.

The marriages of the first six children as printed in *The Lookout* agree with the Frederick County bonds, so it is probable that the names mentioned in the mother's will were the youngest, and also that the others had gone to "the Western Country."

Jesse Moore, b. 4 Sept. 1766; d. 26 Sept. 1853; m. Miss Brent of Winchester, Va.

116　III　Innis, died before 1823; m. Rachael Touchstone; she m. (II), Henry Neville; issue (BRENT)—

　　　　1 William, m. —— Ebert, dau. of Martin Ebert.

　　　　2 Sarah, m. 1833, Carr W. Baylis.

　　　　3 Catherine, m. 18 June 1833, Joshua Hudson.

+117　IV　Charles, died by 1829; m. Rachael Moore.

+118　V　Elizabeth, m. 2 April 1804, Wm. Green (Fr. M. B.).

119　VI　Mary, m. 16 March 1800, Presley Talbott (Fr. M. B.).

119a VII　William, m. Prudence Lowry, 17 Jan. 1795 (Faquier County M. B.).

119bVIII　Ann, m. Phillip Baxter.

119c IX　Frances, m. John Connelly.

119d　X　Catherine, m. Jesse Moore.

119e XI　Hannah, m. Dr. Thomas Williams.

119f XII　Henry.

119gXIII　Sarah, spinster.

[52] Capt. HUGH⁴ BRENT (Charles³, Hugh², Hugh¹), was born 3 Nov. 1739, in Overwharton Parish, Stafford County, Va.; d. 1813, near Paris, Ky., where he migrated *circa* 1791. M. 19 Oct. 1764, Elizabeth Baxter. She was b. 17 Oct. 1746. Hugh Brent was a member of the Committee of Safety, captain of the county militia for Prince William County, and Gentleman Justice of the Prince William court. While living in Prince William County, he was granted land in Faquier, 22 April 1774. Elizabeth Baxter was the daughter of Margaret (——), who m. (I) —— Baxter and (II) —— Smith (King George County Wills, B. 2, p. 169).

Children:

+120　I　Mary, b. 26 June 1767; d. 2 Jan. 1812; m. Hugh McIlvain, who was b. 26 Aug. 1767.

121　II　Margaret, b. ——; d. ——; m. Capt. Thomas Young of the Rev. Army, and moved to Kentucky.

+122　III　Innis Baxter, b. ——; d. ——; m. Catherine Thomas of Richmond, Va.

[79]

+123   IV   Hannah, b. 10 April 1769; d. 15 Sept. 1837; m. 15 Dec. 1785, Col. Duval Payne of Fairfax or Faquier Counties. He was b. 15 Dec. 1764; d. 4 June 1830.

+124   V   Hugh, b. 18 Jan. 1773; d. 16 July 1848, in Paris, Ky.; m. "three times, but only Miss Langhorne bore him children"—24 Dec. 1798, Elizabeth Trotter Langhorne, of Lynchburg, Va. She was b. 11 July 1782; d. 1 Oct. 1817.

[53] Capt. WILLIAM[4] BRENT (Charles[3], Hugh[2], Hugh[1]), was born 24 May 1742 in Overwharton Parish, Stafford County, Va., and died in Faquier County, Va. His will was written 13 Feb. 1793, and probated 23 June 1800. He married* Hannah Neale, daughter of Christopher and Ann (Osborne) Neale, and granddaughter of Daniel and Ursula (Presley) Neale, *circa* 1765. On 29 April 1769, he is granted land by the Exors of Col. Armstead Churchill. William Brent is referred to in Hayden, as "captain."

The eight children below are from the will of William Brent. In a note I am giving the data as printed in *The Lookout.†*

Children:**

125   I   Christopher Neale, who died unmarried. He was a gallant soldier in the U. S. Army, and served against the pirates of Morocco.

126   II   George†, probably married —— Lewis: "she (Ann Lewis) had a sister who married George Brent, and a cousin —— Moxley, who married —— Green" (Hayden, p. 271).

127   III   Thomas.

---

*In *The Index to Kentucky Wills*, by Mrs. King, there is listed in Scott County, Book "B," 1809-1817, a will of Hannah Brent. However, the clerk of this county writes me that he cannot find the will.

**The following is the list of children of William and Hannah (Neale) Brent as printed in *The Lookout*, Feb. 1917: William Thomas, m. Nellie Peyton; Christopher N., d. unmarried; George, m. Miss Parsons; John Heath, m. Lucy Baylor; Anna, m. Dr. Henry Peyton; Mary Waddy, m. Col. Joseph Blackwell; Elizabeth Marye, m. 1811, Col. Eppa Hunton; Betsey, m. Col. Hunter of Faquier County; George, m. Miss Cresap of Washington County, Va.; ——, m. Mr. Graham of Faquier County, Va.; Hannah Innes, m. Mr. Hampton.

†The notes of the late Wm. A. Brent, state that George Brent m. a Miss Graham, and that his progeny live at Cumberland, Md.

+128   IV   William, b. Aug. 1777; d. 1851, in Trimble County, Ky.; m. Elizabeth Simmons of Faquier County, Va.

129   v   Alexander, probably died unmarried, as his estate is appraised 3 Jan. 1807, as "one negro boy."

+130   VI   Anne, b. ——; d. ——; m. 15 Nov. 1796, in Faquier County, Henry Peyton, son of Yelverton and Elizabeth (Heath) Peyton, of Stafford County, Va.

+131   VII   Mary Waddy, b. 1785; d. 1822; m. in Faquier County, 25 Oct. 1802, Col. Joseph Blackwell, widower. He was born 1755; d. 15 Sept. 1823 at his residence near Elk Run, Faquier County, Va.

+132   VIII   Elizabeth Marye, b. 1792; d. 1866; m. in Faquier County, 22 June 1811, Eppa Hunton. He was born 1787; d. 1830.

[64] Capt. HUGH⁵ BRENT (James⁴, Hugh³, Hugh², Hugh¹), was born *circa* 1728 in Christ Church Parish, Lancaster County, Va., and died 7 Feb. 1778, in Lancaster County. He married (I), 6 Sept. 1750, Susannah Payne, daughter of George and Frances (Edmonds) Payne; m. (II) 26 Oct. 1761, Easther Shearman, daughter of Martin Shearman; m. (III) 30 Jan. 1766, Judith Kenner, relict of Brererton Kenner, and dau. of Capt. Willoughby and Sarah (Eskridge) Newton. Judith Brent died 22 Jan. 1785. Capt. Hugh Brent was one of his Majesty's justices for Lancaster County, a member of the Committee of Safety, County lieutenant, and Tobacco Inspector, with Fortunatus Sydnor, for both Lancaster and Northumberland counties. He was a vestryman for Christ Church, and also church warden.

     Capt. Hugh Brent took the Oath of the Government and to qualify himself for a Commission—16 March 1767 (*L. Order Book*).

Children, 1st marriage:

+133   I   James, b., *cir.* 1751; d., will written 13 May 1791; probated 17 Dec. 1792; m. (I) 9 Sept. 1771, Sally Butcher of Northumberland County; m. (II) 25 May 1780, Elizabeth Hunt, widow of John Hunt, and dau.

of Epapphroditus and Mary (Brent, 72) Lawson. Eliz. (Lawson-Hunt) Brent m. (III) 1795, Thomas James.

134   II   Frances, b. ——; d. ——; m. 16 Feb. 1775, John Maxwell and had, at least—

      1 Elizabeth, m. 7 Jan. 1796, Geo. Waddy (L. M. B.).

+135   III   Sarah, b. ——; d. ——; m. *cir.* 1775, John Berryman, widower.

136   IV   Lieut. Newton, b. ——; d. ——, 1795; m. 14 April 1779, Ann Steptoe Lawson, dau. of Thomas Lawson. Newton Brent was a lieutenant in Rev. Army.

Children:

    1 Jane, m. 28 Jan. 1700, Robt. M. Robertson (L. M. B.).

    2 Lettice, m. 11 Dec. 1801, Thos. G. Robertson (L. M. B.).

    3 Ann, m. 5 Sept. 1800, Richard Glasscock (L. M. B.).

    4 Peggy.

+137   V   George, b. *cir.* 1755; d., will written 23 Jan. 1821; probated 16 Feb. 1824; m. (I) 15 Jan. 1784, Sarah Ann Simmons; m. (II) 13 Feb. 1802, Judith Carter, wid., of Northumberland County. She m. (I) 1786, Richard Yerby; (II) 1799, James Carter of Amherst County. She was originally Judith George of Northumberland County.

Children, second marriage:

138   VI   Katherine, b. *circa* 1763; d. ——; m. George Glasscock by 15 July 1784.

Children, third marriage:

139   VII   Charlotte, b. 6 Nov. 1766; d. ——; m. 15 March 1782, Joseph Stephens.

140   VIII   Prescilla, b. 7 Oct. 1768; d. ——; m. 15 Aug. 1787, George Stephens of Orange County.

+141   IX   Hugh, b. 16 May 1775; d. 16 Feb. 1814; m. (I) 9 Jan. 1796, Mary T. Lawson. She d. 25 Jan. 1797. M. (II)

5 Dec. 1799, Alice Martin. She was b. 29 April 1784; d. 12 Aug. 1855.

142　x　Martin, b. 6 Oct. 1776; d.* ——; m. 29 Dec. 1796, Ann Chilton.

143　xi　Kenner, b. 7 May 1778; d. s. p. 1796.

[65] SARAH[5] BRENT (James[4], Hugh[3], Hugh[2], Hugh[1]), was born *circa* 1730, in Christ Church Parish, Lancaster County, Va. She wrote her will 25 Feb. 1778, and it was probated 19 March 1778. She married 4 May 1747, Anthony Kirk, brother to James Kirk. Anthony Kirk's will is written 30 Dec. 1763; probated 20 Jan. 1764. He names wife, "Sarah, my great Bible," and sons James and Thomas; "loving wife," brother James Kirk, and Mr. Hugh Brent, Exors. Sarah Kirk, in her will, names son Thomas the "entire estate, and then to my grandchildren," Anthony, Mary and Catherine Kirk, and Sarah Griggs. Lancaster marriage bonds show that Judith Kirk, dau. of Sarah K. married 6 May 1768, Thomas Griggs, Thomas Kirk's will was written five days before his mother's and probated the same day. He leaves his whole estate to his "loving mother," and then to his brother James Kirk and his children.

Children (KIRK):

144　i　James, m. 19 May 1768, Lucy Carter, dau. of Edward and Katherine (MARTIN-Brent) Carter.

145　ii　Thomas, d. s. p. 1778.

146　iii　Judith, m. 6 May 1768, Thomas Griggs.

[66] ELEANOR[5] BRENT (James[4], Hugh[3], Hugh[2], Hugh[1]), was born *cir.* 1732, in Christ Church Parish, Lancaster County; d. ——; m. 5 Nov. 1750, Capt. William Stamps of Goochland County. Cannot find his will there. The William Stamps who d. 1772 in Faquier County, names wife "Ann," and "all of my children,"

---

*There is an appraisement of the estate of one Martin Brent in Scott County, Ky., Will Book "K," p. 288, *circa* 1848.

without listing their names. Stokeley Brent(70), names John, Newton, Catherine, and Mary Stamps; Douglas Register gives only Catherine and James. It is also possible that this family went to Kentucky with the Curds.

Children (STAMPS):

147	I	Catherine, b. 17 Oct. 1757 (D. Reg.).
148	II	James, b. 6 Jan. 1760 (D. Reg.).
149	III	Newton.
150	IV	John.
151	V	Mary.

[67] LUCY[5] BRENT (James[4], Hugh[3], Hugh[2], Hugh[1]), was born in Lancaster County, Va., *circa* 1734, and died in Mercer County, Ky. She married in Lancaster County, Va., 7 April 1758, John Curd (John[2], Edward[1]), of Goochland County, Va., the match, in all probability, having been made by Capt. William Stamps who married her sister eight years earlier, as he is on the bond. John Curd was born *circa* 1726, in Henrico County, Va., and died before 1819, in Mercer County, Ky.

Lucy (Brent) Curd seems to have been worshipped by all of the Kentucky Curds, looked upon as a sort of Godmother, and for that reason the name Brent has been given not only to all of her direct descendants, but also to the Curds who carried no Brent blood.

The children of Lucy Brent and John Curd were born in Goochland County (formed from Henrico 1727), and were registered by the Rev. William Douglas in the register of St. James Northam Parish Church, of which John Curd was Vestryman; the name of Merryman B. Curd, being the only exception. He must have been born during the journey, or shortly after the arrival in Kentucky.

John Curd moved with his family to Kentucky 1780, settling on the south bank of the Kentucky River, at the mouth of Dix River, in what was first Lincoln County, but was later cut off to form Mercer County. Here he established a public ferry authorized

[84]

by law, being one of eight so authorized in Kentucky by the Virginia Assembly. This ferry became the gateway to the settlement at Harrodsburg, and at the present writing, a ferry is still in operation at this point. The road from the ferry to Harrodsburg, and on to Lexington, was known as "Curd's Road," and was so called until the Harrodsburg turnpike was built. He took up large grants of land in Jefferson, Fayette and Lincoln Counties, the first three counties to be formed out of the County of Kentucky. All of his children and those of his brother Joseph (with one exception) eventually settled in Central Kentucky and are the ancestors of a large part of the Kentuckians bearing the name Curd. It is said that he was an intimate friend of both Daniel Boone and Governor Patrick Henry and that under the Governor's direction he served many important missions in the Kentucky section of Virginia. For this work he was granted 1650 acres of land in Kentucky by Gov. Patrick Henry, and 600, by the Virginia Legislature.

There were three John Curds living in Goochland County, Va. at the beginning of the Revolution and writers frequently confuse the three and their military service in the Revolution. The elder John son of John[2] Curd and his wife Elizabeth Price removed from Virginia to Kentucky during the progress of the Revolution. There does not seem to be any record of his having served in the Continental army prior to his removal to Kentucky where he was a member of the Lincoln County militia and saw service under at least three different captains. In company of Capt. John Martin under command of Col. Stephen Trigg, April 21 to May 23, 1781, 33 days. In company of Capt. Samuel Scott, under command of Col. Benjamin Logan, Feb. 22 to March 22, 1782, 29 days. In company of Capt. John Smith under command of Col. Benjamin Logan, Oct. 22 to Nov. 23, 1782, 33 days. (Pay rolls on file Va. state Library). The second John was son of Edward[3] Curd and his wife Mary Morris. He was captain of militia 1778-1781 (Heitman, p. 181) and was Colonel of the Goochland militia following the Revolution. The third John was son of John[3] Curd and his wife Lucy Brent. He enlisted as private in Continental Army 1776 and was appointed Major of the Goochland militia May 1780.

[85]

Children, births only, from Douglas Register (CURD):

+152   I   James, b. in Goochland County, Va., 24 June 1759; d. Jassemine County, Ky., *cir.* 1821; m. 30 Aug. 1791, Mary Ann Perkins, daughter of Capt. Benjamin Hughes Perkins; she was b. 6 May 1770; d. 1850.

+153   II   John, b. in Goochland County, Va., 23 Nov. 1760; d. Logan County, Ky., 10 Sept. 1838; m. 10 July 1787, Ann Williams Curd, dau. of Richard Curd. She was b. 11 July 1762; d. 20 Sept. 1846. John Curd served in the Rev. Army under Washington, was wounded at the battle of Germantown, taken prisoner by the British and carried to New York, where he was exchanged and again reenlisted.

154   III   Elizabeth, b. in Goochland County, Va., 25 Feb. 1762.

155   IV   Nancy, b. Goochland County, Va., 5 Feb. 1764; m. in Lincoln County, Ky., 23 March 1782, James Hoard.

156   V   Catherine, b. in Goochland County, Va., 29 Jan. 1766; m. in Lincoln County, Ky., 31 Dec. 1782, William Bradshaw.

+157   VI   Newton, b. in Goochland County, Va., 31 Nov. 1767; d. 25 Aug. 1822, in Mercer County, Ky., two miles north of the town he founded; m. 25 March 1789, Ann Elizabeth Hatcher, dau. of Thomas Hatcher; she b. 1761; d. 1831.

158   VII   Mary, b. in Goochland County, Va., 10 Sept. 1769; d. in Trimble County, Ky., 30 June 1833, "in her 60th year" (?); m. 30 Sept. 1785, Samuel Pryor, and moved to Trimble County, Ky., *circa* 1800.

+159   VIII   Price, b. in Goochland County, Va., 14 Aug. 1771; d. in Fayette County, Ky., 7 Feb. 1814; m. Fanny Allen, dau. of Richard Allen.

+160   IX   Daniel, b. in Goochland County, Va., 14 Oct. 1773; d. 18 April 1843, at Glasgow, Barren County, Ky.; m. Fanny S. Trigg, dau. of Haiden Trigg of Bedford County, Va.

+161   X   Woodford, b. in Goochland County, Va., 15 Dec. 1775; d. *cir.* 1822; m. 10 Oct. 1800, Jenny West, dau. of Charles West.

+161a XI Merryman B., b. 12 May 1780, probably in Kentucky, as he is not listed in the *Douglas Register;* d. in Trimble County, Ky., 2 Oct. 1841; m. 12 April 1804, Polly Kay, dau. of John and Mary Kay of Fayette County, Ky.

[68] Maj. JOHN[5] BRENT (James[4], Hugh[3], Hugh[2], Hugh[1]), was born in Lancaster County, Va., *cir.* 1739; d. 1781, in Charlotte County, Va. M. *circa* 1760, Margaret Caldwell of Charlotte County. His widow afterwards married a Mr. Sublett. She was probably a daughter of David Caldwell (w. 1769). In 1776, Capt. John Brent is allowed a warrant for deficiency in his former account of waggonage on the Cherokee Expedition. He is of the 4th regiment. He was member of the Committee of Safety of Charlotte County, 1775-76, and member of House of Delegates 1780. After much litigation, his heirs are issued Land Warrant No. 9027 for 1333 1/3 acres, 21 Feb. 1843.

John Brent was granted 2,000 A., 5 June 1780, on Rolling Fork water course, in Kentucky. He was granted 100 A. by warrant No. 889 for three years service as a soldier in Virginia Line, 20 June 1783; 200 A. by warrant, in 1765, "during war soldier in Virginia Line," 15 Sept. 1783; 200 A. by warrant 4531 during war, soldier in Virginia Line, 3 Aug. 1791" (Jillson's "Old Kentucky Entrees and Deeds," p. 178).

Children, from Land Warrant:

+162 I James, b. 2 July 1762; d. 11 April 1819, in Charlotte County; m. Ann Patrick.

163 II Thomas Caldwell, d. in Rockingham County, North Carolina before 1835.

164 III Jane, m. 1 May 1780, John Smith of Charlotte County (Tyler Quart.)

165 IV Elizabeth, m. Samuel Rogers; she was living in Nicholas County, Ky., 27 Aug. 1834.

166 V Catherine, m. (I), Nathaniel Rogers; (II), —— Henderson.

167 VI Nancy, m. William Cobb.

[87]

168 VII   Margaret, m. Liberty Green.

169 VIII   Sarah, m. Robt. Hughes; she was living in Jefferson County, Ky., 6 Dec. 1834.

[72] MARY[5] BRENT (William[4], Hugh[3], Hugh[2], Hugh[1]), was born in Northumberland County, Va., *circa* 1738, the daughter of the first William in her grandfather's list of children (see will of Hugh Brent, 1748-50), and died after 1778. She married before 3 Sept. 1765, Epapphroditus Lawson, who died in Lancaster County, between 16 Jan. and 18 June 1778.

In obedience to an order of Northumberland County Court, we have Examined Mrs. Elizabeth Brent's Account of Administration on the Estate of her dec'd Husband William Brent, and do find that there will be due to Epapphroditus Lawson who Intermarried with the Daughter of the sd. Dece'd on the Death of the sd Elizabeth Brent Eight pounds fourteen Shillings and Eleven pence half penny And we do also Award and direct that the sd Elizabeth deliver unto the sd Lawson within Two Months from this day Fifteen yards of good Negroe Cotton and Twenty one yards of good Oznabrigo. And of this we make our Report this 3rd day of September 1765 Signed by George Ball, Thos. Edwards, Anthony Sydnor (*Northumberland Book* 6, p. 641).

Will of Epapphroditus Lawson, dated 16 Jan. 1778, probated 18 June 1778, names wife Mary, all estate during her widowhood or natural life; daughter Elizabeth Hunt. At the death of wife all of his estate to be equally divided among all of my children, allowing two negroes and bed already given unto my daughter Elizabeth Hunt to be a part of her estate. To son Epapphroditus Lawson, land after decease of my wife. Ext., wife Mary; wit: Richard E. Lee, Henry Lawson, Lawson Hathaway (L. W. B. 37, p. 133).

Hugh Brent (11), in his will 1748-50: I give unto my granddaughter *Mary Brent* daughter of my deceased son *William Brent*, two ewes in full for her part of my estate having provided sufficiently for her Father heretofore.

Children from his will, probably others (LAWSON):

    I   Eppa.

    II   Elizabeth, m. (1) 22 Dec. 1774, John Hunt, and left

issue; m. (II) 25 May 1780, James Brent(133—see his line). She married (III) 7 Sept. 1795, Thomas James.

[75] SARAH[5] BRENT (Hugh[4], Hugh[3], Hugh[2], Hugh[1]), was born *circa* 1748, in White Chapel Parish, Lancaster County, Va.; d. —— in Loudon County, Va.; m. 16 Oct. 1764, Thomas Chinn, Jr., son of Thomas Chinn and his first wife, probably Sarah Mitchell (Thomas Chinn m. 12 Nov. 1735, Sarah Mitchell: Lancaster M. B.). Thomas Chinn, Sr., in his will 1767, Lancaster County, mentions son Robert; son Thomas "all my land in Loudon County . . . together with all appurtenances, stock, and household furniture that is on the plantation"; Rawleigh, Easther and Susannah, "my three youngest children." Thomas Chinn and his wife Sarah, moved to Loudon County, before 1767.

Children, from Wm. A. Brent's notes (CHINN):*

170	I	Thomas, called "Tankerville," m. 12 Dec. 1789, Arnett Moore (F. M. B.).
171	II	Robert.
172	III	Hugh, b. 13 Nov. 1769; d. 23 July 1817; m. 17 Dec. 1789, Margaret Ash, daughter of Frances Ash; she was b. 12 Aug. 1768; d. 27 June 1816.
173	IV	Susan.
174	V	Sarah, m. John Upp.
174a	VI	Catherine, m. Rueben Murray and left issue.
174b	VII	Judith.
174c	VIII	Betsy, b. 3 Oct. 1782; d. 23 Dec. 1799.
174d	IX	Richard, b. 15 May 1774; d. 7 Sept .1800.

*"The following was copied by Wm. A. Brent from two handsome full-length slabs in the old Chinn graveyard, north of Mount Defiance, near Middleburg, Va.—'Here is interred the body of Betsey Chinn, daughter of Thomas Chinn and Sarah his wife, who was b. 3 Oct. 1782 and departed this life the 23 of Dec. 1799, . . . in the bloom of youth . . . Richard, son of Thomas Chinn and Sarah his wife . . . b. 15 May 1774 . . . d. 7 Sept. 1800 . . . In Mem . . . Susannah Sherman . . . b. 2 Aug. 1778 . . . d. 22 Jan. 1803.' The latter is just a head-stone." Thomas Chinn, Sr., probably m. (II), Ann Edmonds, relict of Robert Edmonds, and dau. of Edwin Conway, 11 July 1752. He was son of Rawleigh Chinn and Esther Ball (Joseph[2], William[1]). Esther Ball was half-sister to Martha, mother of Geo. Washington.

[76] JUDITH[5] BRENT (Hugh[4], Hugh[3], Hugh[2], Hugh[1]), was born in White Chapel Parish Lancaster County, 17—; d. ——; m. 17 June 1765, John Bailey; he d., will was written 3 Oct. 1783; probated 19 Feb. 1784, in Lancaster County. In the first census he is listed in 1783 as having "nine whites and twelve blacks." In the census of 1785, Judith Bailey has "10 White souls, 1 Dwelling and 6 Other buildings."

Children, from his will (BAILEY):

175   I   Sally, b. *cir.* 1768; d. ——; m. 18 Aug. 1794, William Carpenter (L. M. B.).

176   II   Molly, b. *cir.* 1769; d. before Dec. 1817; m. 7 June 1794, Thomas Shearman; he m. (II) 17 Dec. 1817, Elizabeth (Brent) Mitchell, wid.

177   III   Hugh, b. *cir.* 1770; d. ——; m. (I) 8 Jan. 1798/9, Frances Chowning; m. (II) 18 May 1801, Sally M. Shearman; Thomas Shearman, Sec. (L. M. B.).

178   IV   Charles, b. *cir.* 1772; d. ——; m. (I) 2 April 1802, Mary Chowning Dunaway, dau. of Samuel and Nancy Dunaway, b. 18 March 1781; m. (II) 28 Sept. 1814, Esther Brown (L. M. B.).

179   V   Catherine, b. *cir.* 1775; d. ——; m. 22 Dec. 1803, James Robb (L. M. B.).

180   VI   Jesse, b. (*cir.*) 1777; d. ——; m. 18 Oct. 1804, Lucy Carter (L. M. B.).

181   VII   John.

181aVIII   Judith Brent, b. 1784, posthumously; d. ——; m. 13 March 1803, Beverly Daniel (L. M. B.).

[95] SARAH[5] BRENT (James[4], William[3], Hugh[2], Hugh[1]), was born 14 Feb. 1773, in Lancaster County, Va.; d. 29 Feb. 1848, in Augusta County, Va., and is buried by her husband in the old cemetery at Tinkling, Springs; m. *circa* 1795, at "Wellington," Nelson County, Va., William Dold, son of Philip Dold, and —— Miller, dau. of Henry Miller, founder of the Miller Iron Works on Mossy Creek, Augusta County. Wm. Dold was b. 1771; d. 3 July 1856.

Henry Miller married Hannah Winter, dau. of William and Ann (Boone) Winter, an aunt of Daniel Boone. Elizabeth Winter, a sister of Hannah Winter m. Abraham Linkhorn, grandfather of President Abe Lincoln (Waddell's *Annals of Augusta County*).

Philip Dold's will (Augusta County, W. B. 13, p. 91, written 2 July 1819; probated Dec. 1819), does not name his wife. His children named are, Jesse, who was captain of the only mounted Virginia troops in the War of 1812 (Waddell). William, above; Elizabeth, m. 22 May 1795, William Donaldson of Tennessee; Nancy, m. 1 Feb. 1798, Luther Morgan, of Tennessee, an ancestor of Gen. John H. Morgan, Mrs. Basil Duke, and Mrs. A. P. Hill; Martha, m. 1 March 1798, Robt. McDowell of Virginia; Catherine, m. 24 Nov. 1798, John Lawrence of Tennessee (marriages from Augusta County marriage bonds).

Children (DOLD):

I   Harriet, b. 20 July 1803; d. 19 June 1878, and is buried in the old cemetery northeast of Waynesboro, Va.; m. Joseph Morrison. He was b. 7 Nov. 1795; d. 11 Sept. 1872. They had at least, Sam'l D. Morrison.

II Elvira, b. 29 Nov. 1804; d. 28 April 1890; m. William Brooks, b. 25 July 1789; d. 11 Nov. 1857.

Children (BROOKS):

1 James Milton Brooks, b. 27 May 1826; d. 7 March 1909; m. 8 May 1854, Catherine J. Shields; b. 2 June 1831; d. 7 May 1899; both buried at Bethel Church, near Staunton, Va.

2 Wm. Howard, b. 17 March 1829; d. 27 Feb. 1861, at Theological Sem., Columbia, S. Carolina; buried at Waynesboro, Va.

3 Estilene, m. Lorenzo Dow Shaw.

4 Addison.

5 John D.

6 Samuel.

7 Annie, m. —— Coons.

8 Mary, m. —— Gill.

[91]

    9 Sally, m. —— Cummings.

III   Elizabeth, m. Frederick Burns.

IV   Samuel Miller, b. 22 Aug. 1798; d. 1883; m. Elizabeth McFadden, and lived in Lexington, Va. Samuel Miller Dold was in the War of 1812 at the age of fourteen (Waddell).

Issue (DOLD):

    1 Fanny, m. Crockett Luther Peirce and lived in Christiansburg, Va.

    2 Dr. Samuel M., m. Sue Heneberger of Harrisonburg, Va., and had at least Dr. Wm. Elliott Dold of New York and Mrs. Charles G. Maphis of University, Va.

    3 William, m. Mary Porter, and had Laura E. Dold, who m. Maj. Wm. H. Sands of Richmond, Va.

V   Dr. Addison, b. 31 May 1808; m. Angelina M. Frazier.

VI   Dryden, m. and left a family in Texas.

[96] JAMES[5] DOGGETT BRENT (James[4], William[3], Hugh[2], Hugh[1]), was born 1 Nov. 1774 in Lancaster County, Va.; d. 7 Sept. 1849, at "Wellington," Nelson County, Va.; m. 13 Feb. 1809, Frances Brent, his second cousin, daughter of William and Ellinor (Brumley) Brent of Lancaster County, Va. She was born 30 Nov. 1787; died 20 June 1848, at "Wellington."

Children, from his diary:

    182   I   Adeline, b. Dec. 1809; d. 17 July 1889; m. 12 Dec. 1854, John Thornhill; b. 20 March 1807; d. 21 March 1875; no issue.

    183   II   William T., b. 20 Oct. 1811; d. u. m. April 1839, in Texas.

+184   III   James Haines, b. 30 Aug. 1813; d. 13 Jan. 1902; m. 24 June 1850, Mildred Pierce; she died in autumn of 1906.

    185   IV   Frances Ellen, b. 3 Oct. 1815; d. Feb. 1859; m. 18 Aug. 1842, Archer A. Hall.

Children (Hall):

1 Robt. A., b. 5 Aug. 1843; d. 2 Nov. 1862 in the Confederate Army.

2 Wm. B., b. July 1845; d. 1861, in the Confederate Army.

3 Mary E. Y., b. 6 May 1852; d. 5 April 1890; m. Nelson Bryant; no issue.

186   v   Fidelia A., b. May 1818; d. 3 Feb. 1869; m. 19 Nov. 1851, William A. Staples; d. Feb. 1894, "over ninety years of age," in Missouri.

Children (Staples):

1 Walter Brent Staples, d.s.p. Oct. 1855.

2 Hortense, d.s.p. *circa* 1920, spinster.

3 Jessie

+187   vi   Hugh Littleton, b. 9 March 1820; d. 25 June 1879; m. 1 Jan. 1850, Missouri (Jones) Clarkson, wid.; she was b. 1828; d. 26 June 1886.

+188   vii   Sarah Ellen, b. 23 Aug., 1822; d. 25 Sept., 1844; m. 3 Oct. 1839, Egbert O. Shields.

+189   viii   Landon Newton, b. 13 Oct. 1824; d. 29 May 1909; m. 8 Dec. 1847, Mary Louise Vaughan of Amherst County; b. 17 Nov. 1828; d. 24 May 1897.

190   ix   Margaret M., b. 25 Feb. 1827; d. 2 April 1861; m. 30 Nov. 1853, William R. Hill, of Amherst County.

Children (Hill):

1 Emma Julia, b. Oct., 1854.

2 James Delaware, b. Sept., 1856.

3 William

4 Margaret

[101] WILLIAM[5] BRENT (Thomas[4], George[3], Hugh[2], Hugh[1]), was born 22 Oct. 1743, in Lancaster County, Va.; and died; his will was written 30 Aug. 1829, and probated 19 Oct. 1829, in Scott County, Ky. He married in Lancaster County, Va., *circa* 1770, Elizabeth ——.

Ann Brent, relict of Thomas Brent . . . her eldest son William . . . 14 May 1783 (L. D. & W. B. 21, p. 16). William Brent and his wife Elizabeth, and Anne, his mother of the Parish of Wiccomoco . . . sell land where Brent now lives to William Yerby, 21 Aug. 1789 (L.D. & W. B. 21, p. 181).

The surname of his wife is not known. She had probably died before he wrote his will, as she is not named in it. His mother, Anne Brent in her will written 1794, names dau. Judith Sullivant, brother John Yerby, late husband Thomas Brent Sr., and granddaughters Jane and Judith Kent. William Brent probably moved to Kentucky about 1790. He is listed in the census of 1785 as living in Lancaster County, Va. See notes—Thomas Brent (104).

Children, from his will (W.B. "E," p. 179, Scott County, Ky.)*:

I   Richard Brent

II   Isaac Brent

III   Anne Cave (Henry Cave's w. probated in Scott County, Ky., 1809).

IV   Fannie Williams

V   Prescilla (?)

VI   Alcy Collins (her trustees to be Richard Cave of Missouri, and James Y. Kelly, of Ky.).

VII   Betsy Self

VIII   Joan (?)

IX   (daughter), m. —— Neale, and had—
    1 Elizabeth Neale

X   (daughter), m. —— Bealert, and had—
    1 Molly Bealert.

[102] GEORGE⁵ BRENT (Thomas⁴, George³, Hugh², Hugh¹), was born in Lancaster County, Va., 4 Nov. 1745, and died; his will was written 15 Sept. 1785, and probated 14 Nov. 1785, in

---

*This connexion has been proven negatively, and the above data is given as a part of this work with the hope that it might help someone with more facts to connect the line positively.

Shelburne Parish, Loudon County, Va. He called his plantation "Wilbourne." He married 19 Dec. 1772, Johanna Wale, daughter of George and Sarah (——) Wale, of Lancaster County, Va. Johanna Brent married (11), —— Lewis, probably the James Lewis who was named in her husband's will as one of the Exors. She died 1827, between the 9 April and 14 May. She names her granddaughter, Patsy Newton Wrenn; her son *Hugh Brent*, his one-quarter part in trust for his four children; her daughter Sarah Powell*, her one-quarter part in trust for her present children; son *Willis Brent*, his four present children when they reach 21 years of age, and son-in-law Thomas Wrenn in trust for his present children when they reach 21 years or day of marriage.

Ann Brent, widow of Thomas (41), and mother of George (102), gives to her son George Brent of Loudon County, slaves, 25 Oct. 1784 (L.D.B. 21, p. 37).

George Brent, in his will, mentions land in Kentucky; he probably saw service in the Revolutionary War.

Children, from his Bible**:

191 1 Sarah, b. 22 Jan. 1774; d. ——; m. —— Powell, and had: (POWELL)

  1 George Brent, b. 29 Nov. 1790.

  2 Bartella, b. 26 Feb. 1792.

  3 Julien, b. 18 Jan. 1794.

---

*Sarah Brent, above, evidently married a son or grandson of Eleanor[5] Peyton (Valentine[4], Henry[3], Henry[2], Henry[1]) and William Powell, Jr. William Powell, Jr., names a daughter and granddaughter "Sarah Powell" in his will, 1787 . . . "Wm. Powell, gent., an incorporator of the 2nd Charter, Va. Company of London, who paid £25 subscription, came to Virginia with Gates 1611; was the gunner of James City; member first House of Burgesses 30 July 1619. Pace first told him of the plot, revealed by chance, for murdering the colonists 21 March 1622. He was afterwards employed to take revenge on the Indians, and was probably killed by them on the Chickahominy, between 20 and 24 Jan. 1623 (Brown's *Genesis*).

**"In response to your letter Sept. 27th, am enclosing transcription of birth and death records as appearing in a Bible which belonged to my grandfather Allen Smith Wrenn (this Bible belonged originally to Thomas Brent, 41, his great, great, great grandfather) of Middletown, Ohio. One page of this Bible, carrying unknown entries, was stolen during my grandfather's time by someone who went to the house and asked permission to look up the records in this Bible . . . My grandfather Allen Smith Wrenn was born in Westchester, W. Va. . . . My own father, Thos. A. Wrenn, died Sept. 17th, 1918." (From letter written by Thomas Newton Wrenn, of South Norwalk, Conn., 1934.)

4 Amey Currell, b. 14 May 1795.

5 Amery, b. 28 (?) Oct. 1796.

192   II   Caty, b. 4 Oct. 1775; d. 22 Sept. 1822; m. Thomas Wrenn, ——, probably a son of James and Catherine (Brent) Wrenn (48), and of the John Wrenn line of Lancaster County. Thomas Wrenn died 9 Sept. 1834, probably in Middletown, Ohio, and had, at least:

(WRENN)

1 Patsy Newton

2 Allen Smith, b. ——, in Westchester, West Va.; m. ——; d. ——, in Middletown, Ohio. He had at least:

    I Kate B. Wrenn (living 1934), spinster

    II Thos. A., d. 17 Sept. 1917; and had at least— Thos. Newton Wrenn of Conn.

193   III   Thomas, b. 3 July 1777, not named in mother's will, 1827.

194   IV   Willis, b. 20 May 1780; d. ——; m. ——, and had four children by 1827.

195   V   Martin, b. 12 March 1782; d.——. [There is an est. appraisement in Scott County, Ky., of one Martin B. It might be this one or Martin B. (142). It is dated 1848.] Not named in mother's will, 1827.

+196   VI   Hugh, b. 30 July 1784; d. 1 Nov. 1852; m. 23 Dec. 1809, Elizabeth Ash Chinn.

[104] THOMAS[5] BRENT (Thomas[4], George[3], Hugh[2], Hugh[1]), was born 17 April 1750 in Lancaster County, Va.; d. 10 May 1832, in Georgetown, Ky. He married (I) 20 Oct. 1774, Judith King, widow, with the consent of James Pollard. The marriage bond describes him as "Thomas Brent Jr." M. (II) Lucy Brent, dau. of George Brent (42), and his wife Margaret Simmons, 18 Feb. 1779; m. (III) Sarah —— probably in Kentucky. She was born 26 Aug. 1765; d. 7 Sept. 1821.

In the census of 1783, Thomas Brent* of Lancaster County is

---

*"Mr. Thomas Brent, younger brother of William Brent, moved long since to Kentucky with Aunt Elizabeth Hathaway, Capt. Lawson's wife's youngest sister. . . . who is now married, but not known to whom. She has children"; from a letter written by Lawson Hathaway (1790-1845), *circa* 1830. This Lawson Hathaway is NOT the son of Capt. John Hathaway (Wm. A. Brent's notes).

listed as having "four whites and six blacks." In the 1785 census, he is not listed. He must have gone to Kentucky during this interim. Miss Allie Lee Brent of Lee County, Va. writes me that she has her great-grandfather's family Bible . . . that after the marriage of his son Thomas William Brent, he moved from Scott City, Ky. (now Georgetown) to Henderson, and had a large dry-goods store . . . "my grandfather had a sister Lizzie Brent who married an Atkins at Scott City, Ky. I know this by an old letter." The dates of birth and death and the third marriage are from her Bible, and the date of birth of Thomas Brent agrees with the date as inscribed in the Bible owned by Mr. Smith Wrenn of Middletown Ohio.

Children:

+197 I Thomas William, b. 1 May 1794, at Scott City, Ky.; d. 24 Nov. 1875, in Lee County, Va.; m. 12 Aug. 1817, Susan Tarlton Keith, daughter of Alexander D. Keith of Markham, Faquier County, Va.

198 II Elizabeth, b. ——; d. ——; m. (I) ——, —— Atkins, of Scott City, Ky.; (II) —— Dehoney.

198-a III (daughter), m. James McManning ("to James McManning and children, 5 shillings, as they have already received their part": from Thos. Brent's will).

[105] VINCENT[5] BRENT (Thomas[4], George[3], Hugh[2], Hugh[1]), was born 6 May 1753 in Lancaster County, Va.; d., his will was written 27 April, and probated 16 Sept. 1799, in Lancaster County, Va.; m. (I) ——; (II) 24 June 1786, Margaret Steptoe Lawson; Thomas N. Lawson, Sec.

He gives to his son Charles Brent, slaves, 1783. Charles was a minor at that time. Lancaster Land Causes 15 Oct. 1809, give as the legal heirs of Vincent Brent: Nancy Brent, Sarah N. Brent and Caty L. Robertson.

Vincent Brent was one of the Gentleman Justices of Lancaster Co. 1795.

[97]

Children, 1st marriage:

199   I   Charles*, b. 5 Nov. 1779; d. s. p. after 1799.

200   II   Arthur, probably d. s. p.

Children, 2nd marriage:

201   III Katherine Lawson, m. 3 May 1809, Andrew Robertson.

+202   IV Ann Steptoe, b. ——; d. ——; m.(I) 24 March 1814, James Brent Jr., son of William and Ellinor (Brumley) Brent; m. (II) 11 Dec. 1828, John Merridith, widower. He died 1834.

203   v   Sarah Newton.

[110] GEORGE⁵ BRENT (George⁴, George³, Hugh², Hugh¹), was born 7 July 1766 in Lancaster County, Va.; d. 11 Nov. 1814; m. 18 Feb. 1792, Sarah Edmonds, dau. of Col. Elias Edmonds of Lancaster County, an officer in the Revolution of 1776. George Brent served in the War of 1812, Capt. Hugh Brent's Co., 92nd Regiment.

Children:

+204   I   George, b. 1794; d. Feb. 1861, "in 68th year"; m. (I) 29 Aug. 1816, Catherine Tapscott, daughter of John and Mary (Spilman) Tapscott, who m. 8 Sept. 1786; b. 1792/3; d. 19 Nov. 1840, "in 48th year of her age." M. (II) 22 May 1843, Hannah G. Curtis, second dau. of Charles and Ann (George) Curtis, who m. 21 Nov. 1789. She was born 17 Nov. 1792; d. 22 Nov. 1852; m. (III), 31 March 1853, Ann N. (Hubbard) Leland, wid. of Leroy Leland.

205   II   Charles, b. 9 Jan. 1793; d. Feb. 1793.

+206   III Elias Edmonds, b. *circa* 1798; d. 1843; m. 1 April 1824, Elizabeth C. Edwards. She died 1843.

---

*The Bible of Thomas Brent, father of Vincent(105), contains the following data:

      Ann Brent, my granddaughter, b. 3 Feb. 1776.
      Charles Brent, my grandson, b. 5 Nov. 1779.
The entry of the death of this same Thomas Brent is: "departed this life on Saturday Morning, 13 October 1781.
                        (signed)   M. Vint. Brent."

+207   IV   William Hartwell, b. 27 Feb. 1800; d. 8 May 1843; m. 20 Nov. 1823, Catherine M. Carter, only dau. of James and Mary (Bond) Carter.

208   V   Elizabeth, b. 2 Feb. 1796; d. 4 April 1854; m. her cousin, Kenner Brent (209) (see his line).

[111] CHARLES[5] BRENT (George[4], George[3], Hugh[2], Hugh[1]), was born *circa* 1768, in Lancaster County, Va.; d. 27 Dec. 1814, in Lancaster County, Va.; m. Dec. 1791, Catherine Kirk, dau. of James Kirk and Lucy Carter. She was born 1770; died 1806. Lucy Carter was daughter of Edward Carter and Catherine (MARTIN–Brent) Carter, and James Kirk was the son of Anthony Kirk and his wife Sarah Brent (65).

Charles Brent was a soldier in the War of 1812, Capt. Hugh Brent's Co., 92 Va. Reg.

Children, from Lancaster Land Causes:

+209   I   Kenner, b. 4 March 1796, in Lancaster County, Va.; d. 27 Nov. 1878, in Ellison Township, Illinois; m. (I) 29 Jan. 1816, Elizabeth Edmonds Brent, dau. of George (107) Brent and Sarah (Edmonds) Brent; m. (II) *circa* 1867, Ann N. (HUBBARD–Leland) Brent, wid. of George Brent (204).

+210   II   Charles S., b. 1802; d. in Missouri; m. 18 July 1825, Sally McTyre; moved to Missouri 1835-6.

211   III   James Kirk, b. *circa* 1800; d. without issue; m. 27 July 1821, Lucy C. Garlington of Lancaster County, Va.

212   IV   Margaret, died in infancy.

[117] Col. CHARLES[5] BRENT (Charles[4], Charles[3], Hugh[2], Hugh[1]), was born at "Winter Hill," Frederick County, Va., *circa* 1765, and was dead by 1829. He married Rachael Moore. He was a colonel in the Va. State militia, and a pall-bearer at Col. Morgan's funeral. He was recorder in Winchester 1808-10, mayor of Winchester 1809, and justice 1811.

Children:

+213   I   Henry Moore, b. ——; d. 15 Oct. 1875; m. (I) Caroline Isabelle Sharrard, who was b. 10 March 1807; d. 11 May 1846; he m. (II) Harriett E. Baker, b. 10 Sept. 1820; d. 9 April 1873.

+214   II   John G., b. ——; d. *circa* 1860 in Henry County, Ky. He m. (I) ——; m. (II) *circa* 1821, Nancy Sidebottoms.

215   III   Charles Inness

216   IV   Emily, m. 1 Sept. 1840, Andrew I. O'Bannon; he is buried in the Riely lot in Winchester, Va.

+217   V   Catherine Moore, b. 21 July 1811; d. 8 March 1862; m. *circa* 1830, James P. Riely, in Frederick County, Va.

218   VI   Elizabeth, b. ——; d. ——; m. 11 Dec. 1816, David Bryarly.

218-a   VII   Sally, b. 23 June 1800; d. 29 March 1818.

218-b   VIII   Mary Ann, b. ——; d. ——; m. 6 Sept. 1830, Richard M. Snyder or Sydnor.

218-c   IX   Susan, b. 3 Dec. 1816; d. 20 Dec. 1910, at Winchester, Va., a spinster.

[118] ELIZABETH[5] BRENT   (Charles[4], Charles[3], Hugh[2], Hugh[1]), was born in Faquier County, Va., 1783 and died 1856. She married William Green in Frederick County, 2 April 1804 (Fr. M. B.). William Green was the son of Moses Green, who married in Faquier County 13 Feb. 1765, Mary Blackwell. She was the daughter of William and Elizabeth (Crump) Blackwell.

Moses Green was the son of Robert Green, who came to Virginia 1717, at the age of 22, and his wife Eleanor Dunn, and grandson of William Green, an English yeoman in the body guard of William, Prince of Orange. Robert Green settled near Brandy (now Culpeper Co.), and his will was probated in Orange County 1748. He was a member of the House of Burgesses in 1736, and was one of the first vestrymen of St. Mark's Parish (Green).

William Green was born in Faquier County, 1784, and died 1824.

[100]

Children, from data presented by Judge John Paul (GREEN):

    I   James, born 1809.

   II   Charles*, born 1810; died 1863; m. (I) 1835, Rebecca Lane; m. (II) 1845, Anne Cunningham.

  III Marianna, b. 1812; d. unmarried.

  IV Maria, b. 1813; m. Howard Rhodes.

   V Robert, m. Adelaide Jacobs, and died in Hannibal, Mo.

  VI William N., m. Elizabeth Langhorne, relict of Allen Stockwell.

 VII Octavia, d. u. m.

VIII George A., b. 1820; d. 1891; m. (I) Elizabeth Talbott; m. (II) Laura Stillwell.

  IX Moses, b. 1822; d. 1870; m. Mary Bowen.

[120] MARY[5] BRENT (Hugh[4], Charles[3], Hugh[2], Hugh[1]), was born 28 June 1767, in Stafford County, Va.; d. 2 Jan. 1812, in Kentucky; m. ——, Hugh McIlvaine, who was born 26 August 1767.

Children, (McILVAINE):

219   I John Brent, b. 5 March 1801; d. 9 Oct. 1888; m. 23 June 1825 Charlotte Victoria Montell Vremont, of Millersburg, Ky. She was born 7 April 1808; died 12 Dec. 1892.

         Children, (McIlvaine):

         1 Hugh, b. 1828; m. Ann Gangon.

         2 John Banks, b. 8 June 1833; m. Clara Lovell Bowen.

         3 Charlotte Vremont, b. 10 June 1835; m. Capt. W. Hehn.

         4 Henry Rogers, b. 26 May 1842; m. Mattie Campbell; d. 1902.

---

*Charles Green, second child above, had at least Katherine Seymour Green, who married Judge John Paul, Sr., of Harrisonburg, Va., and left issue, at least the present judge of the Western Dist. of Virginia, John Paul, Jr., and Charles Paul.

[122] INNES[5] BAXTER BRENT (Hugh[4], Charles[3], Hugh[2], Hugh[1]), was born ——; died ——, in Lexington, Kentucky; m. ——, Catherine Thomas, of Richmond, Va.

He was a deputy sheriff *circa* 1795, and owned considerable real estate in Lexington, and also in Henderson County, Ky., 1804. As his wife is not mentioned in any of his recorded transactions, she was dead by 1800.

Children:

220   I   George, d. s. p., Henderson County, Ky.

221   II   Hugh, d. s. p., Henderson County, Ky.

222   III   Caroline Imlay, b. 15 Feb. 1794; d. 30 Aug. 1829; m. 26 March 1812, Jacob Bugg Hopkins, who was b. 11 Feb. 1790; d. 1849, a son of Gen. Samuel Hopkins and Elizabeth Bugg, who were m. in Mecklenburg County, Va., 10 Jan. 1783.

222-a   IV   Julien.

[123] HANNAH[5] BRENT (Hugh[4], Charles[3], Hugh[2], Hugh[1]), was born 10 April 1769, in Prince William County, Va.; died 15 Sept. 1837 in Kentucky. She married 15 Dec. 1785, Col. Duval Payne, at Goose Creek Church, Fairfax County, and emigrated to Kentucky in 1789. Col. Payne was born 15 Dec. 1764; d. 4 June 1830, a son of Col. William Payne, of the Rev. Army, who was a son of Hugh Payne (Kerr's *Hist. of Ky.*, Vol. V, p. 279).

Children (PAYNE):

223   I   Penelope, b. 19 Sept. 1786; d. ——; m. ——, Daniel Vertuer.

224   II   John, m. (I) Eliza Sprigg; (II) Letitia Whitman.

225   III   May, m. John Morris.

226   IV   Margaret Y., spinster.

227   V   Innes, m. (I) Miss Logan; (II) Eliza Somers.

228   VI   Hugh Brent, m. Amanda Davis.

229   VII   Luanda, m. Wm. Pierce Bayly.

230 VIII Elizabeth Baxter, m. John Trotter Langhorne.

231 IX Susan Clark, m. Samuel Bonde.

232 X Thomas Young, m. Elizabeth Tureman.

233 XI Duval*, m. (I) Miss Taylor; (II) Mary Jane Wilson, dau. of Hamilton Wilson.

234 XII Benjamin, d. young.

235 XIII Alicia Ann, m. James Bonde.

[124] HUGH[5] BRENT (Hugh[4], Charles[3], Hugh[2], Hugh[1]), was born 18 Jan. 1773, in Prince William County, Va.; d. 16 July 1848, in Paris, Kentucky. He married 24 Dec. 1798, Elizabeth Trotter Langhorne, who was born 11 July 1782, and died 1 Oct. 1817. She was the daughter of John and Sarah (Bell) Langhorne, and granddaughter of Maurice and Elizabeth (Trotter) Langhorne, and also granddaughter of David Bell and Judith (Cary) Bell.

Hugh Brent went to Kentucky in the autumn of 1789 with his brother-in-law, Capt. Thomas Young. His father and the remainder of the family came two years later. He resided in Lexington until 1792, when he moved to Paris, Ky. He married three** times, but only Miss Langhorne bore him children. From the Henry County Marriage Bonds, below, he evidently married four times. He is styled *Sr.* and *merchant* in his marriage to Susan Randolph (HARRISON) Lewis, widow.

Children (by Langhorne marriage):

+236 I Thomas Young Trotter, b. 21 July 1801; d. 5 May 1863; m. (I) Elizabeth Arnold; (II) Almyra Taylor.

---

*Duval Payne d. in Independence, Mo. He had at least E. D. Payne, b. 2 Feb. 1847, who returned to Campbell County, Ky., and had John Howard Payne, b. 27 April 1889, in Campbell County, Ky.

**Hugh Brent married Mary Burke; John Burke, bondsman: 23 Dec. 1795 (Henry County, Ky., M. B.). Hugh Brent married Ann Kelly; Wm. McClain, bondsman: 8 Nov. 1818 (Henry County, Ky. M. B.). Hugh Brent, Sr., married Susan Lewis, 31 Jan. 1826 (Bourbon County, Ky., Marriage Records). The Susan Lewis referred to in this bond was the wid. of Chas. Lewis of Lynchburg, Va., and was Susanna Randolph Harrison before her first marriage. She died by 1860 (*Cabells and their Kin*, by Brown).

+237 II Hugh Innes, b. —— 1803; d. —— 1845; m. (I) 13 Oct. 1824, Margaret Armstrong; (II), 1826, Margaret Chambers.

238 III Jack Langhorne, died unmarried.

+239 IV Charles Scott, b. 28 Jan. 1811; d. 16 Feb. 1881; m. (I) Sue Taylor; (II) 10 Feb. 1835, Matilda Chambers; (III) Mrs. M. H. (Page) Ford.

+240 V Sarah Bell, m. Isaac Lewis.

+241 VI Elizabeth Langhorne, m. Henry Clay Hart.

[128] WILLIAM[5] BRENT (William[4], Charles[3], Hugh[2], Hugh[1]), was born in Faquier County, Va. Aug. 1777, and died in Trimble County, Ky. 1851.* He married Elizabeth Simmons, who was born in Faquier County, Va., and moved to Washington County, Ky., 1798. Washington County at that time included what is now Marion County, "and I believe they must have lived in the part that is now Marion County. In 1803, they moved to Henry County, Ky., now Trimble, and resided there until his (William Brent's) death, 1851. They had eleven children, four sons and seven daughters . . two sons and three daughters we know nothing about. The following names of children were given me by my father."**

Children:

+242 I Sanford, b. 5 July 1800, "the eldest son"; d. 1890; m. 7 Dec. 1826, Nancy Scott, dau. of Levi and Nancy (Carter) Scott.

  II John Newton, m. 17 March 1834, America Staten, and left issue.

  III Eliza.†, m. —— McAllister.

  IV Matilda, m. —— Staten.

  V Nancy, m. John Teague, 26 March 1827.

---

*From *Kentucky History*, by Perrin, Battle and Kniffin (6th edition).

**From a letter written me by Mrs. Caroline Brent Stephenson of Crawfordsville, Ind., a great-granddaughter of the above. These two references are my only proofs of this connexion.

†Elizabeth Brent m. Dudley Richardson, 6 Dec. 1827 (Henry County, Ky. marriages).

VI Adeline, m. —— Caplinger.

VII Sarah,* m. 9 March 1830, Henry Roberts; "Wm. Brent, father."

VIII Martha,* m. 6 March, 1837, Noah D. Williams; Eliz. Brent on the bond.

IX ——.

X ——.

XI ——.

[130] ANNE[5] BRENT (William[4], Charles[3], Hugh[2], Hugh[1]), was born *circa* 1775; she is not mentioned in her husband's will, so died before he did, 1815. She married 15 Nov. 1796, Henry Peyton, son of Yelverton and Elizabeth (Heath) Peyton of Stafford County. Hayden states that Henry Peyton was Inspector of Tobacco for Stafford County 1796 to 1803, after which time he was reappointed.

Children, from Hayden (PEYTON):

243 II Henry Peyton (Hayden states that the Rev. Henry Peyton, minister of the Methodist Episcopal church, moved to Boonsville, Missouri).

[131] MARY[5] WADDY BRENT (William[4], Charles[3], Hugh[2], Hugh[1]), was born —— 1785 in Faquier County, Va.; d. —— 1822; m. 25 Oct. 1802, Col. Joseph Blackwell, widower. He was born 1755, and died 15 Sept. 1823, age sixty-eight, at his residence near Elk Run, Faquier County. His first wife was Ann Grayson Gibson, dau. of Col. John and Mary (Brent) Gibson: married 14 Aug. 1787. Mary (Brent) Gibson was the daughter of Hugh Brent (11) and his second wife, Elizabeth Morris.

Col. Joseph Blackwell entered the gallant 3rd regiment of Va. Continental troops a cadet with James Monroe, and served throughout the war. During the struggle

---

*These two marriages are from Henry County, Ky., Marriage Bonds, and are not proven as far as the parentage of the two brides is concerned; however, the inclusion here ought to help other searchers interested in this line.

he was in the battles of Harlem Heights, Princeton, Trenton and Brandywine, and at Charleston, South Carolina, where he was taken prisoner. For his good conduct on these several occasions he was repeatedly promoted until he arrived at the rank of captain, shortly after which the treaty of 1783 was concluded, and Capt. Blackwell returned to Faquier, the county of his birth.

He held the commission of justice of the county court, colonel of the 85th Reg., and was twice commissioned high sheriff of the county.

He was brother-in-law of Col. John Green. His brothers were Captains Samuel, William and Thomas Blackwell. His sister married Col. William Edmonds. (Hayden).

Children, from Hayden, [BLACKWELL—see Mary Brent (29)]:

246   I   Sally Innes, b. 10 Oct. 1804; d. s. p.; m. 30 May 1841, Major Charles Stone, who married her sister Mary Waddy 1832.

247   II   Mary Waddy, m. 12 April, 1832, Maj. Charles Stone, of Stafford County, Va., and had

Children (STONE):

1 Capt. John, killed at Corinth, Miss.

2 Mary.

248   III   Alexander Christopher, b. 24 Dec. 1813; m. 15 Feb. 1838, Eliza. Ann, daughter of Perry and Lorraine (Stucky) Earickson, Jefferson County, Missouri. She was born 13 Nov. 1821.

Children (BLACKWELL):

1 Charles Eppa, educated at West Point; Capt. C. S. A.; mortally wounded at Wilson's Creek.

2 Mary Laura, m. W. M. Eads, at Las Vegas, New Mexico.

3 Perry Erickson, d. s. p.

4 Arthur Malcolm.

5 Isaac Perry.
And four daughters.

249   IV   Joseph Addison, b. 3 March 1816; m. Mary Harrison, and had two children, who died young.

[132] ELIZABETH[5] MARYE BRENT (William[4], Charles[3], Hugh[2], Hugh[1]), was born 1792 ——; died —— 1866; married 22 June 1811, Eppa Hunton, a captain in the War of 1812. He was born —— 1787; died —— 1830, in Faquier County, Va. His will is dated Jan. —— 1830, and recorded 23 Aug. 1830. He names a brother Charles as Exor., and leaves his estate to his family, but does not name them.

Children, (HUNTON):

250	I	Virginia, m. —— Butcher.
251	II	Judith Ann, m. Martin Butcher.
252	III	Silas Brown, m. (I) Margaret Ann Rixey; (II) Mrs. Isaac, nee, Montague.
253	IV	Elizabeth Marye, m. Joseph Morehead.
+254	V	Eppa, b. 1823; d. 1908; m. 1848, Lucy Caroline Weir.
255	VI	George William, m. (I) Virginia Perry; (II) Rebecca Adams; no issue.
256	VII	Mary Brent, m. Maj. Thomas Foster; no issue.
257	VIII	Hannah Neale, m. John Hampton, and had Elizabeth: d. s. p.

[133] JAMES[6] BRENT (Hugh[5], James[4], Hugh[3], Hugh[2], Hugh[1]), was born *circa* 1751 in Lancaster County, Va., and died 1792. His will was written 13 May 1791, and probated 17 Dec. 1792. He married (I) Sally Butcher of Northumberland County, 9 Sept. 1771. She was most probably the relict of William Butcher (will probated 1768); on 11 Nov. 1771, James Brent is possessed with his wife's part of her deceased father's estate, excepting the widow's dower, in the hands of Wm. Nutt, Exor. William Butcher married —— Nutt, daughter of John Nutt of Northumberland County (N. W. B. 5, p. 509). John Nutt, d. 1768.

He married (II) 25 May 1780, Elizabeth (Lawson) Hunt, wid. of John Hunt. She married (III) 7 Sept. 1795, Thomas James. She was the daughter of Eppa Lawson and Mary Brent (72).

James Brent was Church Warden of Christ Church 1783, and a member of the vestry when it was incorporated in July 1783.

[107]

Children, from his will, and that of his dau. Elizabeth; I have not been able to separate the issue by the two wives, but believe that Susannah, Sarah Nutt and James are by the first marriage.

258　ɪ　Susannah, m. 21 Nov. 1796, Spencer George Jr.

259　ɪɪ　Sarah Nutt, m. 19 May 1817, Bartley James.

260　ɪɪɪ　Mary Lee, m. 17 July 1809, John Degge, and had at least:

　　　　ɪ　James Brent Degge, who m. Eliz. Towill, dau. of Thos. and Ann (Lee) Towill, and was living in Alabama 19 Dec. 1842.

+261　ɪv　James, m. 17 June 1805, Frances Hunton.

+262　v　William, m. 19 Aug. 1809, Eliz. L. Hall.

263　vɪ　Elizabeth, d. unmarried, 1814.*

264　vɪɪ　Richard Hall, b. posthumously, 1792.

[135] SARAH[6] BRENT (Hugh[5], James[4], Hugh[3], Hugh[2], Hugh[1]), was born *circa* 1750, in Lancaster County, Va.; d. after 1802, the marriage date of her youngest daughter. She married John Berryman, widower, *circa* 1775. He is spoken of as "Capt. John Berryman," in the Lancaster County records, and was the son of William Berryman of Westmoreland County, whose will was probated 1784. John Berryman's first wife was Martha Newton, daughter of Capt. Willoughby Newton.

John Berryman, in his will, mentions land in Prince William County owned jointly with Mr. Wm. Grayson, and land at Dumfries; Mrs. Frances Maxwell to raise children in case his wife dies before they reach maturity; "to be decently interred by the side of my dec'd wife." James Brent and Wm. Meredith, Exors.

Hugh Brent (64), in his will 1778, names among other children, his daughters, Frances Maxwell and Sarah Berryman, and son James Brent.

---

*Will of *Elizabeth Brent*, 12 April 1814: 17 Oct. 1814; I lend to my friend Thomas James during his natural life, two negroes, and at his death to my brother Thomas James; to Brother John Hunt, one quarter part of my mother's third of my father's estate; also one quarter to my brother *James Brent*; one quarter part to my brother *Richard Hall Brent* and *Mary Lee Brent*; one other quarter to my nephew James Brent Degge; brother John Hunt, Exor.

In Va. County Records, Vol. 1, Spottsylvania County, I find:
"Geo. B. Berryman* and wife Alice, to Martin Brent of Lancaster
County . . ." The above Martin is a half-brother of Sarah (Brent)
Berryman, but Geo. B. Berryman is not named in John Berry-
man's will. John Berryman's will was written 16 Feb. 1786; pro-
bated 16 March 1787.

Children, from John Berryman's will (BERRYMAN):

265   I   Gibson

266   II   Richard

267   III   James, "youngest son."

268   IV   Sarah Foote, m. 3 Sept. 1788, Yarrat Hughlett. She
is described in the bond as "daughter of Sarah Berryman."

269   V   Martha, m. 10 Jan. 1795, John D. Everitt; she probably died before 1800, as he married again 1 Jan.
1800, Alice G. Harrison.

270   VI   Frances Bushrod, "youngest daughter," m. 24 Feb.
1802, George Glasscock. She is described in the bond
as "daughter of Sarah Berryman."

[137] Lieut. GEORGE[6] BRENT (Hugh[5], James[4], Hugh[3], Hugh[2],
Hugh[1]), was born *circa* 1758, in Lancaster County, Va., and died
there 8 Jan. 1824. He married (I) 15 Jan. 1784, Sarah Ann Simmons, daughter of Elizabeth Simmons (w. 1774), Martin Shearman, Sec.; m. (II) 13 Feb. 1802, Judith** (GEORGE-Yerby) Carter,
widow; no issue by this last marriage.

He was lieutenant in the Revolutionary War:
Executive Dept., March 4th, 1833. The heirs of George
Brent are allowed Land Bounty for his services as lieuten-

---

*JOHN BERRYMAN of Spottsylvania County, Va., will written 18 Feb. 1799;
probated 25 Sept. 1799, Scott County, Ky., Bros: Newton, Francis, Josias. Nep-
hews: Wm. Monroe, Josias Berryman Jr., son of Newton B., Francis B.; Nieces:
Eliz. B., dau. of Gerrard B., Winifred B.; Sisters: Winifred Monroe, Eliz. B. (dec'd).
Exors: Newton, Josias and Francis Berryman (bros.). Wit: Sherod Horn, Martin
Brent, Peter Hicks. [These Berrymans are evidently by the John and Martha
(Newton) Berryman marriage.]

**Judith Brent, thrice a widow, mentions in her will: dau. Elizabeth Coppedge,
wife of Cyrus Coppedge; son John Yerby; son Charles Yerby, and his two sons
Thomas and Charles Yerby (Northumberland County B. 27, p. 37).

ant in the State line for three years. (Signed) John Floyd, governor.

"Lancaster County, Va., March 18th, 1833. Cyrus Coppedge made oath as also did Isaac Brent, that Newton Brent, son of George Brent, dec'd, died intestate and without issue, and that George P. Brent and Catherine Pollard are his only heirs. Attest, Robt. T. Dunnaway.

Capt. Henry Lawson for George Brent a loan office certif (icate) for 400 lbs. being money due to the loan office by sd Lawson for a negro fellow that belonged to Sarah Ann Simmons wife of sd Brent that was condemned and executed for felony in the County of Lancaster (W. B. 22, p. 33).

Children:

271   I   Frances, d. s. p.

272   II   Catherine, m. 28 Sept. 1818, James Pollard, and had (POLLARD)—

    1 William

    2 Nancy H., m. Thomas Pinckard, of Northumberland County, 17 Jan. 1842.

    3 Catherine, m. Chatham Flowers.

    4 Sarah Ann, m. Archibald Stott.

273   III   Newton, d. s. p.

+274   IV   George P. Brent, m. 5 May 1818, Harriett Slater, of Fredericksburg, Va.

[141] Capt. HUGH⁶ BRENT (Hugh⁵, James⁴, Hugh³, Hugh², Hugh¹), was born 16 May 1775, in Lancaster County, Va., and died there 16 Feb. 1814. He married (I), 9 Jan. 1796, Mary T. Lawson, who died 25 Jan. 1797. He married (II), 5 Dec. 1799, Alice Martin. She was born 29 April, 1784; died 12 Aug. 1855.

Hugh Brent* was a captain in the 92nd Va. Reg., in the War of 1812; James Kirk was appointed captain after his death.

---

*All printed genealogies have made Hugh Brent of Stafford County, captain of the 92nd Va. Reg. That Hugh had moved to Kentucky by 1789, and the 92nd Va. Reg. was a Lancaster County military unit.

Children, first marriage:

+275   I   Isaac, born 31 Oct. 1796; d. 1848; m. 8 March 1819, Mary Dameron, of Wiccomicco Parish.

Children, second marriage:

276   II   Judith Newton, b. 12 Nov. 1802; m. 28 Nov. 1821, Thomas L. Lawson. He died before 21 June, 1841, leaving (minors)—(Lawson)

     1 Elizabeth C. Lawson.

     2 Marian L. Lawson.

277   III   Kitty Ann, b. 20 Nov. 1804; d. 13 March 1812.

278   IV   Hugh, b. 17 March 1806; m. Mrs. Jane Jones, of Heathsville, Va.

279   V   Wm. Martin, b. 27 March 1808; d. 17 Oct. 1821.

280   VI   Kenner Joseph, b. 22 March 1812; d. 19 July 1831.

[152] JAMES[6] CURD (Brent—Lucy[5], James[4], Hugh[3], Hugh[2], Hugh[1]—Curd—John[3], John[2], Edward[1]), was born in Goochland County, Va., 24 June 1759, and died in Jessamine County, Kentucky about 1821. His gravestone says he died 11 Aug. 1822, but his inventory was taken 21 Nov. 1821; m. in Mercer County, Ky., 30 Aug. 1791, Mary Ann Perkins, b. 6 May 1770; d. 1850; she was the daughter of Capt. Benjamin Hughes Perkins and Mary A. Curd.

Children (Curd):

   I   Willis, b. in Kentucky, 7 Jan. 1793; d. in Missouri Aug. 1866; m. (I) 8 Nov. 1827, Mary Scott, dau. of Joseph Scott; she was b. 11 Sept. 1802; d. 24 Nov. 1845; m. (II) May 1849, Celia South.
Issue, by first marriage (Curd):

     1 Mary A., b. 5 April 1832; d. 29 July 1845, unm.

     2 James W., b. 18 April 1834; d. 24 Dec. 1875; m. (I) 16 Oct. 1860 or 61, Jane Church; m. (II) 8 June 1870, Lucy McFarland, of Ralls County, Mo.

     3 Nancy Price, b. 20 June 1837, in Clark County, Mo.; d. 15 July 1915; m. 26 March 1857, Willis Caldwell Mitchell.

4 Jane, b. in Clark County, Mo. 11 March 1839;
d. 25 Jan. 1888; m. March 1864, William D. Pegram
of Montgomery County, Mo.; he was b. Aug.
1837; they had one child: Curd Pegram, b. in
Moberley, Mo., 1871; d. 1875.

5 Catherine, b. in Clark County, Mo. 10 May 1842;
d. 22 May 1871; m. June 1870, William Leach of
Montgomery County, Mo.; he was b. 1838.

II Mary A. (Polly), b. 21 Oct. 1794; d. 1835 (?); m. 26
April 1821, Courtney R. Lewis.

III Catherine Brent, b. 27 May 1796; d. 29 Feb. 1874;
m. 21 May 1820, Benjamin C. Johnson, widower.

IV Sarah, b. 23 March 1798; d. v. p.

V Lucy Brent, b. 11 March 1800; d. 1822 unmarried.*

VI William, b. 17 June 1802; d. 1822, unmarried.*

VII John Hughes, b. 1804; d. 10 Oct. 1869; m. (I) 19
June 1827, Emily C. Hickman; m. (II), Sept. 1842,
Deborah Freeland; b. 1821; d. 1860.
Issue, second marriage (CURD):

1 Diana, b. 11 Sept. 1843.

2 Mary Ann Brent, b. 30 Nov. or Dec. 1844; m. 28
Aug. 1877, Samuel L. Woody, who was b. Oct.
1838; d. 20 Oct. 1905.

VIII Elizabeth Nichols, b. 15 Sept. 1806; d. 1822.*

IX Benjamin Perkins, b. 10 April 1810; d. 19 Nov. 1888;
m. 18 Sept. 1832, Mary Ann Bryan, b. in Fayette
County, Ky. 18 Aug. 1812; d. 22 Dec. 1887; she was
dau. of Lewis Bryan. They moved to Missouri *circa*
1832.

Issue (CURD):

1 Lewis Bryan, b. Lewis County, Mo., 25 June 1833;
d. 2 Feb. 1867, unmarried.

2 Nancy Price, b. 9 Sept. 1834; d. 24 Nov. 1834.

---

*Jessamine County, Ky. Court Records show inventories of the estates of
Lucy Curd, Elizabeth N. Curd, and William Curd all dated 24 Aug. 1824. It is
probable that these three children died during an epidemic which raged in Kentucky
in 1822. In settlement of their estates, allotments were made to Willis Curd, Courtney R. Lewis, John Curd, James Stephen Curd, Benjamin Curd, Nancy Price
Curd and Mrs. Mary Ann Curd (B. "C," p. 390).

3 Mary Ann, b. 1 Sept. 1835; d. 14 Nov. 1845.

4 James, b. 11 Jan. 1838; d. 27 Feb. 1915; m. 20 Sept. 1866, Margaret J. Feagan.

5 Eliza. Barckley, b. 15 March 1839; d. Columbus, New Mexico, Jan. 1926; m. 18 Nov. 1858, Dr. Hubbard Kavanaugh Hinde, b. 6 Jan. 1834; d. Dec. 1915.

6 Thomas Edward, b. Marion County, Mo., 15 April 1844; d. 3 March 1905; m. 15 March 1871, Estelle Leeper, b. 26 Feb. 1852.

7 William Brent, b. 3 Dec. 1849; d. Kansas City, Mo., 13 May 1916; m. 3 Dec. 1873, Celeste Belle Harriman, dau. of John Harriman of Chillicothe, Mo.

x James Stephens, b. 6 March 1812; d. unmarried.

xi Nancy Price, b. 1814; d. 1833, unmarried.

[153] Major JOHN[6] CURD (Brent—Lucy[5], James[4], Hugh[3], Hugh[2], Hugh[1]—Curd—John[3], John[2], Edward[1]), was born in Goochland County, Va. 23 Nov. 1760 (his gravestone says 10 Sept. 1760, which is an error). He died in Logan County, Ky., 10 Sept. 1838. He married in Goochland County, Va., 10 July 1787, Ann (Nancy) Williams Curd, b. 11 July 1762, d. 20 Sept. 1846, daughter of Richard Curd and Sarah Downer. They came to Kentucky, settling first in Warren County, later removing to Logan County. He enlisted in the Continental Army in 1776 from Goochland County Va., served as private in 9th Va. Reg., Co. of Capt. Samuel Woodson, Col. George Matthews. He was wounded at the Battle of Germantown, 4 Oct. 1777, taken prisoner, carried first to Philadelphia and then to New York, and held until the summer of 1778, when he was exchanged and returned to the army, and then discharged by Gen. Peter Muhlenburg. He later reenlisted, and again served for a period under Col. George Matthews. In May 1780, he was commissioned Major of a Goochland County Company of Militia. His wife Nancy survived him, and was allowed a pension on her application, executed 7 Feb. 1839, at which time she was living with her son Richard at Bowling Green, Ky. John

[113]

and his wife are buried in the Maple Grove Cemetery at Russellville, Ky., their remains having been removed there from the old Baptist Cemetery near that point. The inscription on his tomb reads:

Major John Curd

Mr. Curd espoused with zeal the cause of our glorious Revolution and after a life of virtuous and honorable toil mingles in Heaven (it is hoped) with kindred spirits of that eventful period.

He was a member of the Kentucky Legislature of 1800, representing Warren and Barren Counties.

Children (CURD):

I   Sarah (Sallie), m. 29 Aug. 1810, Samuel H. Curd, b. 10 July 1786, son of Edmund Curd and Elizabeth Coghill.

II Richard, m. Logan County, Ky., 26 Sept. 1812, Elizabeth Moorehead. He removed from Logan County to Warren County, Ky., where he died 1857, without issue; his will dated 27 March 1856; probated Dec. 1857; names wife Eliza. M., and adopted dau. Richardelle Thomas, wife of F. G. Ragland.

III Polly Smith, b. 7 April 1794; d. 26 July 1864; m. 19 May 1812, Spencer Curd, son of Edmund Curd.

IV John Brent, m. 15 Jan. 1818, Louisa C. Slaughter. He settled in Christian County, Ky. The only record found of his children is in a deed of trust for their benefit from their grandfather, John Curd; deeds dated March 1823, and 25 Dec. 1824, Christian County, Ky. records. He died prior to 1838.

Issue (CURD):

1 John Spencer Curd

2 Edward S.

3 Sally Ann McLaughlin Curd, m. 15 May 1838, R. H. Davidge.

4 Lucy Brent Curd (this is problematical), m. 12 Feb. 1846, Edmund H. Curd, of Logan County, Ky.

v Lucy Brent, m. in Logan County, Ky., 20 Sept.
1821, Robert Slaughter. Both Robert and his wife
were dead by 1826, leaving a son Richard H. Slaughter, born *circa* 1822-23.

vi Elizabeth, b. 6 Feb. 1802; d. 13 Oct. 1866; m. 7 Aug.
1821, Col. Samuel Poindexter, b. 17 April 1794; d.
31 Sept. 1875. They are buried at Russellville, Ky.

vii Fanny, b. 9 March 1804; d. 26 June 1834; m. Samuel
Mathis. She is buried at Elizabethtown, Ky.

viii William Elliott, b. 30 April 1807; d. 15 Dec. 1847; m.
in Russellville, Ky., 16 Jan. 1831, Ann Maria Ely,
who was born 8 April 1805, and died 23 July 1881.

Issue (CURD):

1 Elizabeth C., b. 6 April 1834; d. 23 Dec. 1915; m.
Charles W. Nourse, b. 21 Jan. 1834; d. 24 July 1897.

2 Mary, m. Eli Robinson.

[157] NEWTON[6] CURD (BRENT—Lucy[5], James[4], Hugh[3], Hugh[2],
Hugh[1]—CURD—John[3], John[2], Edward[1]), was born in Goochland
County, Va., 31 Nov. 1767, and died in Mercer County, Kentucky,
25 August 1822. He is buried in the Curd cemetery near Curds-
ville, about three miles north of Burgin, Ky. He married 25 March
1789, Ann Elizabeth Hatcher, daughter of Thomas Hatcher, and
his first wife, Sarah Porter. Ann E. Hatcher was born 12 June
1761, and died 29 May 1831. The division of the estate of Newton
Curd, 18 Dec. 1822 (W. B. 7, p. 176, Mercer County, Ky.), names
children below, with the exception of Lucy, who died 1813. His
gravestone says he died 25 Aug. 1822, aged 57 years.

Children (CURD):

1 Sarah Porter, b. 1791-2; d. Jan. 1877; m. her cousin
Stephen Curd, b. 1786; d. Dec. 1876. He was son of
Joseph Curd.

ii Elizabeth Hatcher, b. 1793; m. (i) 4 Feb. 1810, John
West; m. (ii) Brice L. Bradshaw.

iii Sophia Weston, b. 1794; d. March 1878; m. Leonard
T. McCoun, b. 16 Nov. 1800; d. 25 March 1822.

Their daughter, Rebecca McCoun, b. 25 April 1822, d. 25 March 1901, m. Robert Slaughter Curd.

iv Thomas, b. 1796; d. 1878; m. Patsy Cox.

v Lucy Brent, b. 23 Nov. 1798; killed by lightning 23 July 1813.

vi William, b. 1800; d. 1869; m. Lucinda Coghill.

Issue (Curd):

1 Ann Catherine, b. 1825; m. Aaron Voris.

2 Elizabeth Sutton, b. 1826; m. S. L. Bradshaw.

3 William Jr., b. 1829; m. Susan Askins.

4 Thomas J., b. 1831; m. 4 Dec. 1869, Mary L. Sallee.

5 Newton S., b. 1835; m. Lucy E. Munday.

6 Littleton, b. 1837; m. Sarah F. Adams.

7 John Henry, b. 1840; d. in Confederate Army 1864.

[159] PRICE[6] CURD (Brent—Lucy[5], James[4], Hugh[3], Hugh[2], Hugh[1]—Curd—John[3], John[2], Edward[1]), was born in Goochland County, Va., 14 Aug. 1771, and died in Fayette County, Ky., 7 Feb. 1814. He married Fannie Allen, daughter of Richard Allen. She was born 1780, and died Sept. 1834. Price Curd died intestate, his inventory was taken March 1814 (B. "C," p. 22). Richard Higgins, administrator, makes his report 10 March 1816 (B. "D," p. 136). His children are known from his Est. Div. (B. "D," p. 177), and other records. He settled first in Warren County, Ky., where he was Justice of the Quarterly Court; later he removed to Fayette County, Ky.

Children (Curd):

i Kitty Brent, m. 6 Dec. 1814, William Price. Kitty B. Price was living in Warren County, Ky., in 1843, having inherited land there from her father.

ii John, b. 16 May 1799; d. Feb. 1876; m. (1) 13 May 1824, Elizabeth Caldwell, who died 1864. She was dau. of Geo. and Susan Caldwell. They had an only son, John Caldwell Curd, b. 2 Dec. 1840; m. 1863,

Lydia Downing. John Curd served three terms in the Kentucky Legislature. He m. (II), 17 Oct. 1845, Mrs. Eliza M. Gist. No issue by this second marriage.

III Richard Allen Curd, b. 1801; d. March 1836, son of Price Curd and Fanny Allen. He m. 8 May 1823, Eleanor Hart Hunt, daughter of John Hunt, and sister to the mother of Gen. John Hunt Morgan, and to Charlton Hunt, one of the early mayors of Lexington, Ky. His will was dated 3 March 1836, and proved the same month. In it he names his wife Eleanor, and states that his children are to be educated, but does not name them. The children are named in their mother's will, dated 9 April 1868, when all except one were married.

Issue (CURD):

1 Catherine H., m. 20 June 1844, John B. Tilford.

2 Frances Price, b. 1825; d. 1885; m. 7 Nov. 1844, Charles Scott Bodley.

3 Richard Allen Jr.

4 Eleanor H., m. 3 Nov. 1853, J. C. Wickliffe.

5 Theodosia A., b. 1836; m. 26 April 1870, Col. William Douglas Pickett, C. S. A., and died shortly afterwards; had one child: Wm. Douglas Jr., b. 1871; d. 1874.

6 John W., died in the Mexican War. His will was proven 12 Sept. 1849.

IV Lucy Ann, m. Harrison E. Daniel of Jessamine County, Ky.

V Polly, m. 6 Feb. 1827, Samuel Harvey.

VI William P., m. 14 Jan. 1830, Mary A. McGowan, dau. of D. McGowan (Magowan). They had one child, a dau., Nancy, who m. 29 August 1850, Robert B. Shelton. William Curd was proprietor of the "Curd House," one of Lexington, Kentucky's early hostelrys, which stood at the corner of Vine and Mill Streets for many years.

[160] DANIEL[6] CURD (BRENT—Lucy[5], James[4], Hugh[3], Hugh[2], Hugh[1]—CURD—John[3], John[2], Edward[1]), was born 14 October 1773, in Goochland County, Va. He died 18 April 1843, in Barren County,

[117]

Kentucky. He married at Glasgow, Ky., 1799, Fannie S. Trigg, who was born 28 Jan. 1785, daughter of Haiden Trigg, who came to Kentucky from Bedford County, Va., where he married 12 Aug. 1783, Martha Gatewood, with the consent of her father, James Gatewood. Haiden Trigg was one of the first Justices of Peace of Barren County, Ky. Daniel Curd's will was dated 5 Oct. 1841, and probated May 1843 (B. 3, p. 207—Barren County, Ky., wills).

Children (CURD):

1 Haiden Trigg, b. in Glasgow, Kentucky 26 April 1804; d. in Louisville, Ky., 24 Feb. 1859. He married 26 Feb. 1830, Martha Ann Edmunds, b. 7 Dec. 1813; d. 21 June 1868. She was daughter of Capt. William Edmunds and his wife Polly Ann Penn, who came from Amherst County, Va., where they were married 27 March 1805, John Penn Sr., guardian (Amherst County M. B.).

Issue (CURD):

1 John Tomkins, b. 1 March 1831; d. 5 April 1841.

2 William Edmunds, b. 21 April 1833; d. Jan. 1872; m. 4 Oct. 1855, Elizabeth Cunningham. She died 10 Aug. 1884, without issue.

3 Mary Fanny, b. 24 Feb. 1835; d. 8 Jan. 1808; m. 31 Jan. 1856, George R. Miller.

4 Lucy James, b. 4 April 1837; d. 28 June 1908; m. 12 Nov. 1868, Daniel Flavel Wilkin.

5 Daniel, b. 14 Sept. 1839; d. 24 March 1841.

6 Martha Ann, b. 23 July 1843; d. 4 Aug. 1869; m. June 1869, Morton B. Howell, of Nashville, Tenn. She was his second wife.

7 Sarah Holman, b. 26 June 1845; d. Nov. 1881; m. June 1865, James Steele.

8 Elizabeth Capers Trigg, b. 9 Sept. 1848; m. 3 Nov. 1870, Morton B. Howell of Nashville, Tenn.— his third wife.

9 Haiden Trigg, b. 10 Jan. 1850; d. 4 Aug. 1889; m. June 1878, Annie Joyes, dau. of Patrick Joyes, of Louisville, Ky.

10 Charles Paine, b. 20 Sept. 1851; d. 4 June 1906; m. 1880, Selene Harding of Nashville, Tenn.

11 James Pryor, b. 3 June 1855; d. Sept. 1913; m. Elizabeth Swearengen.

II John Brent, b. 27 Dec. 1806; d. *circa* 1852. He married Helen Chaplin, dau. of William Chaplin and his wife, Betty Perkins. He went to Mercer County, then to Pulaski County, Ky.

Issue (CURD):

1 Elizabeth, m. John Crawford.

2 Alanson Trigg, m. Rebecca Woods.

3 William Chaplin, m. Belle O. Saunders. They lived at Somerset, Pulaski County, Ky.

4 Sarah Ann, m. Maj. Alderson Keene.

5 Martha Jane, m. J. B. Gragg.

III Alanson Trigg, d. 1836, unmarried; will dated 12 Aug. 1836; probated Oct. 1836.

IV Elizabeth C., b. 14 June 1808; d. 7 Feb. 1887; m. 7 July 1829, John J. Snoddy.

V Patsy, m. 1824, Schuyler Murrell, son of Samuel Murrell.

VI Haviliah Price, b. 1817, in Barren County; d. Cave City, Ky., 18 July 1884; m. 1851, Letitia Y. Mosby, daughter of Thomas Mosby and Judith Martin, of Woodford County, Ky.

Issue (CURD):

1 Daniel Trigg, b. 23 June 1856; m. 13 Nov. 1878, Kate R. Wilson.

2 Elizabeth Irby, b. 3 Feb. 1863; m. 16 Dec. 1885, George Thomas Tucker.

3 John Brent, b. Nov. 1865; m. 1887, Syrene Petty

4 Oscar Frank, b. 18 Oct. 1868; m. 14 Jan. 1891, Kate E. Grimes.

5 Clara Winn, b. 5 April 1871; m. 21 Dec. 1887 William G. Overstreet.

6 Cyrus Haiden, b. 12 April 1873; m. (1) 27 Aug. 1895, Rufie Ivy, dau. of Jesse W. Ivy and Margaret Walker; lives at Holly Springs, Mississippi.

[119]

vii Lucy Brent, m. 1 Jan. 1831, Woodford Martin.

viii Mary Ann Willia, b. 1824; d. 1888; m. 12 Nov. 1849, Franklin Dickey.

ix Beverly Daniel, b. 26 Dec. 1826; d. 16 Aug. 1898; m. 2 Nov. 1849, Mariah L. Stark, who was b. 3 Dec. 1830, and d. 15 Nov. 1891. She was dau. of Theophilus Stark, of Culpeper County, Va. Beverly Daniel Curd and his wife are buried at Cave City, Ky.
Issue (CURD):

1 Fanny Lucinda, b. 1853; m. 21 May 1872, Hardin Young Davis.

2 Lucy, b. 1855; d. unmarried.

3 Patty W., b. 1857; d. unmarried.

4 Daniel, b. 20 March 1862; d. 30 Oct. 1918, unmarried.

5 Edwin W., b. 1864; d. 1923; m. Anne M. Smith, b. 1868; d. 1933; lived at Cave City, Ky.

6 Mary Elizabeth, b. 4 Jan. 1867; m. 1887 Eugene Ford.

7 Bunny, b. 31 Jan. 1869; m. 1885, Henry C. King. They live in Oklahoma.

8 Theophilus, b. Sept. 1871; d. unmarried.

[161] WOODFORD[6] CURD (BRENT—Lucy[5], James[4], Hugh[3], Hugh[2], Hugh[1]—CURD—John[3], John[2], Edward[1]), was born in Goochland County, Virginia, 15 Dec. 1775. He married 10 Oct. 1800, in Jessamine County, Kentucky, Jenny West, daughter of Charles West. He moved to Jefferson County, Ky., settling in that part cut off to form Oldham. He died *circa* 1821-2.

Children, from the settlement of the estate of John Curd, when they were given lands on Harrod's Creek, Jefferson County, later Oldham County, Ky., 8 May 1823 (B. 5, p. 395, Jefferson County, Ky.) (CURD):

1 Lucy Brent, m. 20 Aug. 1821, Coleman Buckner, who d. 10 Jan. 1852.

II Fanny E., m. 9 March 1824, James B. Ward.

III Adaline (Malvina Adaline), m. 19 Dec. 1829, James Metcalfe.

IV John W., m. 20 Aug. 1839, Mary Jane Ashby, daughter of John Ashby.

V Emily P., m. 13 Dec. 1833, James Taylor Thornton.

VI Mary J., m. 23 June 1835, John H. Baldock.

VII Patsy P., m. 16 Dec. 1839, James H. Button.

[161-a] MERRYMAN⁶ B. CURD (Brent—Lucy⁵, James⁴, Hugh³, Hugh², Hugh¹,—Curd, John³, John², Edward¹), was born (either in Goochland County, Va., or just after the arrival of his parents in Kentucky), 12 May 1780. He died in Trimble County, Ky. 2 Oct. 1841. He married in Fayette County, Ky., 12 April 1804, Polly Kay, born 11 April 1780, and died in Crawford County, Illinois, 20 March 1858. She was the daughter of John and Mary Kay of Fayette County, Ky. Merryman Curd's marriage is recorded in both Fayette and Jessamine Counties, Ky. Because he is not listed in the Douglas Register, I am giving the following references to prove that he was a son of John and Lucy Brent Curd.

(B. "H," p. 27, Jessamine County, Ky.) 12 July 1823 . . "whereas I, Merriman B. Curd of Jessamine County State of Kentucky have given unto my children all of my property to wit, thirteen negro slaves, all of my tract of land whereon I now live containing 350 acres, it being a part of John Curds 820 acre survey above the mouth of Dick's River and adjoining Bradshaw, Curds etc. . . . . all of my stock of horses, cows, sheep . . . household goods, also all of my crop now on the plantation . . . also what is willed to me and my wife Polly by John Kay. . . . . The said children by their guardians Robert Kay, William A. Leavey and Richard A. Curd of Fayette County, John Green of Lincoln County, and Willis Curd and Samuel H. Woodson of Jessamine County, and James Birney, Sr. of Mercer County, do agree to pay all just debts of their father M. B. Curd, take the property above mentioned and maintain their father and mother jenteely, allow them the same and every (comfort) they

[121]

formerly enjoyed. As witness my hand the 12th day of July 1823. Test. Edward Bradshaw, Benjamin Bradshaw, Filed 29 Feb. 1824."

(B. "H," p. 34, 22 March 1824) . . . "Merryman B. Curd and wife Polly to Benjamin Bradshaw 333 acres . . . $3,333.00 . . . adjoining lands of Newton Curd deceased, upon which the said Merryman B. Curd at present resides." Test—Willis Curd, C. R. Lewis, John Curd, J. Higbee Jr.

Our next record of Merryman B. Curd is from the Deed Books of Oldham County, Ky. (B. "C," p. 497, 29 Feb. 1836).

Between Robert Wickliffe of Lexington, Ky., on the one part and John Curd and William T. Curd of the other part, witnesseth: that whereas the said Robert Wickliffe did agree to convey to Merryman B. Curd or his order a certain tract of land situated in the county of Oldham on the Ohio River and the said Merryman B. Curd has by his order dated the 5th day of Feb. 1836 ordered and requested said Wickliffe to convey to the said John Curd and William T. Curd 319 acres, parcel of the original tract, in consideration of the premises and the further consideration of four dollars per acre heretofore paid to said Wickliffe by the said Merryman B. Curd, said Wickliffe conveys to John and William T. Curd. . . .

Our fourth record of Merryman B. Curd is in Trimble County, Ky., 6 Jan. 1834, when he pays a surveyor named Strother for having made a survey of lands on the Ohio River belonging to Robert Wickliffe which Merryman had evidently proposed purchasing from said Wickliffe. Then, D. B. "A," p. 8, 13 March 1837, Robert Wickliffe of Lexington, Ky., deeds land to Samuel Trotter Curd and Augustine Lewis Curd, of the County of Trimble, and for description of this land, refers to the plat made by Strother for Merryman B. Curd. 5 Sept. 1842; Augustine L. Curd sells his part of this land to Evan M. Garrett of Trimble County, and on 1 March 1843, Samuel Trotter Curd sells his share to the same Garrett. In book "B," p. 79, 17 Oct. 1843, is the following: Samuel T. Curd and Augustine L. Curd, of Trimble County, Ky., to Milburn Abbott of Bethlehem in the State of Indiana, for one dollar in hand paid and for the consideration that said Abbott, as the attorney in fact of

[122]

John Hawkins of Jessamine County, Ky., has compromised a claim of said Hawkins against said Curds.

These families eventually left Trimble and Oldham Counties, some going to Missouri, others to Indiana and Illinois. The fact that Merryman B. Curd owned one third of the John Curd 820 acre tract, and that the other two thirds was owned by Newton, son of John, and by William Bradshaw and his wife Catherine Curd, son-in-law and daughter of John Curd, together with the fact that Merryman named his first son JOHN, and the further fact that when he left Jessamine County he settled in Oldham County, alongside the family of his brother Woodford, and that the name Merryman, through the marriage of Susannah Merryman, daughter of Richard Merryman, to William Payne, and the son by this marriage, Merryman Payne's marriage with Catherine Brent, leads one to believe that he must have been a son of John Curd of Dix River. The reason his birth was not registered in the Douglas Register, as were those of the other children, is probably due to the fact that his family moved to Kentucky about the time of his birth. The following list of children of Merryman B. Curd has been sent by Mr. R. A. Curd, of Indianapolis, Ind., and is taken from the family bible.

Children (CURD):

I John M., b. 19 April 1805; d. Marion County, Indiana, 19 April 1837; m. in Oldham County, Ky., 11 Jan. 1836, Rebecca Baldock, dau. of James Baldock.

II Mariah Etna, b. 28 Jan. 1807; d. 19 Aug. 1841; m. in Oldham County, Ky., 9 Jan. 1827, Henry H. Neighbours.

III William T., b. in Jessamine County, Ky., 18 Jan. 1809; d. 4 Feb. 1875; m. in Oldham County, Ky., 19 April 1830, Elizabeth Moreland, who was b. 3 Nov. 1808; d. 19 Nov. 1888, dau. of Jesse Moreland. Issue (CURD):

 I James Moreland, b. 1 March 1831; m. and had issue.

2 Merryman Brent, b. 22 March 1832; d. 18 Jan. 1917; m. 8 Feb. 1855, Margaret Jennings.

IV Francis H., b. 29 Dec. 1810; d. Aug. 1832.

V Robert I., b. 27 Sept. 1812; d. Sept. 1833.

VI Sarah Ann, b. 12 Jan. 1814; d. Aug. 1834.

VII Samuel Trotter, b. in Jessamine County, Ky., 8 May 1816; d. Stoddard County, Mo., 1866; m. in Trimble County, Ky., 14 Oct. 1837, Lucy (Lucens) Moreland, dau. of Jesse Moreland. Oct. 10, 1859, he sold the last of his land holdings in Trimble County, Ky., to Elijah Chandler, and moved to Stoddard County, Mo., settling six miles east of Puxico, at the present site of Curdton, where he bought land 2 Jan. 1860. He died intestate 1866, and his estate was ordered sold at public sale 13 Aug. 1866, and when sold was purchased by his son Samuel P. Curd.

Issue (CURD):

1 Jesse A., b. 1840; d. 1895; m. Rosetta J. Hammons.

2 Samuel Price, b. 5 Dec. 1842; d. 8 Aug. 1893; m. 28 Feb. 1867, Mary E. St. John.

3 Newton, b. 1859; d. 1923, unmarried.

4 Josephine, m. Jesse Jackson, and living at Marble Hill P. O., Lutesville, Mo.

5 Sarah Jane, m. James G. Gaines.

6 Mary Jane, m. —— Gaines.

7 Emily, m. —— Bess.

VIII Andrew Price, b. 21 April 1816; d. Sept. 1835.

IX Augustine Lewis, b. in Jessamine County, Ky., 7 March 1820; he moved to Trimble County, Ky., where he married Lucinda ——. He is supposed to have moved later to Indianapolis, Indiana.

Issue (CURD):

1 John

2 James

3 Howard, and probably others.

X Polly, b. 12 Nov. 1821; d. 1823.

[162] JAMES[6] BRENT (John[5], James[4], Hugh[3], Hugh[2], Hugh[1]), was born 2 July 1762, in either Lancaster or Charlotte County, Va.; died 11 April 1819, in Charlotte County, Va.; m. —— Ann Patrick.

Stockley Brent (70), in his will, 1764, leaves to his nephew James Brent, son of his brother, John Brent, a horse and other property.

Children:

281 I Martha, m. Capt. George Hannah, and had—(HAN-NAH):

      1 Joel W. Hannah.

      2 Julia Ann Hannah, m. Samuel Thomas.

282 II Julia, m. Edward Cary Allen, and "lives in North Carolina"; she was b. 9 April 1791; d. 22 Jan. 1881; and had—(ALLEN):

      1 Wm. H. Allen, b. 10 Jan. 1816; d. 4 Nov. 1892; m. Emaline Allen, and had—

         1 Julia Brent Allen, b. 24 April 1850; d. 19 Jan. 1919; and probably others.

[184] JAMES[6] HAINES BRENT (James[5], James[4], William[3], Hugh[2], Hugh[1]), was born at "Wellington," Nelson County, Va., 30 Aug. 1813; d. in Nelson County 13 Jan. 1902. He married 24 June 1850, Mildred Pierce. She died in the fall of 1906.

Children:

+283 I Franklin Pierce, b. 14 Sept. 1852; d. 11 Aug. 1927; m. Mattie Buxton Porter.

284 II Sarah, d. v. p.

285 III Florence, d. v. p.

286 IV John Thornhill, b. Dec. 1856; m. Betty Kent, and has several children living.

287 V Jacob, d. v. p. 1881.

288 VI Minnie, d. v. p. 1891, twenty-six years old.

289 VII Lucy, m. Kimbrough Anderson, and has three children.

290 VIII Genoa, m. Charles Witt, and had several children.
291 IX Betty E., b. 4 Aug. 1858; d. 1906; m. J. L. Shelton, and had several children.
292 X Annie, d. s. p.
293 XI Otis, d. s. p. 1902.
293-a XII James D., m. Ruby Fitch, and left issue.

[187] HUGH⁶ LITTLETON BRENT (James⁵, James⁴, William³, Hugh², Hugh¹), was born at "Wellington," Nelson County, Va., 19 March 1820; died in Nelson County, Va., 25 June 1879. He married 1 Jan. 1850, Missouri C. (Jones) Clarkson, widow; b. 1828; d. 26 June 1886.

Children:
294 I Metellus, b. *circa* 1852; d. 1924; m. 14 Jan. 1874, his cousin, Susan Witt and had—
    1 Mary Weta, d. 16 Sept. 1931, spinster.
    2 Hugh, d. 1922, and left one son.
    3 Claude, b. 1883.
295 II Wm. Kossuth, b. 21 Dec. 1856; d. 27 Dec. 1861.
296 III J. Claude, b. 22 Sept. 1858; d. 22 April 1874.

[188] SARAH⁶ ELLEN BRENT (James D.⁵, James⁴, William³, Hugh², Hugh¹), was born at "Wellington," Nelson County, Va., 23 August 1822, and died 25 Sept. 1844, in Warren County, Ky. She married 3 Oct. 1839, Egbert Oswald Shields, tenth child of James Shields and Elizabeth Higginbotham. He was born in Nelson County, Va., 30 May 1818, and died in Howard County, Missouri, 8 Feb. 1883.

Children (SHIELDS):
    1 Henry Constantine, b. in Warren County, Ky., 20 July 1840, and died in Howard County, Mo., 27 Dec. 1928; served in the Confederate Army, was county surveyor and county judge.

II   Frances Ellen, b. in Warren County, Ky., 11 April 1842; d. in Amherst County, Va., 14 Nov. 1905; married 26 Aug. 1858, Dr. James Walter Washington La Fayette Vaughan, and had (VAUGHAN)—

    1 Dr. Geo. Tully, m. 27 June 1883, Maria Venable, and left issue.

    2 Corinne, m. Edward Hoffman, and had one son.

    3 (dau.), m. —— Burks, and had issue.

III   Eugenia Landon, b. in Warren County, Ky., 7 Sept. 1844; d. in Nelson County, Va., 17 Feb. 1905; m. Dec. 1864, Shadrack Levi Carter, son of Thomas Carter and Eliz. A. Moore; b. 6 Sept. 1840; d. 7 Feb. 1924; he was Lt. 49th Va. Reg., C. S. A. Issue (CARTER)—

    1 Thomas, m. and had issue.

    2 Robert, m. and had issue.

    3 Cleveland, unmarried.

    4 Judson, m. and had issue.

    5 Eugenia, m. Frank Anderson and had issue.

    6 Christine, m. W. Cabell Higginbotham.

    7 Lessly, m. Minnie Brent (411); no issue.

EXCURSUS—VAUGHAN

1 *John Vaughan*, living in King George County, Va., 1705, married a Miss Loving; his son—

2 William, b. *circa* 1730, m. Girnetta Riddle of Culpeper County, Va. His son—

3 George, b. in Culpeper County, 1772, m. (I) 1795, Sukie Loving; m. (II), 1817, Alice Nevil, wid.; he d. in Missouri, 1846; his son—

4 George, b. in Nelson County, Va., 1801; d. there 1876; m. Mary C. Edmunds, dau. of Roland Edmunds and his wife Elizabeth Nevil, dau. of Col. James Nevil, of Amherst County (See NEVIL excursus that follows.)

EXCURSUS—NEVIL

1   *John Nevil*, came to St. Marys, Maryland on the *Ark and Dove*, 1634; m. M. B. Thornley; their son—

2   James, b. *circa* 1640, m. Elizabeth ——, and moved to Isle of Wight County, Va., where he was killed in an Indian massacre 1740; they had—

3   John, m. Margaret ——, and had—

4   James, b. 1686; d. 1752, in Albemarle County, Va. They had—

5   James, b. 1728, d. in Amherst County, 1784; m. Mary Lewis. He was captain of Albemarle Militia in French and Indian Wars (Hening), Sheriff of Amherst County, Major, Lt. Col., Col., and County Lieutenant prior to and during the Rev. War, for Amherst County. They had—

6   Elizabeth Nevil, b. 1767; m. 1789, Roland Edmunds, b. 1775; d. 1840; they had—

7   Mary C. Edmunds, b. 1805; d. 1875; m. 20 Oct. 1825, Capt. George Vaughan, who was b. 1801, and d. 1877. They were the parents of Mary Louise Vaughan, wife of Landon Newton Brent, Sr. (189).

[189] LANDON[6] NEWTON BRENT (James[5], James[4], William[3], Hugh[2], Hugh[1]), was born 13 Oct. 1824, "at 10 o'clock Wednesday night," at "Wellington," Nelson County, Va., and died there 29 May 1909, in his 85th year. He married 8th Dec. 1847, Mary Louise Vaughan of Amherst County, daughter of George and Mary C. (Edmunds) Vaughan, and great granddaughter of Col. James Nevil and his wife Mary Lewis. She was born 17 Nov. 1828, and died 24 May 1897.

Col. James Nevil was captain of Albemarle militia in French and Indian Wars 1757-8; sheriff of Amherst County; major, lieutenant-colonel, colonel and County Lieutenant in the Revolutionary War.

[128]

"Capt. George Vaughan died 27 Aug. 1877, seventy-six years old" (from Landon N. Brent's diary).

Landon Newton Brent served in the army of the Confederacy. From his diary: 26 March 1862—"Our cause is a little gloomy, but not hopeless. . . . I am packing up today to start for the seat of War . . . time is pressing . . . and the great Day of Retribution will right all things, and I shall turn my face from my home and fireside with a full consciousness of having tried to do my duty—of having been a faithful husband, father and master."

Children:

     I   Ulla Bona, d. v. p. 1855, six years old.

+297   II   Kendall Carroll, b. 6 Aug. 1851; d. 24 Feb. 1931; m. (I), 2 Feb. 1872, Florence Hall, in the state of New Mexico; m. (II), *circa* 1875, Beneranda Chivez, in old Mexico.

298   III   Mary Washington, b. 24 Sept. 1853; d. 11 June 1915; m. 20 Dec. 1876, John Will Witt; he d. 15 Nov. 1924; they had (WITT):

       1 Margaret, d. v. p.

299   IV   Adeline Thornhill, b. 23 Nov. 1856; m. 16 Dec. 1874, Henry Patteson; he was b. 12 June 1851; d. 2 June 1904. She changed her name to Ulla Bona, in 1865, and was called "Tumps." She died 11 Nov. 1934, and is buried at "Wellington." Issue (PATTESON):

       1 Brent, m. and has issue.

       2 Vaughan, m. and has issue.

       3 Claude, m. and has issue.

       4 Mary, m. L. A. Patteson, and has issue.

       5 Eugene, d. v. p.

       6 George, m. Veve Brent, and has issue.

       7 Craig, m., and has issue.

       8 Charles, m. and has issue.

       9 Ulla, m. T. C. Witt; no issue.

      10 Elsie, m. G. R. Higginbotham and has issue.

300   v   Betty Shearman, b. 1 April 1858; d. 7 May 1935; m. 4 Dec. 1876, Jas. Penn Fitzpatrick, son of Judge Thomas P. Fitzpatrick and Mary Ann Carrington. He d. 22 Oct. 1935.

Issue (Fitzpatrick):

1 Thomas, m. Martha Pitzer, and has infant son.

301   vi   George William, b. 16 July 1860; d. 23 Nov. 1936; m. (i) 26 Nov. 1884, Virginia Harvey; (ii), 1 Aug. 1908, Annie Mays.

Issue, 1st marriage—

1 Russell Stuart, d. v. p.

2 Aldice Craig, m. and has issue.

3 Mabel, m. Geo. Norris, and has one dau.

4 Geo. William, m., and no issue.

5 James Shearman, m., and has issue.

6 Corinne Vaughan, m., and has issue.

7 Richard Harvey, m. Charlotte Whitehead, and has four children.

8 Carrie Bryant, m. and has issue; lives in California.

9 Aurelia, m. Frank Cavedo, and has three sons.

10 Franklin Pettit, d. v. p.

11 Isabelle Anderson, m. and has 1 son.

12 Hazel Tully, m. and has issue.

Issue, 2nd marriage—

13 Doris.

14 Ulla.

15 Margaret Edmonds, m. Joseph Bryant and has issue.

16 Mary Calvert.

17 Helen.

302   vii   Landon Newton, Jr., b. 4 Nov. 1862; d. 20 Jan. 1930; m. 23 Dec. 1885, Frances Henderson Clarkson; b. 1862; d. 14 May 1933.

Issue—

1 Frank.

2 Landon, m. and has issue.

3 Fanny Hall, m. and has issue.

4 Robert, d., a corporal in 80th Div., at Camp Lee, Va., 1917–18.

5 Ashby Pelham, m. Clara Irvine, and lives in Phila.

6 Thomas, m. and living in California.

7 (dau.), m. —— Hughes.

8 (dau.), m. —— Duffield.

303 VIII James Pinckney, b. 21 Jan. 1865; d. 21 Dec. 1910; m. (I) 23 Nov. 1887, Willie Bowles of Roanoke, Va.; m. (II) Lottie Turpin.

Issue, 1st marriage:

1 Aurelia V., b. 1 Sept. 1888; moved to Phoenix, Arizona, *circa* 1905.

2 Ida Hall, b. 16 June 1890; moved to Phoenix, Arizona, *circa* 1905.

Issue, 2nd marriage:

3 William Sydney, m. Ethel Harrison Cooper, of Clarke County, Va., 1 Oct. 1930.

304 IX Fanny Hall, d. v. p. 1872, five years old.

+305 X Robert Craig, b. 14 Aug. 1869; d. 30 July 1921; m. 23 Dec. 1890, Lelia Bunting, of "Pilgrim's Rest," Norfolk County, Va.

306 XI Sherwood Lindsey, b. 2 June 1871; d. 1926; m. Ella Henry, and left issue.

307 XII Cameron, b. 29 Sept. 1873; m. 22 Aug. 1891, Annie Ballard, of Fluvanna County, Va.

Issue—

1 Norma, d. v. p.

2 Landon, d. v. p.

3 Mamie, m. Harvey Townsend; no issue.

4 Christine, m. Norman Coates, of Winchester, Ind., and has one son, Norman Jr.

5 Randolph Haig, d. v. p.

[196] HUGH[6] BRENT (George[5], Thomas[4], George[3], Hugh[2], Hugh[1]), was born in Loudon County, Va. at "Wilbourne," 30 July, 1784. He died at "Brenton," near Upperville in Faquier County, Va., 1 Nov. 1852. He married 23 Dec. 1809, Elizabeth Ash Chinn, daughter of Hugh and Margaret (Ash) Chinn, who married 17 Dec. 1789. Elizabeth Chinn was granddaughter of Thomas and Sarah (Brent) Chinn who were born in Lancaster County, Va. Thomas Chinn was left "land in Loudon" by his father, Thomas Chinn, 1767. Sarah (Brent) Chinn was daughter of Hugh (20) and Catherine (Martin) Brent.

Children:

308   I   James F., b. 23 Dec. 1810; d. April 1840; m. in Missouri, 3 April 1836, Martha Holmes; no issue.

309   II   Mary Ash Hitaffer (the "Hitaffer" might signify that she was a widow; she is listed as Mary Ash in the birth records; as Mary Hitaffer in the Faquier marriage bonds), b. 21 Aug. 1813; m. 26 Jan. 1837, Meredith A. Robinson, who died Jan. 1839, in Lawrenceville, Illinois. They had (ROBINSON)—

1 Ann Elizabeth, b. 3 Oct. 1837; m. 1858, in Quincy, Ill., —— Benton, and had (BENTON)—

1 Hugh Brent.

2 Meredith A., b. 1 July 1839.

+310   III   Lafayette, b. 11 Jan. 1816; d. 1895; m. 17 Feb. 1840, Juliet P. Johnson,

311   IV   Burr Chinn, b. 12 Feb. 1818; m. (I) Ann Lane of Quincy, Ill.; (II) her cousin, Sue Meade; he died childless in New Orleans.

[197] THOMAS[6] WILLIAM BRENT (Thomas[5], Thomas[4], George[3], Hugh[2], Hugh[1]), was born at Scott City, now Georgetown, Ky., 1 May 1794, most probably by his father's third marriage. He died 24 Nov. 1875, in Lee County, Va. He married Susan Tarlton Keith, daughter of Alexander D. Keith, Markham Station, in Faquier County, Va., "Aug. 12th, in the year of our Lord, 1817, Tuesday Evening, six o'clock, by Elder Benjamin Dawson, at

home. . . . Later on my grandfather and his family drifted down into Lee County, Va., before the Civil War. My aunts use to tell me of Eastern Va. and the relatives, Brents, Keiths and Dawsons. They spoke of Burr, Hugh and Fayette Brent. . . . When I was twelve years old a Mr. Lawrence Brent from Eastern Va. was through our country and called to see my aunts" (from a letter dated 1 July 1934, written me by Miss Allie Lee Brent of Lee County, Va., who has her grandfather's Bible—the source of this line).

*Susan Tarlton Keith Brent was born 9 March 1796 in Faquier County, Va., and died April 22nd, half past five in the morning, 1858, in Lee County, Va.

There was a Thomas Brent who was Commander of the C. S. N. *Savannah* during the Civil War.

Children, from his Bible, now owned by his granddaughter, Miss Allie Lee Brent, Gibson Station, Lee County, Va.:

312   I   Alexander Keith, b. 21 July 1818, Tues. night; d. 2 Sept. 1866, Montgomery, Alabama.

313   II   Sally A., b. 1 Feb. 1820; d. 27 Oct. 1825.

314   III   Caroline, b. 10 Oct. 1821; d. 14 Nov. 1821.

315   IV   Nancy Keith, b. 3 April 1823; m. 28 Sept. 1854, John Hurst, in Lee County, Va.; she d. 25 March 1894.

316   V   Mary Isham Randolph, b. 17 March 1825; m. 3 Aug. 1848, John Brown, by Elder Taylor, in Lee County, Va.

317   VI   Elizabeth M., b. 7 Sept. 1826; m. 22 Oct. 1856, John B. Jackson of Morristown, Tenn.; she d. 30 Oct. 1871, in Morristown, Tenn., and is buried in Lee County, Va.

318   VII   John M., b. 7 Sept. 1826; m. 23 Jan. 1856, Virginia Hurst, in Claiborn County, Tenn.; d. 9 Oct. 1904. She died 17 April 1890, and left issue.

319   VIII   Catherine K., b. 26 Jan. 1829; d. 17 July 1829.

*Mrs. J. T. Brent, of San Jose, Cal., writes me that Thos. W. Brent and his wife, Susan Keith were cousins.

319-a IX Anderson K., b. 26 Jan. 1829; d. 20 Dec. 1829.

320 XI Louise Charlotte Marshall, b. 14 Dec. 1830; m. 18 Sept. 1851, Samuel P. Hobbs, by Rev. Williams, in Lee County; she d. 14 April 1903.

321 XII Thomas Jr., b. 27 Feb. 1833; d. 16 July 1846, Tuesday night 12 o'clock, and buried at Ebenezer church on Chucky River in Green River, Tenn.

322 XIII Susan K., b. 4 July 1835; d. Nov. 1871.

323 XIV Rebecca, b. 24 May 1838; d. 13 Nov. 1876.

[202] ANN[6] STEPTOE BRENT (Vincent[5], Thomas[4], George[3], Hugh[2], Hugh[1]), was born in Lancaster County, Va., *circa* 1790; d. in Lancaster County ——; m. (I) 24 March 1814, James Brent Jr. (91), no issue; m. (II) 11 Dec. 1828, John Meredith, widower. He died 1834.

Ann S. Meredith vs. Margaret S. Meredith, et als.—suit for dower and sale.

> . . . your oratrix Ann S. Meredith, wid. of John Meredith, dec'd, whose will is recorded in Lancaster County . . . left considerable land . . . his main tract to his eldest son, Thomas James Meredith, who was admnr. John Meredith also owned 95 A., which he purchased from *Sarah N. Brent*, it being a part of a tract formerly belonging to your oratrix's father, *Vincent Brent*, which tract passes to John Meredith's three youngest children, namely, Margaret Meredith, Thomas Meredith and William V. Meredith. 15 Sept. 1834 (P. 222, Lancaster Land Causes).

Children, Lancaster Land Causes (MEREDITH):

324 I Margaret, m. James A. Palmer.

325 II Thomas W. Meredith.

326 III William V. Meredith.

[204] GEORGE[6] BRENT (George[5], George[4], George[3], Hugh[2], Hugh[1]), was born in Lancaster County, Va., 1794; died Feb. 1861, "in 68th year," in Lancaster County. He married (1) 29 Aug. 1816, Catherine Tapscott, daughter of John and Mary (Spilman)

Tapscott, who were married 8 Sept. 1786; d. 19 Nov. 1840, "in 48th year of her age"; m. (II) 22 May 1843, Hannah G. Curtis, second daughter of Charles and Ann (George) Curtis, who were m. 21 Nov. 1789; b. 17 Nov. 1792; d. 22 Nov. 1852; m. (III) 31 March 1853, Ann N. (Hubbard) Leland, wid. of Leroy Leland.

George Brent's first two wives are buried at "Brookvale," Lancaster County, Va. His third wife married his cousin Kenner Brent (209), and died in Illinois.

Children, first marriage:

327   I   Thomas, d. Feb. 1847 "in 29th year."

328   II   Richard H.

+329   III   Sarah, m. (I) 26 Dec. 1839, Chas. Simmonds; (II) 15 Nov. 1845, Hilkiah Ball.

+330   IV   Alice, m. her bro.-in-law, Hilkiah Ball, son of Hilkiah Ball and Hannah Gaskins Ball, dau. of Rev. David Ball.

331   V   Elizabeth Jane, d. Sept. 1842, "in her twentieth year."

Children, third marriage (no children by second marriage):

332   VI   Charles Benjamin, m. —— Davison, and died in Hodgeman County, Kansas.

333   VII   Mary E., m. —— Cox.

334   VIII   Georgia Ann, m. Fitzhugh Brent (435), and died in Illinois, 1919.

[206] ELIAS[6] EDMONDS BRENT (George[5], George[4], George[3], Hugh[2], Hugh[1]), was born *circa* 1798 in Lancaster County, Va., and died there, 1843; his will was written 5 Dec., and probated 23 Dec. 1843. He married 1 April 1824, Elizabeth C. Edwards; she died 1843.

Children:

335   I   Joseph W., b. 1 April 1825; killed in battle as a member of 9th Va. Cav., C. S. A., 12 Aug. 1861; m.

29 April 1856, Mary Jane Lee, dau. of John Lee of Northumberland County, and his wife Elizabeth Ball.

Issue:

1 Betty Blanch, d. young.

2 George Joseph, d. young.

336 II Elias E., Jr., b. 24 Aug. 1827; d. of wounds received in battle during the Civil War, near a Dr. Hatcher's home in the vicinity of Richmond, Va., and is buried in the yard there.

337 III Lucy E., b. 6 Sept. 1830; d. 18 April 1913; m. (I) Geo. Brent; (II) R. B. Mitchell, and had (MITCHELL):

1 Molly, m. —— Anderson.

2 Bessie, m. John D. Haddox of Rappahannock County.

3 Nina, m. Robert Wiles, of Northumberland County.

4 G. S. Mitchell (1868–1898), m. Claudia Stoneham.

+338 IV William Hartwell, b. 3 March 1834; d. 1 March 1910; m. 1861, Ann Marie Leland.

339 V Frances E., b. 26 May 1838; d. 31 Dec. 1910; m. 26 May 1858, Geo. D. Alderson of Paducah Ky., and had (ALDERSON)—

1 Georgia.

2 Fanny E.

3 Mable.

4 Joseph.

[207] WILLIAM[6] HARTWELL BRENT (George[5], George[4], George[3], Hugh[2], Hugh[1]), was born in Lancaster County, Va., 27 Feb. 1800, the "fourth son of George Brent." He died in Northumberland County, Va., 8 May 1843; m. 20 Nov. 1823, Catherine M. Carter, only daughter of James and Mary (Bond) Carter. She was born 10 Nov. 1808, and died 22 Feb. 1878.

Children:

+340 1 Sarah E., b. 10 Nov. 1825; m. 26 Dec. 1843, Maj. Charles N. Lawson of Northumberland County.

341   II   Mary B., b. 30 Oct. 1827; m. 27 Jan. 1845, George R. Waddy.

342   III   William, b. 21 March 1830; d. 15 July 1833.

343   IV   Elizabeth E., b. 25 Oct. 1832; d. 26 July 1833.

+344   V   Elias Carter, b. 20 Jan. 1835; d. 7 Dec. 1888; m. 6 Jan. 1859, Elizabeth Fitzhugh Payne, dau. of George Payne and Jane Fitzhugh of King George County.

+345   VI   Catherine A., b. 17 June 1837; d. 1887; m. 1855, Major Chas. N. Lawson, her bro-in-law.

346   VII   Novella, b. 4 Feb. 1841; d. 4 Aug. 1843.

347   VIII   Williamette H., b. 22 Aug. 1843; d. 10 Nov. 1884; m. 12 April, 1866, Jas. O. Harding, and had (HARDING)—

    1 George.

    2 Wilbur.

    3 Clara.

[209] KENNER[6] BRENT (Charles[5], George[4], George[3], Hugh[2], Hugh[1]), was born in Lancaster County, Va., 4 March 1796; d. 27 Nov. 1878 in Ellison Twp., Illinois, where he moved from Virginia in 1835–36. He married (I) 29 Jan. 1816, Elizabeth Edmonds Brent, daughter of George and Sarah (Edmonds) Brent, and granddaughter of Col. Elias Edmonds of Lancaster County, Va., an officer in the Rev. War. She was born 2 Feb. 1796, and died 4 April 1854, the mother of fourteen children.

Kenner Brent married (II) *circa* 1867, Ann N. (HUBBARD—Leland—Brent), widow of Leroy Leland, and also of George Brent, taking her and her three children, by her marriage with George Brent, back to Illinois. He enlisted when a youth in Armstrong's company of artillery, 92nd. Va. Reg., War of 1812.

Children (the first eleven were born in Lancaster County, Va.), 1st marriage:

348   I   James Kirk, b. 24 Dec. 1816; d. young.

+349   II   Elias Edmonds, b. 28 June 1818; d. 1863; m. 2 July 1845, in Warren County, Ill., Elizabeth Ann Sovereign.

[137]

+350 III William Prettiman, b. 4 Jan. 1820; d. 22 April 1880; m. 3 Oct. 1850, Margaret E. Jamison, dau. of James and Mary (——) Jamison, of Illinois.

+351 IV David Cralle, b. 12 Oct. 1821; d. 16 Feb. 1897; m. 7 March 1850, Jane Catherine Brown.

+352 V Catherine Kirk, b. 25 June 1824; d. 24 Jan. 1897; m. 20 Sept. 1849, Samuel S. Jamison, and moved to Texas.

+353 VI Elizabeth Edmonds, b. 5 March 1826; d. 18 April 1863; m. 24 Nov. 1848, William B. Jameson.

+354 VII Kenner, b. 23 Oct. 1827; d. 8 April 1888; m. (I) *circa* 1850, Elizabeth Virginia Simpson; (II), 14 Feb. 1870, Mary Anne Dempsey.

355 VIII James Kirk, b. 6 Aug. 1829; d. 1911; m. (I) 4 April 1854, Martha Coleman; (II) Mary McClelland; (III) Mary Louise Brent, dau. of Richard W. H. Brent son of (262) of Muscatine, Iowa, 20 Sept. 1892, in Kansas City, Mo.: no issue.

Children, 1st marriage:

1 Norvella, b. 1857; m., in Iowa, James Dickson, and had (DICKSON)—

  1 Myrtle.

2 Laura, m. a Mr. Davidson: no issue.

3 Walter, d. in infancy.

+356 IX Paul, b. 15 June 1831; d. 1906; m. 13 Aug. 1857, Phoebe Moore, dau. of Andrew and Margaret (Cleckner) Moore.

357 X Lucy Thornton, b. 17 March 1833; d. 10 March, 1916, in Iowa; m. 7 Nov. 1861, Alexander A. Campbell.

Children (CAMPBELL):

1 Samuel Martin, b. 29 July 1866; d. 16 June 1918, unmarried.

2 Jessie, d. 12 May, 1934, unmarried.

3 Elizabeth, m. T. J. Clause, and lives in Le Mars, Colorado.

358 XI Mary Virginia, b. 17 May, 1835; d. unmarried.

359 XII   Charles, died in infancy.

360 XIII   George Whitfield, b. 4 March 1840; d. 1922; never married. "He enlisted in the War of the Rebellion 14 Feb. 1865, in Co. "H", 49th Illinois Vol. Inf., which was assigned to the Army of the Cumberland, and fought in all the battles in which his regiment was engaged. He was promoted to corporal 21 Dec. 1865. He was discharged at Selma, Alabama, 21 Jan. 1866, and returned home immediately . . . where he resides with his two spinster sisters, Virginia and Sarah."

360-a XIV Sarah Frances, b. 15 Sept. 1842; d. 1890, unmarried.

[210] CHARLES[6] S. BRENT (Charles[5], George[4], George[3], Hugh[2], Hugh[1]), was born in Lancaster County, Va., 1802; d. in Missouri, probably Hickory County. He married 18 July 1825, Sally McTyre. "They left for Illinois in 1835, stopping at Fort Dearborn that winter, and went to Illinois, and from there to Hickory County, Mo."

Children:

    I   Robert.
    II   Augustus.
    III   John.
    IV   James, moved to Oklahoma.
    V   Catherine, b. 25 May 1843; d. 16 Aug. 1925; m. Ira Amrine, of Quincy, Mo.
    VI   Margaret, b. 15 Dec. 1845; d. 27 Oct. 1915; m. 1866 Lyman W. Stiltz, and had twin daughters.
    VII   Marcus, b. 4 Oct. 1848; d. 11 Sept. 1934; m. 22 Feb. 1874, Mary Jane Tummons, and had six children.
    VIII Sarah, m. Henry Laller, and had three children.
    IX   Charles.

[213] HENRY[6] MOORE BRENT (Charles[5], Charles[4], Charles[3], Hugh[2], Hugh[1]), was born at "Winter Hill", near Marlboro, in Frederick County, Va., *circa* 1800, and died there 15 Oct. 1875.

[139]

He married (i) *circa* 1827, Caroline Isabelle Sharrard. She was born 10 March 1807, and died 11 May 1846. He married (ii) *circa* 1848, Harriett E. Baker, who was born 10 Sept. 1820, and died 9 April 1873. He was appointed, a captain of an artillery company in Frederick County 8 August, 1821.

Children, 1st marriage:

    I   Charles Lewis, b. 15 March 1829; d. 29 Oct. 1881; m. Mary Sharrard Myers, a niece of Judge Sharrard. She was born 18 Oct. 1835; d. 13 Jan. 1890. They had—

        1 Harry, died in Oklahoma, and left issue.

        2 E. Sharrard, b. 20 June 1862; d. s. p. 16 Aug. 1898.

        3 Carrie, b. 8 Nov. 1864; d. 10 Sept. 1923; m. —— Rogers, and had two children.

        4 Nanny Lewis, unmarried.

        5 Harriett, unmarried.

    II   Henry Moore, Jr., m. (i) Nancy Lewis, b. 1846; d. 26 Jan. 1868; m. (ii) Ella Wright, and died in St. Louis, Missouri. Lt. Henry M. Brent, Jr., C. S. A. was ordinance officer at Richmond, Va. They had

        by 1st marriage—

        1 Harriett.

        2nd marriage—

        2 Edwin.

        3 Carter.

        4 Bessie.

    III Edwin Sowers, b. 12 May 1829; d. 14 Nov. 1921; m. 28 Oct. 1869, Fanny Evalina Baker, dau. of Geo. W. and Emily (Streit) Baker. She was b. 1833; d. 1924. No issue.

Children, 2nd marriage:

    IV Carrie Moore Brent, b. Sept. 1849; d. s. p. 15 Nov. 1876.

[214] JOHN[6] G. BRENT (Charles[5], Charles[4], Charles[3], Hugh[2], Hugh[1]), was born at "Winter Hill," Frederick County, Va. *circa* 1790, and died in Henry County, Ky., *circa* 1860. (This line* is proven negatively, and is included here because there was no other *John Brent* who could have fitted in from the records searched). He married (i) ——; (ii) *circa* 1821, Nancy Sidebottoms.

Children, first marriage:

  i John, moved to Wisconsin.

  ii Greenberry, moved to San Jose, California.

  iii Mahalia, prob. m. 22 March 1841, Millouck Tucker.

  iv Ailsa, m. 17 Oct. 1847, John M. Mills or Miles.

  v Nancy, m. 8 March 1837, John B. Porter.

  vi James, moved to Pensacola, Florida.

  vii ——.

  viii ——.

  ix Allen, b. 16 Nov. 1819; m. 11 Feb. 1842, Abigail McManie, dau. of William McManie.

+361 x Harrison, twin of Allen; m. 3 March 1842, Mary Walker.

Children, second marriage:

+362 xi Lawson Fields, b. 1827; d. 1906; m. Fanny Corbin Mitchell.

  xii Thomas.

  xiii ——(dau.).

  xiv ——(dau.).

[217] CATHERINE[6] MOORE BRENT (Charles[5], Charles[4], Charles[3], Hugh[2], Hugh[1]), was born at *Winter Hill*, Frederick County, Va. 21 July 1811, and died 8 March 1862, and is buried

---

*In regard to the Brent history, I don't know that I can help you much for my information begins with my grandfather *John Brent*, and is very meager concerning him . . . he lived and died in Henry County, Ky., and was married twice . . . his second wife was Nancy Sidebottoms, but could not find out to whom he was married first . . . only that she died young, leaving five day old twins, *Allen* and *Harrison Brent*, the youngest of ten children. (From a letter from Benjamin F. Brent, Bardwell, Ky., 1934.)

in Winchester, Va. She married *circa* 1830, James P. Riely. He was born 12 Sept. 1808; died 21 Aug. 1859.

Children, from tombstones (RIELY):

 I Thomas A., b. 23 Sept. 1831; d. 27 Feb. 1858.

 II Chas. Brent, b. 24 April 1833; d. 10 June 1900.

 III J. Chapelier, b. 8 July 1835; d. 24 Feb. 1895; m. Bettie Bell Myers, who was b. 23 Jan. 1832; d. 13 April 1907; no issue.

 IV James P., b. 22 Sept. 1840; d. 1 Jan. 1888.

 V W. Brent, b. 14 Jan. 1843; d. 14 Nov. 1873.

 VI ——.

 VII ——.

[236] THOMAS[6] YOUNG TROTTER BRENT (Hugh[5], Hugh[4], Charles[3], Hugh[2], Hugh[1]), was born 21 July 1801, in Paris, Bourbon County, Ky. He died 5 May 1863, in Louisville, Ky.; m. (I) 25 Jan. 1827, Elizabeth Susan Arnold; (II) 19 Dec. 1837, Almyra Dalrymple Taylor, in Winchester, Ky. She was born 17 Sept. 1817, and died 21 June 1854, the daughter of Maj. Jonathan Taylor and his wife, Mary Ashby.

Children, first marriage:

  I America, d. young.

+363 II Susan, b. Jan. 1829; m. William T. Haggin.

364 III Hugh, m. 30 Nov. 1853, Sallie Elizabeth Burbridge of Scott County, Ky., and had—

   1 Robert, of St. Louis, Mo.

   2 Lewis, of St. Louis, Mo.

365 IV Mary Ellen, m. Byron Gates.

Children, second marriage:

366 V Thomas Young, b. July 1841; m. Mrs. Jane Clemens.

367 VI Jack Langhorne, b. 4 July, 1843; d. Dec. 1900; m. Mary Frances Berry, dau. of Peter and Mary Wash-

ington (Berry) Berry, who was dau. of John[2] Washington Berry (Thomas[1]) and Ann Taylor, dau. of Lieut. Jonathan Taylor of the Rev. War, and his wife Ann Berry (*Va. Mag.*, Vol. XXV). Issue—

1 Judge George A. Brent, of Louisville, Ky.

2 Mary Berry.

3 Fannie Langhorne.

368 VII Sarah Bell, d. young.

369 VIII Jonathan Taylor, b. 19 Oct. 1846; m. Mrs. Emma DeVinney.

370 IX Almyra Bell, b. 21 March 1848; m. S. J. Rogers.

371 X Lucy J., b. 28 July 1849; m. 31 Dec. 1868, Dr. Edward Rush Palmer; he died 6 July 1895; and had

(PALMER)—

1 Belle, m. E. K. Rand.

2 Jack Brent, d. s. p.

372 XI Marion Fielder, b. 1850; d. s. p.

[237] HUGH[6] INNES BRENT (Hugh[5], Hugh[4], Charles[3], Hugh[2], Hugh[1]), was born in Paris, Bourbon County, Ky., 1803; d. 1845; m. (I) 13 Oct. 1824, Margaret Armstrong; (II) in 1826, Margaret Taylor Chambers, daughter of Gov. John Chambers and Hannah Lee Taylor, one of the pioneers of Mason County, Ky., from New Jersey.

Children, second marriage:

373 I Elizabeth Langhorne, b. 1827; d. 1846; m. 1843, John Esten Cooke, the novelist and poet.

374 II John Chambers, b. 1829; d. 1877; m. Lucy Beale, of Fredericksburg, Va.

375 III Hugh Innes Jr., b. 1832; d. s. p. 1852.

376 IV Thomas Young, b. 1835; d. 1863, was a Maj. in the Confederate Army, and killed in battle with Gen. Morgan's troops; m. 1860, Mary Moore of "Forest Retreat," near Fredericksburg, Va., and had—

1 Mary Chilton, m. Chas. Wm. Dabney, president of U. of Cincinnati, and had two children.

2 Margaret Thomas, m. Joseph Leicester Adkins of Lexington, Ky.

377   v   Margaret Chambers, m. William H. Mackoy, and had (MACKOY)—

1 Harry Brent Mackoy, b. 18 July 1874; m. 18 Nov. 1905, Ruth Barrington Simrall, and had—

I Harry B., Jr., b. 10-18-06.

II Margaret B., b. 7-26-08.

III Ruth S., b. 3-12-16.

378   vi   James Henry, b. 11 Aug., 1842; m. Elizabeth Durrett Chambers, and had five children.

[239] CHARLES⁶ SCOTT BRENT (Hugh⁵, Hugh⁴, Charles³, Hugh², Hugh¹), was born in Paris, Ky., 28 Jan. 1811; d. 16 Feb. 1881. He married (I) Sue Taylor; (II) 10 Feb. 1835, Matilda Chambers; b. in Mason County, Ky., 17 March 1815; d. 28 Aug. 1866, in Paris, Ky.; m. (III) Mrs. M. H. Ford, nee Page; no issue.

"Gen. C. S. Brent recruiting rebels in Paris, Texas, C. S. A."

Children, first marriage:

379   1   Hugh Taylor, m. Caroline Russell.

Children, second marriage:

380   II   John Chambers, b. 5 Feb. 1836; m. Martha Nicholas Ford and had two sons and one daughter.

381   III   Elizabeth Langhorne, m. John Marshall, and had four sons and one daughter.

382   IV   Sprigg, m. Josephine Harris, and had one daughter.

383   v   Belle Hart, m. Charlton Alexander, and had one son, and four daughters.

384   vi   Hannah Chambers, d. v. p., four years old.

+385   vii   Charles Scott, b. 3 March 1844, in Paris, Ky.; d. 3 July 1903 in Baltimore, Md.; buried in Lexington, Ky.; m. 17 Oct. 1871, Elizabeth Todd Young, in St. Louis, Mo. She was born in Fayette County, Ky.

386 VIII Thomas Innes, m. Mary Fleming, and had two sons and four daughters.

387 IX James Arnold, d. v. p. age twenty-four years.

388 X Matilda, m. Frank F. Woodall; two sons and one dau.

389 XI Henry Chambers, m. Binnie Mae Schaeffer; no issue.

390 XII Kelly, m. Marie Dudley Talbott; three sons and three daughters.

[240] SARAH[6] BELL BRENT (Hugh[5], Hugh[4], Charles[3], Hugh[2], Hugh[1]), was born in Paris, Ky., *circa* ——; d. ——; m. ——, Isaac Lewis.

Children, (LEWIS):

391 I Charles Thomas, m. Henriette Gray.

392 II Mary, m. (I) Dr. —— Jackson; (II) Col.—Alexander.

393 III George, d. unmarried.

394 IV John, killed in Civil War.

395 V Jane, d. young.

[241] ELIZABETH[6] LANGHORNE BRENT (Hugh[5], Hugh[4], Charles[3], Hugh[2], Hugh[1]), was born in Paris, Ky., ——, the second daughter of Hugh Brent and Elizabeth Trotter Langhorne. The date of her death and marriage are not in my notes. She married Henry Clay Hart, nephew of Henry Clay.

Children (HART):

396 I Elizabeth Brent.

397 II Nathaniel.

398 III Hugh Brent.

399 IV Henry Clay Hart.

[242] Dr. SANFORD[6] BRENT (William[5], William[4], Charles[3], Hugh[2], Hugh[1]), was born in Washington County, Ky., 5 July 1800, and died 1890 in what is now Trimble County, Ky. He

married Dec. 1826, Nancy Scott, daughter of Levi (1762–1844) and Nancy (Carter) Scott (died 1822). Sanford Brent studied medicine under Dr. John Bright in 1821, and in 1824, graduated with high honors from Transylvania University. Nancy Scott was born 23 Aug. 1807, and died 12 July 1889.

Children:

  I Levi, died in infancy.

  II Elizabeth, b. 1829; m. Jacob Hughley; no issue.

  III William, b. 1832; m. Magdelene Sutton; 4 children.

  IV Roland, b. 1834; m. Eliz. Teague; 4 children.

  V Mary, b. 1836; m. —— McCormick.

  VI Eliza. E., b. 1838; m. James Boyer, and left 4 sons (she was dead by Jan. 1881.)

  VII George, b. 1841; m. Marian McVey, d. by Jan. 1881; left 4 children.

  VIII James, b. 1843; m. —— Mahoney (or Minnie Tingle).

  IX Dr. Isaac Newton, b. 12 Aug. 1845; d. 13 Jan. 1933; m. 9 Sept. 1879, Tinie Quisenberry. She was b. 2 Sept. 1860. They had—

    1 Caroline, b. 7 Aug. 1880; m. 21 Oct. 1901, Dr. Chas. Everett Stephenson, who was b. 29 July 1878; d. 30 March 1908.

  X David, b. 1848; m. Nannie Hardesty: 2 sons.

  XI Harriett, b. after 1850; m. William Walker; lives in Cinn. They had (WALKER)—
    1 Brent.

[254] EPPA[6] HUNTON (BRENT, Elizabeth Marye[5], William[4], Charles[3], Hugh[2], Hugh[1]), was born 1823 and died 1908. He married 1848, Lucy Caroline Weir (1824–1899), daughter of Robert and Clara Boothe (Smith) Weir. Hunton was a distinguished soldier, and rose to the rank of a brigadier general in the Confederate Army. He lived at "Brentsville", and his home was destroyed by Union soldiers. After the Civil War he was a member of Congress and of the Senate.

Children (HUNTON):
> 1 Elizabeth Booth, d. in infancy.
> 11 Eppa, b. 14 April, 1855; m. (1) 1888, Erva Winslow Payne; m. (11) 24 April, 1901, her sister, Virginia Semmes Payne, daughters of Gen. William Henry and Mary Elizabeth (Payne) Payne, and left issue.

[261] JAMES⁷ BRENT (James⁶, Hugh⁵, James⁴, Hugh³, Hugh², Hugh¹), was born in Lancaster County, Va. ——; d. ——; m. 17 June 1805, Frances Hunton, in Lancaster County, Va., daughter of Lieut. Thomas Hunton of Middlesex County, Va., who died 17 Aug. 1792.

> "Lieut. Thomas Hunton of Middlesex County, d. intestate 17 Aug. 1792, leaving children: Polly, John, Frances, Judith M., Eliz., Thomas; Frances m. James Brent, and d. intestate, her children were William B., and Eliz. Porter, wife of Wm. Porter."

Children:
+400   1 William, b. 14 Sept. 1813; d. ——; m. 14 Dec. 1835, Martha C. Ingram, daughter of John Ingram, of Northumberland County, Va.

400-a 11 Elizabeth, b. ——; d. ——; m. William Porter, 12 Jan. 1833.

[262] WILLIAM⁷ BRENT (James⁶, Hugh⁵, James⁴, Hugh³, Hugh², Hugh¹), was born in Lancaster County, Va., ——, and probably died there. He married 19 Aug. 1809, Elizabeth L. Hall, Addison Hall, Sec.

Children (at least):
> 1 Richard William Hall, b. 1810, in Lancaster County, Va.; d. 20 Feb. 1886, in Muscantine, Iowa. The family legend is that he went to William and Mary College, became a staunch abolitionist and a Methodist minister. He was attached to the Baltimore Conference, the Rock River Conference in Ill., and later moved to Muscantine, Iowa in 1853. He m. (1) in Lancaster County, Va., 15 Jan. 1833, Sally M.

Gibson; m. (II) *circa* 1838 in Frederick, Md., Katherine Keiss Miller, of Lancaster, Pa., and had (second marriage):

1 Theodore R., b. 1839, Frederick, Md.; d. 1930, Hinsdale, Ill.; m. 1869, Mary Eliza. Reece, who d. 1886, at Muscantine Iowa, and left issue; he m. (II) 1887, Mary Alice Downs who d. 1934, without issue. Children, 1st marriage—

    I Theodore, b. 30 March 1874.

    II Fanny E., b. 1870; d. 1931.

2 Richard Hall, b. 1842, at Jefferson, Md.; d. 1932, Kansas City, Mo.; m. 1873, Ella Junkin in Kansas City, and had—

    I Waldo J., b. 1874; m. and has two sons.

3 Mary Louise, b. 1845, in Maryland; m. 20 Sept. 1892, James Brent (355), widower; no issue.

4 William Oliver, born 1847 in Dixon, Lee County, Ill.; m. Fannie ——, and had two daughters who live in Pasadena, California.

5 Edmund James, born 1850, in Illinois; d. *circa* 1912, in Seattle, Wash.; m. Fannie Elizabeth Grinstead, at Litchfield, Ill. No issue.

[274] GEORGE[7] P. BRENT (George[6], Hugh[5], James[4], Hugh[3], Hugh[2], Hugh[1]), was born *circa* 1790 in Lancaster County, Va., and died* ——. He married 5 May 1818, Harriett Slater of Fredericksburg, Va., William Wells, security. William James made oath that George Brent resided with him several years, and "that to the best of his knowledge and belief the said George Brent is considerably upward of twenty-one years of age. . . . Harriett Slater is also upward of twenty-one years of age."

William Wells, in his will, 2 Feb. 1819: 8 July 1819, leaves his estate to his wife Sarah Wells. Wit: Joseph Walker, Benj. Clarke and Robt. Lipscomb.

---

*The will of the above George is not in Orange or Madison Counties, nor can I find marriage bonds concerning his daughters except this: Anna Elizabeth Brent m. John Wesley Bond, 27 Oct. 1870 (Madison County). George P. Brent deeds property in 1837, 1846, 1867 and 1870, so evidently died after that date, at a very mature age.

"I, Sarah Wells, of the Town of Fredericksburg . . . unto my sister's daughter, Mrs. Harriett Brent, and her three daughters, Sarah, Elizabeth and Harriett, being the wife and daughters of George P. Brent of Orange County, and the State of Va." . . . Wit: Eliz. C. Lucas, Agnes I. M. Sanford (Will Book "D," P. 385). This will was written 5 Jan. 1846; probated 12 Aug. 1847.

George P. Brent signed a petition Jan. 1832, in Orange Courthouse, to pave the streets of the town. The money was to be raised from a lottery.

Children:

401	I	Sarah
402	II	Elizabeth
403	III	Harriett

[275] ISAAC[7] BRENT (Hugh[6], Hugh[5], James[4], Hugh[3], Hugh[2], Hugh[1]), was born 31 Oct. 1796, and died in Northumberland County, Va., 1848. He married 8 March 1819, Mary Dameron, of Wiccomicco Parish, Northumberland County, b. 1791; d. June 1862; she was a granddaughter of Geo. Dameron and Mary Ann Jones.

Isaac Brent is syled in the Northumberland marriage bonds as "Capt." Isaac Brent. He is listed as being in the 92nd Reg. Va. Militia, Capt. Hugh Brent's Co., the War of 1812.

Children:

404	I	Thomas Oglethorpe, b. 22 Aug. 1822; d. 19 April 1891; m. 24 April 1852, Annie Betts.
405	II	Mary, b. 27 Jan. 1825; d. 14 June 1855; m. 20 Jan. 1841, Rev. Henry Fleet Cundiff.
+406	III	Andrew Jackson, b. 1 Jan. 1827; d. March 1889; m. 22 May 1851, Sally Mason Stith.

[283] FRANKLIN[7] PIERCE BRENT (James H.[6], James D.[5], James[4], William[3], Hugh[2], Hugh[1]), was born in Nelson County, Va., 14 Sept. 1852; d. 11 Aug. 1927, at Christ Church School,

Middlesex County, Va. He married Mattie Buxton Porter, dau. of Capt. John L. Porter, of the Confederate Navy, Dec. 1883.

He was educated at Fleetwood Seminary, Nelson County, Va., first studying Latin and Greek under his uncle, Landon N. Brent. In early life he taught at Norwood School in Nelson County. Among those who studied under him was William Cabell Brown, afterwards Episcopal Bishop of Virginia, who died in London recently. He was noted as a Greek scholar and numbered the late Dr. Basil L. Gildersleeve, long professor of Greek at Johns Hopkins University, among his intimate friends. He also collaborated with the late Armstead Churchill Gordon, a schoolmate and fraternity brother at the University of Virginia, in certain Virginia biographies. He was instructor at Christ Church School at the time of his death.

Children:

407	I	Franklin Pierce, Jr.
408	II	John Pierce.
409	III	Mildred, m. R. A. Savedge, of Waverly, Va.
410	IV	Helen.

[297] KENDALL[7] CARROLL BRENT (Landon N.[6], James[5], James[4], William[3], Hugh[2], Hugh[1]), was born 6 Aug. 1851, at "Wellington" Nelson County, Va., and died 24 Feb. 1931, near Arrington, Nelson County, Va. He married (I) in New Mexico, 2 Feb. 1872, Florence Hall; m. (II) in old Mexico, *circa* 1875, Beneranda Chavez.

He left home in 1869 and went to Mexico Territory and became a member of the border patrol. He returned "home with his family after spending eighteen years in Mexico," 31 Aug. 1887. He was sheriff in New Mexico 1886, and also served in the customs department.

Children, 1st marriage:

411	I	Minnie, m. Lessly Carter, son of S. L. Carter and Eugenia L. Shields (III, 188); no issue.

Children, 2nd marriage:

412 II   Kendall Carroll, m. and had issue. He died 1933.

413 III Landon Haines, m.; no issue.

414 IV   Anna, m. her cousin, Charles Coakley; no issue.

415 V   Veve, m. her cousin, Geo. Patteson, and had issue.

416 VI   Sarah Dold, m. ——, and had issue.

417 VII William, d. v. p.

418 VIII James, living in New York.

[305] ROBERT[7] CRAIG BRENT (Landon[6] Newton, James[5], James[4], William[3], Hugh[2], Hugh[1]), was born at "Wellington," Nelson County, Va., 14 Aug. 1869; d. 30 July 1921, in Roanoke, Va.; m. 23 Dec. 1890, Lelia Bunting, daughter of George Solomon and Harriett (Jordan) Bunting, of "Pilgrim's Rest," Norfolk County, Va. She was born 5 Nov. 1873, and was the granddaughter of Samuel and Margaret (Savage) Bunting. The Bunting and Savage families came from the Eastern Shore of Va. George S. Bunting was a member of Capt. Doyle's Co., in the Civil War.

Children:

419 I   Chester Horton, b. 6 Sept. 1892; m. 30 May 1925, Ruth Moran, daughter of William Grayson and Evalina (Ferguson) Moran of Albemarle County, Va. and had—

   1 Chester Horton, II, b. 30 April 1926.

   2 Sarah Kendall, b. 10 Jan. 1928.

420 II Irl D'Arcy, b. 26 Dec. 1893; m. 11 May 1918, Catherine Hart, of Roanoke, Va. He was captain of Co. "E," 305th combat Engrs., 80th Div., in the World War.

   Issue:

   1 Irl, II, b. 4 Oct. 1820, Flint, Mich.

   2 George Landon, b. 10 July 1922; d. v. p.

   3 Catherine, b. 9 Aug. 1930.

421 III Louisa Harriet, b. 2 March 1896; m. 27 Sept. 1920, John Calvin Shockley, of Stuart, Va.
Issue (SHOCKLEY):
1 Ann Brent, b. 4 May 1925.

422 IV Robert Craig, II, b. 9 Dec. 1897; d. v. p. 28 Dec. 1907.

EXCURSUS—BERNARD

1 *John Bernard*, b. *circa* 1700, in England; came to Maryland *circa* 1720; married a Miss Abney, and afterwards settled on the Rivanna River in Albemarle County (later Fluvanna), Va. He had—

2 John Bernard, b. 16 Nov. 1736; d. 15 Jan. 1824; m. 6 March 1760, Elizabeth Burnett, daughter of John and Sarah Burnett. She was born 4 April 1744; died 30 Aug. 1822, in Albemarle County. He had among others—

3 Major Allen Bernard, b. 29 Jan. 1763; d. 4 July 1834; m. 3 May 1787, Ann Mitchell, who was b. 28 Oct. 1764; d. 1 April 1851. At the time of his marriage he was merchandising in Goochland County. Shortly after this date he moved to Richmond, where he ran a public house (tavern) until 1792, when he moved to the county of Fluvanna, having purchased 1640 acres on the south side of the Rivanna Riv. and Adrien's Creek, including the site of the dwelling in which he was born and opposite the property of the Payne family upon whose premises reposed the remains of his grandfather John Bernard and wife. He moved to Rockfish Gap (west of the now town of Afton) 1820 (see note in L. H. Brent's diary), and later settled on a farm near Greenfield in Nelson County, where he finished his mortal career. Maj. Allen Bernard was a member of the legislature from either Fluvanna or Goochland Counties, and in all probability, an officer in the militia in the War of 1812. He had, among others—

4 Mary Byron Bernard, the second child, b. 31 Dec. 1789; m. (I) 19 Dec. 1807, Samuel Ferguson, who d. 12 July 1827; she m. (II) 5 Dec. 1837, Joel Smith of Nelson County, Va.; she died 1863–4. She had among others—

5 Jesse Bernard Ferguson, b. 27 Feb. 1827; d. 16 July 1909;

m. 20 Nov. 1856, Nancy Burnett, who was b. 28 Nov. 1838; d. 1 April 1931. He had—

6 Evaline Jane, b. 27 Feb. 1863; m. 19 Jan. 1887, William Grayson Moran, b. 1 Dec. 1863; d. 6 Sept. 1926, at "Beverly Manor," in Augusta County. He was manager of the farm and orchard at Miller's School for twenty-five years, and an authority on orchard cultivation and management in the apple belt of Virginia.

EXCURSUS—SAVAGE

Margaret Savage, daughter of William Savage and his wife Elizabeth, married Samuel Bunting, with her father's consent, in Northampton County, Va., 9 Dec. 1820. Her father, William Savage, was born 9 Nov., "in the Yeare of our Lord" 1783, the son of Abel Savage and his second wife, Nancy James. (Abel Savage married (1) Sheba Gunter, daughter of Joseph Gunter, by 1758). William Savage was dead by 27 Nov. 1821, as the following Land Causes will show:

1   JOHN SAVAGE (OF ABEL) VS. (PARTITION SUIT)
    William Savage (of Abel) and Abel Savage (of Abel). That one Abel Savage, father of the sd John, William and Abel, was upon 28 Jan. 1793, seized (of certain lands) . . . ½ of which he left to William and the other ½ to John Savage . . . that at the death of the sd Abel Savage the elder, he left the following children, then born: the sd John and William, and also Jacob, Nancy and Sally Savage, and grandchild Abel, son of his dec'd son Parker Savage, also a widow, to wit: Nancy Savage, who at the time of the death of the testator, was enciente of a child which was born after the death of the testator, to wit: the sd Abel, the defendant, which Abel being unprovided for . . . received share for share with the other children (Accomack Land Causes, 29 Aug. 1803). Nancy Savage, 2nd wife of Abel Savage (w. 1794), was daughter of —— James, and sister of Hetty Mason, wife of Teackle Mason; Elizabeth Warner, wife of Geo. Warner, Jr.; of David James . . . and that Mary Ann and Sally C. Savage are the only children of Nancy Savage, dec'd., who was a sister of the whole blood to the sd Hetty Mason (Accomack Land Causes, 27 Nov. 1821).

[153]

Descendants of Hugh Brent

Family tradition "shows" that the above Abel who married secondly, Nancy James, was the son of one Major Savage. The only Major Savage I can find left no will. He married Peggy daughter of Abel Roberts, of Accomack County. Nor is a Major named in the many other Savage wills.

The Savage Family is the oldest family in America surviving the colonization of Virginia. Ensign Thomas Savage came to the Easterne Shoare, *cir.* 1620, and according to John Pory, an English visitor to the Colonies in 1624:

> This Thomas Savage, it is sixteen years since he went to Virginia, being a boy, he was left with Powhatan for Namontacke, to learn the language, and as the Author Affirmith, with much honestie and good success hath served the publike without any publike recompence, yet had an arrow shot through his body in their service.

Ensign Thomas Savage, an "Ancient Planter," arrived in Virginia on the *John and Francis*", 1607. He was born 1595, and died by 1635. He married Hannah Tyng, who arrived in Virginia 1621, aboard the *Seaflower*. They had at least Capt. John Savage, who was a large landowner, receiving in 1664, one grant of 6,000 acres in Northampton County. Mrs. Hannah Savage, of "Savage's Choice," married (II) Daniell Cugley 1635.

EXCURSUS—BUNTING

The earliest data on this family comes from the "Accomack Tithables," and concerns one William Bunting, who in 1680, pays 2 tithes. He continues on the list until 1695, and then disappears. Whether he is the progenitor of this family, this compiler does not know. The Buntings might have come down from Delaware or Pennsylvania. There was a Solomon Bunting, who from "his declaration," was a soldier in the Rev. War, Capt. John Blair's Company, and in 1820, he is 78 years old, which would place his date of birth at 1742.

Jonathan Bunting died 1763/4, leaving a wife, Polly, and several children. Solomon Bunting died 1787, leaving wife Peggy, and son William "beyond the seas for past four years . . . if he has son by name Solomon, if not to Solomon and his heir by name of Solomon, if not to son Holloway and his heir by name Solomon, if not to son Jonathan and his heir by name Solomon." In the order of probate, Holloway qualified, so he evidently produced the first Solomon! Holloway Bunting died Jan. 1808. He married (1) 12 May 1787, Prescilla Turner, daughter of John Furbush Turner; he married (11) 10 July 1797, Sally White. From his will he had three children by each marriage.

Samuel Bunting, listed in his will as among the three older children, is written in his Bible as being the son of Hollwy and Sally Bunting, and his date of birth, 2 Aug. 1798. He died 7 April 1847. He married 9 Dec. 1820 Margaret, with the consent of her father William Savage. She was born 5 Oct. 1807, and died 1 June 1846. There were seven sons and two daughters. George Solomon Bunting, the third son, was born 4 Jan. 1829, and died 20 April 1917, at "Landale," Norfolk County, Va. He married three times. His second wife was Harriett Jordan, a sister of his first wife. By this second marriage he had Lelia Bunting, who married Robert Craig Brent (305).

[310] LAFAYETTE[7] BRENT (Hugh[6], George[5], Thomas[4], George[3], Hugh[2], Hugh[1]), was born 11 Jan. 1816 at "Brenton," in Faquier County, Va., and died there 1895. He married 17 Feb. 1840, Juliet P. Johnson, daughter of Amos Johnson of "Clover Hill" and his wife Sarah Nutt, who was the daughter of Richard Nutt of Northumberland County, and his wife Elizabeth Hathaway of Lancaster County, Va. Juliet Brent died "Thursday June 13th, about 10 o'clock in the evening, 1889."

Children:

423   1   Joseph Warren, b. 25 Dec. 1840; killed* in battle as a member of Moseby's troops near Upperville, Va., 21 May 1863.

---

*   Hdqs. 7th Va. Cavalry

                                               June 26th, 1863

Captn,
    If anything can be done in the case of the two Brents, who have recently lost a brother in action with the enemy, I would be placed under obligation. The family is in great distress, especially the mother. The horses of both the surviving sons have been recently shot, and it will take some little time to replace them. They desire to remain only a few days at home. It is unnecessary for me to state their character as soldiers. The Confederacy has none superior.

                           Very resptly

                           Yrobtsol

                           Thomas Marshall

                           Lt. Col. commg 7th V. C.

424　II　William A., b. 3 April 1842; d. u. m. 1898. He was a member of the 7th Va. Cavalry, in the Confederate Army.

425　III　Hugh, b. 24 April 1845; d. 25 May 1913; m. 29 Jan. 1883, Sarah J. Bull, daughter of Dr. B. H. Bull, of Baltimore, Md. She was the granddaughter of Col. John S. Berry who commanded the artillery at the bombardment of Fort McHenry in the War of 1812. She died 15 Feb. 1887. Hugh Brent was a member of the 7th Va. Cavalry in the Civil War. They had:

1　Hugh W., m. Helene Vogeler, of Baltimore, and had two sons and one daughter.

2　Harrison, m. Mary Louise Franke, and has two sons.

3　Rawleigh Chinn, m. (I) Nellie Turnbull, of Baltimore; (II) ——, and lives in California.

426　IV　James R., b. 17 March 1847; m. in New Mexico, 24 June, 1886, Charlotta Baca, and left heirs.

427　V　George L., b. 11 Feb. 1851; went to Wyoming, and came back and married, and died at Aldie, Va.

428　VI　Sallie E. A., b. 3 Oct. 1852; d. unmarried.

429　VII　Thomas Randolph,* b. 11 Nov. 1854; d. in California.

430　VIII　Lawrence Decatur, b. 28 Dec. 1848; d. 31 Jan. 1922; m. 11 Dec. 1889, Lila G. Murray, of Faquier County, Va.

Issue—

1　Joseph Warren, b. 25 Aug. 1891.

2　Juliet, m. Howell Bell, of Washington, D. C.

3　M. Murray, m. Marie Helm.

4　Nannie, m. Capt. George A. Patrick.

5　Lawrence, m., 14 June 1929, Martha Carter.

6　Hugh, unmarried.

431　IX　Nannie Josephine, b. 1 Aug. 1857; d. unmarried 1894.

---

*"Brenton," March 18th 1898; Cary Ambler, *The Dell*, Hume, Va., informs me that he saw and stayed with Thomas R(andolph) Brent at the Southern Hotel, El Paso Del Norte, Texas in 1887. That he had lost an arm . . . he also says that he met a man in Mexico who called himself John James Robinson, who was Nick Carter, Chenooni, Mexico (from Wm. A. Brent notes).

[329] SARAH[7] E. BRENT (George[6], George[5], George[4], George[3], Hugh[2], Hugh[1]), was born 11 March 1821, at "Brookvale," Lancaster County, Va. by her father's first wife. She died 12 Dec. 1846 in Northumberland. Married (I) 26 Dec. 1839, Charles Simmonds; m. (II) 15 Nov. 1845, Hilkiah[8] Ball (Hilkiah[7], George[6], David[5], George[4], George[3], William[2], William[1]), widower, the son of Hilkiah and Harriett Ball, who were married 11 Nov. 1811 in Northumberland County. Harriett Ball was the daughter of David Ball (probably not the Rev. David Ball: Hayden). See 330 line.

Children (BALL):
    1 George Summerfield, b. 23 Oct. 1846.

[330] ALICE[7] P. BRENT (George[6], George[5], George[4], George[3], Hugh[2], Hugh[1]), was born 22 May 1825, and died 1 March 1851. She married her brother-in-law, Hilkiah Ball, 12 Dec. 1847. (My notes from Northumberland County state that this Hilkiah Ball was the son of Hilkiah Ball and Hannah Gaskins Ball, daughter of Rev. David Ball; Hayden does not seem to be certain of his data. I offer mine as from family records, which in all probability the Rev. Hayden did not have access to.)

Children (BALL):
    1 Hannah Catherine, born Sept. 1848 (one of twins).
    2 —— (a son) twin of above.

[338] WILLIAM[7] HARTWELL BRENT (Elias E.[6], George[5], George[4], George[3], Hugh[2], Hugh[1]), was born in Lancaster County, Va., 3 March 1834. He moved with his family to Illinois in Sept. 1878, but came back to Lancaster County, Va., 1907, and died there, 1 March 1910. He married 1861, Ann Marie Leland, daughter of Leroy and Ann N. (Hubbard) Leland, of Lancaster County, Va. He is listed as a member of the Lancaster Patrol, in Dec. 1857.

Children:
432   1 Bernard Cameron, b. 1873; m. (I) 15 Oct. 1885, Florence Edwards; m. (II) Mrs. Claudia (Stoneham) Mitchell.

[157]

Issue, by first marriage:

1 H. G. Brent.

2 C. E. Brent.

3 Fay Agnes, m. W. R. Davies.

4 W. L. Brent, m. 1922, Lucretia Hathaway.

433   II   Wm. Earnest, m. Gertrude Bean, granddaughter of Richard Mitchell, of Lancaster County, Va. Issue:

1 Ann Maria Brent.

[340] SARAH[7] E. BRENT (Wm. H.[6], George[5], George[4], George[3], Hugh[2], Hugh[1]), was born 10 Nov. 1825, and died 1853. She married 27 Dec. 1843, Maj. Charles N. Lawson, of Northumberland County, Va., son of Henry Chinn Lawson and his wife Margaret Steptoe Lee, who were married 18 Jan. 1796.

Children (LAWSON):

   I   Margaret Catherine, b. 1845; m. Chas. Betts Payne.

   II   Elliott Winfield, b. 1 Dec. 1847; d. 1933; m. Fanny Hathaway, and had—

      1 Henry.

      2 Charles Nichols Lawson.

   III   James Osborne, b. 1850; d. 1925.

   IV   Mary, b. 1853; m. 1874, John Thomas Payne, b. 1851, and had (PAYNE)—

      1 Fitzhugh.

      2 Leonard, b. 1878; m. 1907, Laura, daughter of Thomas Sargent Brent (478).

      3 Charles Lawson, b. 1881; m. 1905, Jane Chilton.

[344] ELIAS[7] CARTER BRENT (Wm. H.[6], George[5], George[4], George[3], Hugh[2], Hugh[1]), was born in Northumberland County, Va., 20 Jan. 1835, and died 7 Dec. 1888. He married 6 Jan. 1859, Elizabeth Fitzhugh Payne, daughter of George Payne and Jane

Fitzhugh, of King George County, Va. She was born 14 Aug. 1841, and died 25 March 1917. They moved to Illinois, and died there.

Children:

434 I   Florence M., m. 24 Oct. 1883, B. Frank Corzatt.

435 II   Fitzhugh, b. 7 Aug. 1862; m. Georgia Ann Brent, daughter of George (204), and Ann (HUBBARD-Leland) Brent, at Smithshire, Ill., and have one child—

 I Amy, m. Ezra Ross.

436 III Nevada Payne, b. 6 April 1865; m. Frank Hearn.

437 IV   George William, b. 10 Oct. 1867; d. 1867.

438 V   Jane Catherine, b. 2 March 1869; m. 19 Nov. 1919, George Brooks who d. 1933, no issue.

439 VI   Panola Champ, b. 20 Aug. 1872; m. 21 June 1893, Chas. E. Rankin, and lives in Des Moines, Iowa, and had—

 I Capt. Russell L. Rankin.

440 VII Ola May, b. 23 July 1875; unmarried.

441 VIII Mervyn Carter, b. 8 March 1878; d. 1 Dec. 1900.

[345] CATHERINE[7] A. BRENT (Wm. H.[6], George[5], George[4], George[3], Hugh[2], Hugh[1]), was born in Northumberland County, Va., 17 June 1837, and died in Northumberland County, Va., 1887. She married 1855, her brother-in-law, Maj. Charles N. Lawson, of Northumberland County, Va.

Children (LAWSON):

 I   Sarah Ann, b. 1855; d. 1873.

 II   Paulina, b. 1857.

 III Edward Everett, b. 1860; m. Virginia Chase, and had—

  I Wm. Tell, m. Marion Cundiff, 1917.

  2 Edward Everett, b. 1895; m. 1927, Vivian Harper.

3 Francis Wm. b. 1896; d. 1926; m. 1917, Ellinor Ingham, and has two daughters.

4 Rebecca V., b. 1898; m. 1930 Chas. H. McReynolds.

5 Hilda, b. 1900.

6 Katherine Ann, b. 1902; m. 1923, Walter Fawcett.

7 Emma Chase, b. 1905; m. 1926, V. A. Shrine.

8 Paulina, b. 1908; d. in infancy.

IV Thomas Jackson, b. 1863; d. 1925; m. (I) 1889, Lillian Augusta Hathaway, who died 28 May 1900; m. (II) 1915, Gertrude Hall.

Children by 1st marriage—

1 Percy Gage, b. 1890; m. 1916, Virginia Croasdale.

2 Earnest Jackson, b. 1892; m. 1913 Edna Kemp.

3 Catherine Brent, b. 1894; m. 1910 Leslie Henderson.

4 Hathaway, b. 1897; m. 1920 Ala Cundiff.

5 Mary Eleanor, b. 1900, and died in infancy.

6 Augusta, m. 1932 J. P. Dize.

[349] ELIAS[7] EDMONDS BRENT (Kenner[6], Charles[5], George[4], George[3], Hugh[2], Hugh[1]), was born 28 June 1818 in Lancaster County, Va., and died 1863, in Warren County, Ill. He married 2 July 1845, in Warren County, Ill., Elizabeth Ann Sovereign, who was born 10 Sept. 1826.

Children:

1 Homer Irving, b. 30 May 1847; d. Jan. 1920 in Indianola, Warren County, Iowa; m. 1 Jan. 1875, in Ringgold County, Iowa, Nancy Lorimor, and had—

 1 Frederick J., b. 29 Feb. 1876; m. 13 Dec. 1917, Belle Parnham of Audobon, Iowa, and had—

  I Forrest H., b. 24 Oct. 1921.

  II Homer I., b. 24 Oct. 1921.

 2 Lida Luella, b. 6 Nov. 1881; m. Arthur Dain of Ringgold, Iowa; live in Indianola, and have

(Dain)—

  i Elton

  ii Robert

  iii Ione, m. Russell Barker

  iv Bernice

  v Gladys, d. 1933

  vi Elizabeth

3 James, d. in infancy.

4 Perle Ione, b. 23 April 1884; m. 10 June 1908, Dr. W. S. Kyle, and lives in Washington, Iowa, and have(Kyle)—

  i Donald Brent, b. 26 Sept. 1909.

  ii Wm. Shirley, b. 4 June 1913.

  iii James Paul, b. 26 April 1916.

  iv Mildred Ione, b. 21 Sept. 1918.

5 Martin V., b. 16 July 1887; m. (i) Kathleen Spence; (ii) Mrs. Mata (Fultz) Cox: no issue; live in Woodward, Iowa.

  Issue, 1st marriage—

  i Mildred Kathleen.

  ii Helen, d. young.

  iii Lawrence.

  iv Grace.

  v Ralph.

  vi Ruth.

6 Florence Myrtle, b. 23 Oct. 1891; m. Waldon Miller, who d. 1933, in Aurora Ill.; they had—
(Miller)

  i Brent, born in Korea.

  ii Joseph L., b. in U. S. A.

  iii Betty Jean, b. in U. S. A.

ii Coleman F., b. 10 March 1849; d. 17 Dec. 1883; m. Elizabeth McClelland, Ringgold, Iowa, and had—

  1 Walter

  2 Bertram

III Alice Norvella, b. 6 April 1851; m. 7 Nov. 1872, in Warren County, Ill., Milford Allen Bechtel, who was born in Ohio. They had (BECHTEL)—

1 Orpha May, b. 31 Dec. 1873; m. Forrest Tinkham, and had three children; live in Kirkwood, Ill.

2 Archer Edmonds, d. young.

3 Roy Vermon, b. 11 July 1880; m. Anna ——, live at Roseville, Ill., and have two children.

4 Elizabeth Ann, b. 6 Oct. 1885; m. Chester Davis of Kirkwood, Ill., and have a son.

IV Orra Emily, b. 10 Jan. 1853; d. 21 Jan. 1853.

V Mary Elizabeth, b. 1 Feb. 1854; d. 17 Oct. 1854.

VI Charles Wesley, b. 30 March 1856; moved west.

VII Lillian V., b. 28 Oct. 1858; m. Rhonie Herde.

VIII Kate Roselle, b. 12 Nov. 1860; m. Charles Hobson, and died in Nebraska.

IX Emma Edmonds, b. 27 July 1863; m. Edward Bliss, and lives in Ringgold, Iowa.

[350] WILLIAM[7] PRETTIMAN BRENT (Kenner[6], Charles[5], George[4], George[3], Hugh[2], Hugh[1]), was born 4 Jan. 1820 in Lancaster County, Va., and died 22 April 1880, in Warren County, Ill. He married 3 Oct. 1850, Margaret Ellen Jamison, daughter of James and Mary (——) Jamison, who settled in Henderson County, Ill. in 1829, moving from Kentucky. She was born 1 Jan. 1833.

Children:

442 1 Bathania, b. Dec. 1851; d. in Oregon; m. John H. Warfield, of Montgomery County, Iowa, and had (WARFIELD)—

1 George, m. Sadie Hall, and lives in Denver.

2 Harriett, m. Wiley Jerome Huddle, who d. 17 March 1931; they had (HUDDLE)—

I John Warfield.

II Margaret.

  iii Wiley Jerome.

  iv Mary Alice.

 3 Mary, m. Arthur McAllister, and lives in Oregon. They have (McAllister)—

  i Castle

  ii Helen

  iii Robert

  iv Doris

  v Kenner Brent

443 ii Velma, b. 12 Feb. 1854, Warren County, Ill.; m. 22 Oct. 1874, Michael V. Jamison, who was born 12 July 1849. They had (Jamison)—

 1 Cordelia, b. 1 Aug. 1875; m. Henry Crane, and had (Crane)—

  i Crystal

  ii Ludlow

  iii Edwin

  iv Frank

 2 Edwin, b. 10 Aug. 1878; m. Clara ——; no issue.

 3 Estelle, b. 23 Aug. 1880.

 4 Bulah, b. 5 July 1883; no issue.

 5 Martha.

 6 Michael.

444 iii Arthur Jamison, b. 1 May 1862; d. 6 March 1925; m. 9 Dec. 1891, Anna Rebecca Pendarvis, in Warren County, Ill.; they had—

 1 Wilma Louise, b. 3 Oct. 1892; m. 16 Oct. 1923, Theron F. Jennings, b. 1896.

 2 Ruth Eleanor, b. 5 Aug. 1897; d. 17 Sept. 1907.

 3 Mary Virginia, b. 6 Dec. 1899.

445 iv Schuyler Lincoln, b. 1 Jan. 1865; m. 10 Dec. 1890 Elizabeth Orchert in Warren County, Ill. She was born 2 Dec. 1864. They had—

 1 Glenn Wm., b. 11 Sept. 1891; m. 1917, Opal Galbreath, and have two children.

2 John Carl, b. 21 Dec. 1892; m. Lois Galbreath, and have two children.

3 Helen, b. 11 June 1894; m. 31 Aug. 1923, Glenn Davis, and have one daughter.

4 Esther, b. Nov. 1895; m. 10 June 1920, Wilbur M. Patch, and have (PATCH)—

   I Harold Brent.

   II Wilbur.

5 Gertrude, b. 21 July 1902.

446 v Charles Eddie, b. 26 April 1867; m. 4 Oct. 1892, Emma Brown, who died 18 Jan. 1894; m. (II) Mrs. Ella (McGraw) Anderson: no issue by second marriage; by first marriage—

   I Lucille, b. 25 Dec. 1893; m. 1915, R. D. Akers, and lives in California; they have (AKERS)—

      I Brent, b. 1916

      II Joseph, b. 1921

447 VI William Watson, b. 1 Sept. 1869; m. Etta Fordyce, and had—

   I Katherine, m. Paul Mancel, and had (MANCEL)—

      I Rosemary

      II Katherine Eloise

448 VII Mary Ellen, b. 1879; m. John Schuyler Bates, and lives in Berkley Cal.; they had (BATES)—

   I Kenton

   2 Margaret, m. 1934, Roy Trotter

   3 Robert

[351] DAVID[7] CRALLE BRENT (Kenner[6], Charles[5], George[4], George[3], Hugh[2], Hugh[1]), was born in Lancaster County, Va., 12 Oct. 1821, and died in Ellison Twp., Warren County, Ill., 16 Feb. 1897. He was a prosperous farmer and cattle raiser. He married 7 March 1850, Jane Catherine Brown, daughter of William Brown, who moved from Lancaster County, Va. to Warren County, Ill. She was born 1 Jan. 1830, and died 18 Jan. 1907. William Brown died July 1883.

Children:

  I Florence A., b. 6 Dec. 1850; d. 24 Jan. 1857.

  II James C., b. 7 Aug. 1852; d. 22 Jan. 1857.

449 III Elizabeth C., b. 25 April 1854; m. 29 Oct. 1873, Jeremiah H. Warfield (b. 13 April 1845), and had (WARFIELD)—

    1 Alpha David.

    2 Ralph L.

450 IV Jane Augusta, b. 22 Feb. 1856; m. James Watson of Warren County, Ill., and had (WATSON)—

    1 Amy, m. David C. Runkle of MacComb, Ill., and moved to Saskatchewan, Canada 1911.

    2 George, married and living in California.

451 V Wm. Kenner, b. 14 Dec. 1857; m. 1 March 1882, Sarah Ellen Jamison (b. 28 Sept. 1858), and had—

    1 Orpha Augusta, b. 8 Dec. 1883; m. Wm. Libby, and had (LIBBY)—

      I Gaylord, m. Gertrude Duncan.

      II Leland.

    2 Nathan, b. 5 March 1885.

    3 Harry, b. 17 Nov. 1887.

    4 David, b. 13 April 1889.

    5 Clifford R., b. 10 Dec. 1892.

    6 Louis Cecil, b. 18 April 1894.

452 VI Melvin David, b. 8 Jan. 1860; m. 18 March 1891, Nellie May Seymour (b. 4 April 1871), and had—

    1 Ralph Earl, b. 16 Jan. 1892; m. Bessie Spence, and had—

      I Irving

      II Alice

    2 Orman Donald, b. 25 Aug. 1893.

    3 Mabel Ione, b. 4 Nov. 1895.

    4 Ruth

    5 Catherine

    6 Theodore Taft

    7 Ora

453 VII   Thomas H., b. 14 Feb. 1862; m. 17 Feb. 1885, Sarah Eleanora Morris (b. 21 Feb. 1866), and lives in Warren County, Ill. They had—

    1 Lena, b. 23 Jan. 1886; m. Archer O. Bradshaw of Kentucky, and had (BRADSHAW)—

      1 Eleanora

    2 Harry David, b. 14 Dec. 1887; m. Florence Mitchell; live at Galesburg, Ill., and had—

      1 Mitchell.

      11 (daughter).

454 VIII   Miriam L., b. 17 June 1864; m. 6 Sept. 1883, William Allen Fletcher (b. 23 March 1862), and lives in Roseville, Warren County, Ill. They had (FLETCHER)—

    1 Bessie, b. 5 Dec. 1883; m. Emmett J. Boyd of Burlington, Iowa.

    2 Anna Mary, b. 6 April 1885; m. Dr. Guy Rutledge, and lives in Salt Lake City.

    3 Mildred Allen, b. 3 Sept. 1886.

    4 James M., b. 4 June 1888; m. Gertrude Roker.

    5 Gertrude A., b. 10 Sept. 1890; m. Harold Osborne, and lives in Chicago.

    6 Marion Brent, b. 1 April 1896; d. 4 Sept. 1918 at Rambucourt, France. He was Sgt. Battery "D", 123rd Field Artillery.

  IX   Orpha E., b. 1 Nov. 1866; d. 1 Sept. 1867.

455   X   Edmund, b. 26 July 1868.

456   XI   Frank J., b. 15 Oct. 1870; m. (I) Luella Crane, who was b. 3 July 1869; d. 19 March 1901; m. (II) Ada Savage, (1881-1931).

Children—

    1 Ferrand.

    2 Carroll, m. Roy Van Riber.

    3 Frances, m. Ralph Killey.

457 XII   Joseph A., b. 27 Nov. 1872; m. Retta Wilson.

[352] CATHERINE[7] KIRK BRENT (Kenner[6], Charles[5], George[4], George[3], Hugh[2], Hugh[1]), was born 25 June 1824 in Lancaster County, Va., and died 24 Jan. 1897 in Texas, where she moved with her family in 1860, having moved from Illinois to Iowa in 1855, and from there to Texas. She married 20 Sept. 1849, Samuel S. Jamison, who was born 8 June 1827, in Warren County, Ill.

Children (JAMISON):

I   Eugene, b. 12 June 1850; m. Molly Reeves.

II   Leonora, b. 11 Sept. 1851.

III   Cecil, b. 15 April 1853, Henderson County, Ill.

IV   John Kenner, b. 17 Sept. 1854; m. Ella N. Love, who was born 13 March 1870, in Calvert County, Texas. They had—

     1 John Kenner, b. 31 June 1888.

     2 Cecil Brent, b. 20 March 1890.

     3 Jessie Forbes, b. 17 Aug. 1891.

     4 Herschel C., b. 29 March 1893.

     5 Eunice Elizabeth, b. 29 June 1894.

     6 Madison Love, b. 17 Feb. 1896.

     7 Catherine Kirk, b. 17 Feb. 1897.

     8 Ella Norvella, b. 13 April 1898.

     9 Cornelia Ann, b. 29 April 1900.

V   Cecilia S., b. 9 April 1857; d. 18 Feb. 1861, at Burnett, Texas.

VI   Samuel S., b. 2 Jan. 1859; m. 29 March 1884, Mary Humphrey (b. 20 March 1852, in Missouri): they had—

     1 John Samuel, b. 28 Jan. 1887.

     2 Wm. Arthur, b. 3 May 1888.

     3 James Eric, b. 22 June 1890.

     4 Glenna May, b. 12 July 1894; d. 4 Aug. 1894.

VII   Estella C., b. 23 April 1861.

VIII   William Octavius, b. 3 Feb. 1863; m. 19 Nov. 1890,

Fannie Love, who was born 6 July 1866, in Texas; they had—

1 Paul Patton, b. 8 Aug. 1891.

2 Fanny Catherine, b. 12 Dec. 1892.

3 Robert Love, b. 11 Oct. 1894.

4 Ora Etheral, b. 28 Aug. 1896.

5 Mabel Ernealia, b. 10 Aug. 1899.

[353] ELIZABETH[7] EDMONDS BRENT (Kenner[6], Charles[5], George[4], George[3], Hugh[2], Hugh[1]), was born 5 March 1826 in Lancaster County, Va., and died 18 April 1888 in Henderson County, Ill. She married 24 Nov. 1848, William B. Jamison, who was born 20 March 1816.

Children (JAMISON):

    I   Alpheus, b. 30 Oct. 1849; d. 22 March 1882; m. 6 Oct. 1875, Caroline Montieth, and had—

        1 William, b. 24 Sept. 1876.

        2 Alpheus, b. 26 April 1879.

    II   Sarah Alma, b. 5 Nov. 1851; m. 16 Oct. 1871, Joseph Addison Carter of Henderson County, Ill., and had (CARTER)—

        1 Earnest O., b. 10 Aug. 1872.

        2 John Kenner, b. 24 March 1876.

        3 James Jamison, b. 26 April 1879.

        4 Foy Brent, b. 6 July 1885.

    III   Elizabeth Ann, b. 29 Oct. 1854; d. 23 March 1860.

    IV   Joseph Edmonds, b. 3 April 1857; d. 2 May 1863.

    V   Catherine Norvella, b. 27 Aug. 1859; d. 2 June 1860.

    VI   Martha Jane, b. 10 Feb. 1863; m. Marcus Whitman who was b. 2 Aug. 1859, and had (WHITMAN)—

        1 Margarati White, b. 18 Nov. 1891.

        2 Marcus Jamison, b. 3 Oct. 1900.

[354] KENNER[7] BRENT (Kenner[6], Charles[5], George[4], George[3], Hugh[2], Hugh[1]), was born 23 Oct. 1827 in Lancaster County, Va., and died 8 April 1888 in Knox County, Ill. He married (1) Eliza-

beth Virginia Simpson, who was born 15 March 1830; the daughter of Henson and Maria (Magoon) Simpson of Jackson County, Iowa. She was born in Kentucky, and died, 11 March 1867, in Ill. He married (II) 14 Feb. 1870, Mary Anne Dempsey, who was b. 7 March 1846 the daughter of Cornelius and Julia A. (Brown) Dempsey.

Children, 1st marriage:

I   Emma Viola, b. 3 March 1853, in Jackson County, Iowa; d. 11 July 1865, Warren County, Ill.

II   Mary Elizabeth, b. 18 July 1855; d. Sept. 1911, in Williston North Dakota; m. 18 Dec. 1883, Lloyd C. Lemmert. They moved to N. Dakota in the '90s, and had (LEMMERT)—

    1 Leroy, b. 1885; d. 1885, Newton, Kansas.

    2 Ethel V., b. 17 Oct. 1887, Kiowa Kan.; m. Christian O. Rude, Williston, N. Dakota, and had (RUDE)—

        I Helen E.

        II Lloyd.

        III Beverly.

III   Virginia Simpson, b. 9 Jan. 1857; d. Feb. 1922; never married.

IV   Carrie Violinda, 12 Jan. 1859; m. 22 July 1885, Charles I. Freeman (b. 10 April 1855; d. 9 March 1934), of Des Moines; they had (FREEMAN)—

    1 Linda Viola, b. 8 July 1886; m. 20 July 1911, at McKensie, N. Dakota, Benjamin Eugene Braucht (b. 14 April 1887, in Warren County, Ill.), and had (BRAUCHT)—

        1 Eugene Freeman, b. 27 Nov. 1912.

    2 Elsie, d. in infancy (1888).

    3 Ina Elizabeth, b. 14 Sept. 1891.

    4 Harold Brent, b. 28 May 1895; m. (I) Vera Phillips; (II) Rose ——. He was Sgt. Battery "F", 10th Field Artillery, 3rd Div., World War.

    5 Agnes Simpson, b. 1 Dec. 1900; m. Jas. Clifford

Clemmens, and lives at Newton, Iowa; they have (CLEMMENS)—

i Jas. Clifford, b. 8 Sept. 1926.

ii George, b. 25 May 1933.

v Richard Henson, b. 1 Dec. 1861; m. 22 Jan. 1888, Martha Ward (b. 24 Feb. 1866, in Indiana), and had—

1 Leonora, b. 13 Dec. 1888; d. 20 March 1889.

2 Carrie Mabel, b. 3 Jan. 1890; m. (i) —— Nelson; (ii) Paul Klug, and lives in Greensburg, Kan.

3 Charles Kenner, b. 13 Nov. 1895; m. Virginia ——.

vi Kenner, b. 22 Nov. 1863; d. 23 Feb. 1864.

vii Samuel S. Simpson, b. 26 Oct. 1865; d. 20 Oct. 1866.

Children, second marriage:

viii Ada, b. 28 Dec. 1870; m. 17 Oct. 1889, Samuel Albrecht, and had (ALBRECHT)—

1 Samuel E., b. 25 July 1890; m. Mabel Sherlock.

2 Ralph W., b. 31 Dec. 1892; m. Hazel Royal.

3 Myrtle W., b. 24 June 1894; m. Ellis C. Rhymer.

4 Verne Brent, b. 1897; m. Lula F. Day.

5 Joseph M., m. —— Heitman.

6 Mary M., m. Geo. A. Lehr.

ix Julia, b. 17 Oct. 1872; m. Edward C. Cook.

x Emma V., 13 Dec. 1874; m. Robt. Gilmore.

xi Leonora M., b. 23 July 1877; lives in Seattle.

xii Albert C., b. 29 Jan. 1881; lives in Sacramento, Cal.

[356] PAUL[7] BRENT (Kenner[6], Charles[5], George[4], George[3], Hugh[2], Hugh[1]), was born in Lancaster County, Va., 15 June 1831, and died after 1886, in Warren County, Illinois. He married 13 Aug. 1857, in Monmouth, Ill., Phoebe Moore, daughter of Andrew and Margaret (Cleckner) Moore, natives of Pennsylvania, who moved to Ohio soon after their marriage, and later to Ellison

Twp. Ill., (1842). Andrew Moore died 28 Dec. 1842. His widow married (II) John Brown, a native of South Carolina, and an uncle of Gen. Burnside. Phoebe Moore was born 9 Oct. 1836, in Ohio.

Children:

458	I	Ida A., m. Emory Starr; no issue.
459	II	Vesper M.
460	III	Elias G.
461	IV	Eva G., m. (I) Amos Renshbarger; (II) —— Barrick.
462	V	Jessie C., m. Oscar Laws and had two daughters.
463	VI	Paul, Jr., d. s. p.
464	VII	Harry, m. Frances ——, and had two daughters.
465	VIII	Orco, b. 25 March 1860; d. 27 July 1877.
466	IX	Marvin M., d. 29 Aug. 1869.
467	X	David L., d. in infancy.
468	XI	Minnie, d. in infancy.
469	XII	Edwin, d. in infancy.

[361] HARRISON[7] BRENT (John[6] G., Charles[5], Charles[4], Charles[3], Hugh[2], Hugh[1]), was born 16 Nov. 1819. He died in Carlisle County, Ky., 9 June 1895; married 3 March 1842, Mary Walker, daughter of John Walker (b. 29 July 1791; d. 30 July 1860), and his wife Elizabeth Parsons, daughter of James Parsons and his wife Lucy Myrtle, married 1789, in Culpeper County, Va. John Walker married Elizabeth Parsons 1820, in Culpeper County, Va. Mary Walker was born 1825, in Virginia, and died in Carlisle County, Ky., 7 March 1920.

Children:

I John T., b. 10 Jan. 1843; d. 26 Aug. 1930; m. 20 June 1865, Clarissa B. Jones.

II William A., b. 26 Aug. 1844; d. 29 Oct. 1891; m. 7 Oct. 1866, Mary N. Porter.

III Sarah Frances, b. 27 March 1846; d. 14 Feb. 1922; m. 28 Jan. 1866, William Williams.

iv   Amanda E., b. 24 Nov. 1847; d. 9 Aug. 1854.

v   Luther, b. 10 Oct. 1849; d. 1 Nov. 1852.

vi   Benjamin F., b. 4 Sept. 1851; d. 1935; m. (i) 26 Jan. 1873, Phoebe Shaffer; (ii) 22 Sec. 1906, her sister, Elizabeth Shaffer, and left issue.

vii   Mary E., b. 8 May 1854; m. 3 April 1871, Joseph Watson.

viii   James Harrison, b. 27 Dec. 1856.

ix   George Ray, b. 11 Jan. 1859; m. 4 Sept. 1878, Mary Mix.

x   Sanford Newton, b. 23 May 1861; d. 19 Dec. 1919; m. 2 Nov. 1882, Julia Williams.

xi   Joannah, b. 9 June 1864; d. 9 Aug. 1895.

xii   Noah, b. 2 Oct. 1866; d. 26 Sept. 1891.

[362] LAWSON[7] FIELDS BRENT (John G.[6], Charles[5], Charles[4], Charles[3], Hugh[2], Hugh[1]), was born 1827, and died April 1906. He married Fannie Corbin Mitchell, daughter of Harrison Mitchell and his wife Elizabeth Corbin.

Children:

i   John, b. 29 March 1852; m. (i) 8 April 1878, Mollie Cronin of Tiptonville, Tenn.; (ii) Lulu Brent dau. of (318). Living in California.

ii   Ann Elizabeth, b. 12 Sept. 1855; m. 22 Dec. 1873 Wm. U. Hodges, who d. 20 Jan. 1890.

iii   Lewis, b. 27 March 1858; m. Elizabeth Holt, 18 March 1889. She was born 10 April 1870.

iv   Eva, d. s. p.

v   Robert, m. Lilian Payne.

vi   Newton, b. 6 Oct. 1866; d. 20 Feb. 1913; m. Dora Hayes.

vii   James, d. s. p.

[363] SUSAN[7] BRENT (Thomas[6] Y. T., Hugh[5], Hugh[4], Charles[3], Hugh[2], Hugh[1]), was born in Louisville, Kentucky, —— Jan. 1829, and died there. She married 5 March 1851, William T. Haggin.

Children, (HAGGIN):

    I Mary Brent, m. Lucien G. Quigley, and had (QUIG-LEY)—

         1 Sue Brent, m. A. K. Bates.

         2 Thomas, m. Sarah Ingram; no issue.

         3 Eva, m. James Stewart Taylor; no issue.

         4 Brent Haggin, m. 20 March 1924, Julia Elizabeth Otto, and had Judith Brent Innes Quigley, b. New York, 22 April 1926; living in Palo Alto, Cal.

         5 Elizabeth Arnold.

    II Elizabeth Arnold, m. Louis Innes Stewart.

    III Sue Brent, m. Horace T. Price.

    IV Brent, d. u. m., age 28 years.

[385] CHARLES[7] SCOTT BRENT (Charles[6], Hugh[5], Hugh[4], Charles[3], Hugh[2], Hugh[1]), was born 3 March 1844, in Paris, Kentucky. He died 3 July 1903 in Baltimore, Maryland and is buried in Lexington, Ky. He married 17 Oct., 1871, Elizabeth Todd Young; born 27 July 1849; died 2 Oct. 1929. Elizabeth Todd Young was born in Fayette County, Ky. and was married in St. Louis, Mo.

Children:

  470 I Alfred Chambers, m. Annell Tomlinson; no issue.

  471 II Henry K., m. Emily Rogers; no issue.

+472 III Charles Scott, b. 20 Feb. 1881; d. 3 Dec. 1936, at Lexington, Ky.; m. 10 July 1907, Ann Penn Chew Mason, a great-great-granddaughter of George Mason of "Gunston Hall."

  473 IV Elizabeth Todd, m. M. Don Foreman, and had two sons.

[400] WILLIAM[8] BRENT (James[7], James[6], Hugh[5], James[4], Hugh[3], Hugh[2], Hugh[1]), was born 14 Sept. 1813, in either Lancaster or Northumberland Counties, most probably in Lancaster. He died —— in Lancaster County, Va.; married 14 Dec. 1835,

Martha C. Ingram, daughter of John Ingram, of Northumberland County, Va.

Children:

474   I   Sophia Ann, b. 1836; m. 15 Sept. 1853, Col. Benjamin Robinson.

475   II   Frances Helen, b. 1838.

476   III James William, b. 1840.

477   IV William Henry, b. 1844; m. Carrie Hunton.

+478   V   Thomas Sargent, b. 1846; m. Sue Hurst, b. 1851; d. 11 Feb. 1935.

479   VI Martha Gertrude, b. 1848; m. T. B. Hurst.

480   VII Richard Nixon, b. 1851; m. —— Edmonds and moved to Texas.

481   VIII James Madison, b. 1853; m. Elizabeth Eustace.

482   IX Sarah Frances, b. 1857; m. —— Garland.

[406] ANDREW[8] JACKSON BRENT (Isaac[7], Hugh[6], Hugh[5], James[4], Hugh[3], Hugh[2], Hugh[1]), was born in Northumberland County, Va., 1 Jan. 1827; died there —— March 1889. He married 22 May 1851, Sally Mason Stith. He was clerk of the County for many years.

Children:

+483   I   Andrew Mason, b. 2 Oct. 1856; d. 24 Dec. 1926; m. 16 Dec. 1880, Roberta Harper; b. 22 Nov. 1856; d. 2 June 1933.

+484   II Randolph Stith, b. 24 Aug. 1859; d. 28 Oct. 1923; m. ——, Laura Deshields.

485   III Maria Meade, died in infancy.

[472] CHARLES[8] SCOTT BRENT (Charles S.[7], Charles[6], Hugh[5], Hugh[4], Charles[3], Hugh[2], Hugh[1]), was born 20 Feb. 1881, at Paris, Ky.; d. 3 Dec. 1936 in Lexington, Ky. He graduated in medicine at the University of Va., 1906; married 10 July 1907, Ann Penn Chew Mason, granddaughter of Senator James M.

Mason, Confederate Commissioner to the Court of St. James, and great-great-granddaughter of George Mason of "Gunston Hall."

Children:

486   I   Ann Mason, m. John Blanton Winn, Jr., and has twin sons.

487   II   Elizabeth Todd.

488   III   Elizabeth Chew.

[478] THOMAS[9] SARGENT BRENT (William[8], James[7], James[6], Hugh[5], James[4], Hugh[3], Hugh[2], Hugh[1]), was born in either Northumberland or Lancaster Counties, Va., 1846; died before 1935. He married Susan Hurst, daughter of James K. and Athaliah Hurst of Northumberland County, Va. She was born 1851 in Northumberland County, Va., and died in Kilmarnock, Lancaster County, Va., 11 Feb. 1935.

Children:

I   J. H. Brent, of Pasadena, Md.

II   H. Walton, of Washington, D. C.

III   Thomas Sargent, of Kilmarnock, Va.

IV   ——, m. Albert Noblett, of Kilmarnock, Va.

V   Susan, m. 1905, Dr. James Thomas Wayman: born 1847, in Faquier County, Va., and died at Kilmarnock, Lancaster County, Va., 13 Sept., 1933, one of Kilmarnock's oldest and most prominent citizens. During the Civil War he was a member of Moseby's Rangers.

Children (WAYMAN):

1 Dr. T. Brent Wayman, of San Francisco, Cal.

2 John, of Kilmarnock, Va.

VI   ——, m. George W. Noblett, of Kilmarnock, Va.

VII   ——, m. Earnest Bussells, of Kilmarnock, Va.

VIII   Laura, m. 1907 Leonard R. Payne (see 340), of White Stone, Va.

[175]

[483] ANDREW[9] MASON BRENT (Andrew J.[8], Isaac[7], Hugh[6], Hugh[5], James[4], Hugh[3], Hugh[2], Hugh[1]), was born in Northumberland County, Va., 2 Oct. 1856, and died there 24 Dec. 1926. He practiced his profession of medicine there up to the time of his death. He married 16 Dec. 1880, Roberta Harper, of Alexandria, Va.; b. 22 Nov. 1856; d. 2 June 1933, at Heathsville, Va.

Children:

489   I   Meade Stith, b. 11 Sept. 1881; m. 21 March 1918, Helen Wilson.

490   II   Mary Genevieve, b. 29 Jan. 1883; d. 4 Oct. 1885.

491   III   Andrew Jackson, b. 12 July 1884; d. 4 Feb. 1920; m. 5 March 1912, Gussie Reinhardt.

492   IV   John Harper, b. 29 Nov. 1886; m. 26 June 1916, Mary Scruggs.

493   V   Alma Mason, b. 6 Oct. 1889; m. 19 Oct. 1910 Milton M. Neale.

494   VI   Robert Andrews, b. 22 May 1891; m. 10 Feb. 1927, Miriam Lewis.

495   VII   William Seymour, b. 9 Oct. 1893.

[484] RANDOLPH[9] STITH BRENT (Andrew J.[8], Isaac[7], Hugh[6], Hugh[5], James[4], Hugh[3], Hugh[2], Hugh[1]), was born 24 August 1859, in Northumberland County, Va., and died there 28 October, 1923. He was clerk of the county for many years, succeeding his father. He married Laura DeShields.

Children:

496   I   Margery, d. in infancy.

497   II   Laura, d. in infancy.

498   III   Henry Mason, b. 19 May 1885; d. 14 Nov. 1933; m. Nov. 1912, Rose O'Hara, and had—

     1 Randolph Stith

     2 Frances

     3 Laura

     4 Eileen

499   IV   Frederick DeShields, b. 14 July 1890; d. s. p. 18 Sept. 1931.

500   V   John Stith, b. 17 June 1892.

501   VI   Thomas Wheelwright, b. 15 July 1894.

502   VII   Sarah Randolph, b. 24 July 1897; m. 24 July 1931, T. Boyd Taliferro, of Heathsville, Va.

503   VIII   Laurence, b. 18 April 1910; m. Elizabeth Faulkner, of Fredericksburg, Va., 1932; d. 19 Nov. 1933. He was an Episcopal minister at Upperville, Va. at the time of his death.

UNTRACED BRENTS

BELOW are some notes with their sources which I could not absolutely connect with this work. Maybe the future will solve them.

1   WILLIAM D. BRENT, an attorney of Covington, Ky., was born in Hart County, Kentucky, Dec., 1852, son of John D. Brent and Elizabeth (Garvin) Brent. The father, Capt. John D. Brent, was born in Hart County, 1826, and died in 1895; buried at Bowling Green, Ky. He married Elizabeth Garvin, dau. of Valentine Garvin of Rockingham, Va. She was born in Hart County, Ky., 1829, and married in 1847. Joshua Brent, father of Capt. John D. Brent, and grandfather of William D. Brent, was a native of Virginia, who removed to Kentucky and settled in what is now Hart County, in 1783. He married Rebecca Worley, who was born in Fayette County, Ky., 1785, and lived to be ninety years of age (*Kentucky Biographical Sketches*).

2   JAMES B. BRENT, m. Sarah Morgan, 5 Oct., 1807; Wm. Morgan, father. WALKER S. BRENT, m. Parthena Tingle, 22 Oct., 1849; Eli Tingle on the bond (From Henry County, Ky., marriage bonds).

3   MARGARET BRENT, said to have married Henry Moffatt (2nd wife), born 1740. The Brents said to have lived in or near Alexandria, Va. Henry Moffatt lived near Leesburg, Loudon County, Va. They were parents of — (1) Elby Moffatt married John Jordan, and moved to Goshen Twp., Belmont County, Ohio, between 1819-1825, and later to Indiana; (2) Elizabeth Moffatt married William Burr, 1827, Belmont County, Ohio; born near Leesburg, Loudon County, Va., 24 Oct., 1804; died 1892, McConnellsville, Ohio (*Indianapolis Star*).

4   The tax list for Shelby County, Ky., 1792-1795, gives the names of JOHN BRENT and MATTHIS BRENT.

[178]

5 RICHARD BRENT m. Polly Bryant, 26 Nov. 1805 (Bourbon County, Ky.).

6 The Henry County, Ky., tax list has WILLIAM BRENT taxed from 1804 to 1819. Also Joseph Sidebottom from 1801 thru 1821.

7 WILLIAM BRENT, (died intestate), his sale bill, April 1829; Sanford Brent, Admns.; William, Elijah and Newton Brent bought much at sale (Miss Scott's notes, from Henry County, Ky.).

8 WILLIAM BRENT, dec'd, appraisement; (pp. 142 & 167, Will Book "E," 1829–1831, Scott County, Ky.) Isaac Brent, p. 384 of same book.

9 GEORGE W. BRENT m. Cornelia D. Wood, 16 Dec., 1844 (Albermarle County, Va., marriage bonds).

10 JEREMIAH BRENT married Margaret Canterberry, sister of John Canterberry before Nov. 1767. (Chalkley's *Augusta County*, of *Va. Records*, Vol. III, p. 460.)

11 WILLIAM BRENT, resident of Jefferson County, Mississippi, on 2 Aug. 1828, applied for pension, and stated that he enlisted (no date) as a private in Capt. John Stokes' company in the 2nd Va. Reg., was taken prisoner during the siege of Charleston in 1780 but made his escape and was in the interior of South Carolina at the time the troops were disbanded. (Vet. Administration, R. 20335.)

12 JOHN BRENT, b. 21 (?) Nov. 1751, in Virginia; d. 21 July 1833, in Smith County, Tenn.; m. 9 Jan. 1779, Jane —— in Virginia; b. 1763; d. 19 July 1838, in Lawrence County, Alabama at the home of her dau. Elizabeth, the wife of Thomas Hall. Thomas Hall moved to Tenn. Oct. 1848. John Brent enlisted in the fall of 1775 as private in Capt. Morgan Alexander's company* in Col. Alexander Spotswood's Va. Reg.,** and served these officers until

---

*Capt. Morgan Alexander's company was from Frederick County, Va.
**Col. Alexander Spotswood was from Spotsylvania County, Va.

Aug. 1776, when he reenlisted in the same company and regiment, was in the battle of Brandywine, the siege of Mud Island Fort, was wounded in the right side in battle of Monmouth, was at storming of Paulus Hook and was discharged 8 Aug. 1779. Enlisted 2 April 1781, in Capt. Kirkpatrick's Co., Col. Christopher Febiger's Virginia Reg., and was discharged 6 June 1783. He stated that after the Revolution he lived for some time in Virginia and married, that he then moved to North Carolina where he lived until about 1814 when he moved to Tennessee (near Carthage, Smith County, 1818). He had at least — Samuel, b. 1792 (there was a Samuel B., lawyer, in Greensburg, Ky.), Polly, m. —— Johnson and living 1842; Susannah, m. —— Hall, and living 1842; Eliz., b. 1818, m. Thomas Hall, and living 1842; Nancy, b. 1811, and not listed as living 1842; Franky, b. 1814, and not listed as living 1842. (Veterans Administration, R. 1176).

13 JOHN BRENT vs. Archibald Fisher and Susanna, his wife, late Susanna Shaddon, admnx. of Matthew Shaddon, dec'd., 28 May 1767. The bond was dated 20 March 1762 (Augusta County, Va., D. B. 14, p. 22).

FROM JAMES AND LANDON BRENT

NOTES from an account book of JAMES BRENT of "Wellington," Nelson County, Va. (d. 1816), and from parts of the Diary of his eldest son, LANDON HAINES BRENT. Where a name appears with a date, the person was a visitor. THESE NAMES DO NOT APPEAR IN THE INDEX.

A

Abny, William, 1793.

Alexander, Gabriel, of South River, Augusta County, died May 1827.

Ames, Joseph, starts with his family to Tennessee, Feb. 27th, 1831.

Anderson, son of Nelson, is tax appraiser, March 20th, 1826.

Anderson, R. H., has store at Newmarket, Sept. 16th, 1825.

Arkerd, Betsy, daughter of William Arkerd, married William Jones November 3rd, 1825.

Arkerd, William, July 13th, 1827.

Armstead, Mrs. William, daughter of the late Col. Samuel Meredith, was burned up in her house at New Glasgow, Feb. 2nd, 1829.

Aves, Mr. ———, of the town of Hebron, county of Golland (?), State of Connecticut, selling books in place of Asa Northam, April 19th, 1825.

Ames, Alexander, Jan. 1st, 1825.

B

Baber, Killes (Achilles), of Rockfish Gap, died October 1828.

Bailey, Philip, 1791.

Ball, Lewis, 1791.

Ballard, John, 1794; also May 1824.

Ballard, William, 1791.

Barnett, Alexander, 1791.

Barnett, Capt. James, 1796.

Barnett, John, 1796.

Barnett, Nathan: estate administered by John Barnett, Feb. 17th, 1826.

Descendants of Hugh Brent

Barnett, William Sr., 1793.

Barnett, William Jr., 1793.

Barry, Thomas, shoemaker, April 1824.

Beatheal, Joel, Jan. 21st, 1825.

Bell, John, 1792.

Black, James, of Augusta County, died July, 1828, leaving wife, two sons and one daughter, all grown, and a son and daughter married.

Black, Samuel, son of James, above, 1828.

Black, John, son of James, above, 1828.

Black, James, was neighbor of James Brent (d. 1816), when he lived in Augusta (1777–1787).

Blain, Samuel, of Kentucky, March 16th, 1824.

Blunt, Susannah, eldest daughter of Thankful Shields and Charles Blunt, married Mr. Robert Hunter Nov. 11th, 1825.

Boller, John, 1792.

Bradford, William (apothecary), 1805.

Braydon, John, 1792.

Bridge, James, 1792, also Oct. 5th, 1824.

Bridgewater, Joshiah, son of Samuel Bridgewater, late of Rockfish, died October 14th, 1828.

Bridgewater, Charles, 1827 (see Loben).

Bridgewater, Hannah, 1827 (see Rogers).

Bridgewater, Samuel, 1793.

Brock, Harry and James, Feb. 4th, 1824.

Britt, William, 1794.

Brooks, William, (of Augusta County) Nov. 11th, 1826.

Brown, Dr. James M., of New Glasgow, died April 23rd, 1824.

Bryant, David P., April 23rd, 1828.

Burnard (Bernard), "had breakfast at Major Burnard's at Rockfish Gap, October 10th, 1825. Mr. Ferguson, a son-in-law of Maj. Burnard's was there."

Burnett, Edmond, had a sale, May 20th, 1797.

Burnett, Isaac, 1792.

Burnett, Nelson, and his wife stopped by on their way home from John W. Witt's, Dec. 27th, 1826.

Burton, James, 1793.

Burton, Capt. J. H., lives near Newmarket, Jan. 1st, 1827.

Bushner, William, and wife and family, left Col. James Montgomery's for the town of Harrisonburg, Sept. 14th, 1825.

Brent, James, deceased, bought land from Samuel Reed.

Brent, estate of James B., dec'd, divided October 12th, 1826, between Landon H., Kendall C., James D., and Sarah (Brent) Dold.

Brent, L. H. and J. D. "stayed at David Caldwell's on Friday Feb. 2nd, and crossed the mountain on Saturday the 3rd."

Brent, Landon H., put in claim of $6.00 as surveyor of the road, May 27th, 1826.

Brent, Landon Newton, son of James D. and his wife Frances, was born Oct. 13th, 1824.

C

Cabell, Landon, 1791.

Campbell, G. H., April 3rd, 1825.

Carpenter, Mrs. Sarah, 1791.

Carpenter, Thomas, son of "widow Carpenter," 1794.

Carpenter, William, 1791.

Clack, Moses, 1791.

Clark, David, 1793.

Clark, Mrs. David, is midwife, 1793.

Clark, Benjamin, son of David, 1793.

Clark, James, son of David, 1793.

Clark, Nathaniel, brother of David, 1793.

Coffey, Osborn, 1792.

Cole, James, 1791.

Coleman, Mrs. Ann, consort of Hawes Coleman, died Feb. 1st, 1828.

Clark, William, 1791.

Church, William, 1794.

Coleman, Hawes, 1792.

Coleman, John, of Amherst County, Justice of Peace, 1825.

Coleman, wife of J. J., had son born, Sept. 19th, 1825.

Coleman, J. J. started to Kentucky, May 2nd, 1827. He took his family and negroes, Nov. 10th, 1827.

Coleman, Dr. Hawes had a son born June 1827, in Spotsylvania County, by his Lady, formerly Dorothy W. Lewis, daughter of Robert Lewis of Spotsylvania County.

Coleman, Richard Hawes, Sept. 24th, 1827.

Coleman, Richard C., "his Ladye and children, May 31st, 1831."

Coleman, Lee H., son of Richard C. Coleman, above.

Coleman, Thomas, of Kentucky, "at Hawes Coleman's," July 25th, 1824.

Coleman, Walter Lewis, son of Dr. Hawes Coleman, born June 6th, 1827, and died June 8th, 1828.

Camden, John, died Oct. 9th, 1827, at his residence on Piny River.

Camden, John F., Dec. 11th, 1827.

Carter, John M., died June 27th, 1828.

Chewning, James—his sister married Rise Morris.

Chewning, John, July 24th, 1828. His daughter married Rise Morris.

Cleebrooke, John, of Louisa County, "here with William H. Harris," July 5th, 1827.

Clark, James, "his shop," 1796.

Cluff, Betty, had daughter born July 1st, 1827, named Nicey. It died June 23rd, 1829.

Cobbs, Dr. John P., Sept. 24th, 1825.

Collins, Samuel, 1826.

Coffey, Ann, died December 1828; "resident for over seventy years."

Coffey, William, of Tye River, died March 24th, 1828. He was born March 29th, 1740.

Cowin, William, of Alexandria, March 31st, 1826.

Crawford, Nathan, son of Nelson Crawford of Rockfish, died December 20th, 1829.

Curtz, Jacob, "is jailkeeper at Staunton," March 15th, 1829.

D

Daley, Daniel, a nephew of Thomas Beary, married Nov. 6th, 1826, Nancy Harris, daughter of William L. Harris.

Davis, Maj. William, of Augusta County, October 1826.

Dand, William, son of William Dand?, 1793.

Dawson,—"Major Dawson's mill," March 1825.

Detters, Capt. N. "dined at," Oct. 2nd, 1825.

Dillard, Thomas, married Sofe Perry, June 16th, 1824.

Digges, Mrs. Elizabeth, died June 5th, 1828. She was born April 2nd, 1743.

Dinwiddie, Nancy, 1792.

Dinwiddie, Robert, 1792.

Divers, Thomas of Albemarle County, died in the Fall of 1827.

Dold, Eliza, Feb. 22nd, 1830.

Dold, Sarah (wife of Wm. Dold, and sister of L. H. Brent), of Augusta County, "took her sixteen negroes received from the estate of James Brent, dec'd, back to Augusta," 1827.

Dold, William, "was here with Richard Lee," Aug. 16th, 1828.

Duncan, William, administered the sacrament on Sunday Sept. 14th, 1828, to Hawes Coleman; Burgess Witt and wife were there.

Duncan, William, administered the sacrament to his disciples on Sunday, 12th of August, 1827, at the Brick Meeting House in Jonesboro. NOTE: Wm. Duncan preached on Rockfish also.

E

Edmonds, Betty, married John Strickland, August 10th, 1826.

Edmonds, Sarah, had a sale Sept. 20th, 1829, "and she intends to move to Missouri."

Edmonds, William, died March 15th, 1826, "of Rockfish."

Edmonds, Mrs. Sally, January 1826.

Edwards, Lewis, "a blind man from Cumberland County, Pennsylvania," June 1st, 1825.

Elliott, George C., "of Kentucky, was here Winter of 1813."

Emly or Embry, Lucke, died December 1828. A resident over seventy years.

Eskridge, George, March 15th, 1829.

Eskridge, Parson, preached at Jonesboro Sept. 3rd, 1827.

F

Faber, William, 1826.

Fitzpatrick, Maj. Alexander of Rockfish, 1827.

Fitzpatrick, Breckenridge, 1828.

Fitzpatrick, John, baptized by Wm. Duncan at Shelton's Ford on Rockfish, Sept. 24th, 1827.

Fitzpatrick, John, 1793. Had brother Thomas.
Fitzpatrick, Thomas, brother of John, 1793.
Fitzpatrick, John E., cousin of Thomas, 1793.
Fitzpatrick, William, July 18th, 1828.
Franklin, Powhatan, June 1825.
Fortune, John, son of Zachariah Fortune, 1826, Nov. 25th.
Fortune, Richard, Dec. 11th, 1827.
Fortune, Z., Feb. 5th, 1824.
Ferguson, Mr. "son-in-law of Maj. Burnard," 10 Oct. 1825.

G

Garland, Capt. James, returned to the Legislature from Nelson County, April 8th, 1829.
Garland, Samuel M., returned to Legislature from Amherst County, April 20th, 1829.
Goodwin, Ann N., married April 5th, 1825.
Goodwin, Edmund C. Jan. 21st, 1825.
Goodwin, James D., "bought two bales of cotton from," Oct. 30th, 1825.
Goodwin, Mrs. Thomas, consort of Thomas Goodwin, died Jan. 1st, 1829.
Goodwin, Thomas C., moved from Rockfish to Buffalo Springs in Amherst County, Jan. 20th, 1825.

H

Hall, Maj. Alexander, of Augusta County, died March 4th, 1831.
Hale, Leonard, Feb. 4th, 1827 (Hail or Hall).
Hall, Robert M., 1827.
Hall, William—tanyard, 1826.
Hamlet, Mrs., wife of William Hamlet and daughter of David Witt, died August 4th, 1828.
Hardy, Robert, 1789.
Harlow, Nathaniel Jr., 1825.
Harlow, Nathan—his daughter married March 4th, 1824.
Harlow, Rueben, 1793, also Feb. 23rd, 1829.
Harlow, Walter, 1793.
Harlow, William, 1793.

Harmersell, Parson, preached on Rockfish, March 9th, 1828.

Harris, Ann, grandau. of Hawes Coleman, and daughter of the late John W. Harris, died August 24th, 1828.

Harris, Ben. D. wife's funeral preached by Rev. James Boyd, July 20th, 1828.

Harris, John Butler, Dec. 1829.

Harris, Carter B., is son of Wm. L. Harris, 1824.

Harris, Carter B., and wife Mary—son born to, Jan. 13th, 1825.

Harris, Carter Braxton, and wife Polly (Marr) had son, Wm. Lee Harris born October 25th, 1826, at her father's, John R. Marr.

Harris, Carter B., and wife Polly, had son born Dec. 28th, 1828. "This makes the third son born at her father's home."

Harris, Carter B., left with his family for the West, March 14th, 1831.

Harris, "Green Mountain" John, 1793.

Harris, James, son of "Green Mountain" John, 1793.

Harris, Jessie, son of "Green Mountain" John, 1793.

Harris, Joshua, son of "Green Mountain" John, 1793.

Harris, John W., died June 20th, 1828.

Horselly, Wm., succeeded by Col. J. A. Jobling as high sheriff, 1824.

Harris, Mrs. John W., died June 21st, 1828. Buried in same grave with her husband.

Harris, Mary, wife of John W. Harris, died October 18th, 1824. She was daughter of Hawes and Nancy Coleman. She was about thirty-four years old when she died.

Harris, Mary, wife of Ben D. Harris, died March 28th, 1828. She was daughter of Col. James Montgomery.

Harris, Matthew and wife, "John W. Harris' son and daughter also at Hawes Coleman's," Nov. 6th, 1827.

Harris, Matthew, 1795.

Harris, Nancy, daughter of Wm. L. Harris, married Nov. 6th, 1826, Daniel Daley, nephew of Thomas Bearry.

Harris, Polly, "and her three sons," Jan. 26th, 1829.

Harris, Polly T. and sister Jane Marr, March 12th, 1830. Jane Marr has brother Alexander Marr.

Harris, "a Mr. Harris, son of John Harris," June 20th, 1824.

Harris, Sarah, "daughter of Wm. L. Harris, and sister of L. W. Harris, married a Mr. Coleman, June 20th, 1824."

Harris, Mrs. Skilor?, of Albemarle County, died July 1828.

Harris, Wm. Henry, deputy sheriff for Wm. B. Harris, June 23rd, 1827.

Harris, Wm. B. sheriff; John Harris deputy, July 6th, 1828.

Harris, Wm. Lee, 1795.

Harris, Wm. Lee died Wednesday night March 3rd, 1824.

Heulett, William, died May 17th, 1826 at Dr. H. N. Coleman's, and was buried in Spottsylvania County.

Hickoke?, John of Lovingston, Sept. 4th, 1815.

Hight, Matt, 1828.

Hill, William, 1828.

Hockins, Thomas and son Thomas Jr., 1795.

Holbert, William, "a young lad from Essex County stayed all night, July 12th, 1825."

Hopkins, Mr. Arthur, elected from Nelson to the State legislature, April 1829.

Hudgins, William, "going to Kentucky in a few days," Oct. 4th, 1815.

Hughes, Ben, — had a grist mill, 1827.

Hughes, Benjamin, had three sons, viz., Joseph, Benjamin and James, 1829.

Hughes, Benjamin, son of John Hughes, married Feb. 3rd, 1831, Lewandy Parrish, daughter of Samuel Parrish.

Hughes, Mrs. Ben, and Miss. Polly Perry, July 21st, 1828.

Hughes, Capt. James, March 31st, 1824.

Hughes, James B., Aug. 10th, 1826.

Hughes, John, son of Moses Hughes, 1791 and 1793.

Hughes, Moses, the elder of Rockfish, died June 4th, 1824. He was born in 1735. His funeral service was preached Nov. 29th, 1824.

Hughes, Moses, married daughter of Maj. D. R. Clarkson, Feb. 9th, 1828.

Hunter, James A., Sept. 17th, 1826.

Hundley, James, 1791. He has a brother named Nemiah?.

Hundley, Nemiah?, 1794.

Hamilton, Sarah — her daughter married Lawrence Meeks, 12-25-1828.

Hunter, Matthew, April 1824.

Hunter, Robt., "stayed all night with Robt. Hunter in Augusta, and went to Wm. Dold's."

Hunter, Mrs. David, died May 13th, 1831.

K

Kinkaid, Frances, married Geo. Williams, Nov. 14th, 1826.

Knight, William of New Glasgow, died April 22nd, 1824.

Kinney, Chesley, merchant, 1791.

Koontz, Col. of Rockingham — "helped get his wagon over the mountain," Nov. 11th, 1824.

J

Jacobs, Capt. David "was here for breakfast and was very merry with his stories," Sept. 28th, 1824.

Jacobs, Capt. P. C., Sept. 20th, 1827.

Jacobs, Wm. B., Sept. 23rd, 1825.

Jefferson, Thomas, died July 4th, 1826, "on the anniversary of the Declaration of Independence."

Jobling, Col. Jesse A., succeeded Wm. Horsely as high sheriff of Nelson County, Nov. 22nd, 1824.

Jobling, James, 1794.

Johnson, Benjamin, of Warren, 1809.

Johnson, William, 1799.

Johnston, Ben, "James Montgomery's man," June 3rd, 1828.

Johnson, Steven, Feb. 12th, 1826.

Jones, Capt. Charles of Nelson County, Aug. 21st, 1826.

Jones, Mrs. Kitty, Oct. 12th, 1824.

Jones, Thomas, "overseer for W. M. Harris," Feb. 18th, 1826.

Jones, "Capt. Thomas and Charles Jones at Marr's," Jan. 2nd, 1825.

L

Landrom, Thomas, 1805.

London, N., "bought horse-feed from."

Lavender?, George, 1794.

Lee, John H., "a young man from Goochland County," July, 12th, 1825.

Lacky, Samuel, 1792, son Gabriel.

Lacky, Gabriel, son of Samuel, 1792.

Lee, Richard, gave a barbecue July 4th, 1829, "celebrating the 54th year of American independence."

Lee, Richard, 1793.

Lewis, Col. Wm. I (or J.), of Campbell County, died Oct. 1828. He was raised in Augusta County, and married a daughter of Col. Joseph Cabell of Buckingham County.

Littrell, Wm., 1793.

Loben, James, lost a lawsuit to Charles Bridgewater, Oct. 6th, 1827.

Loving, Seaton, married daughter of Joseph Montgomery, Oct. 23rd, 1828.

Lee, Zachariah (see Strickland).

Lowery, Peter, of Rockbridge County, June 24th, 1825.

Loving, William, July 1825.

M

Marr, Alexander, is brother to Jane Marr, 1830.

Marr, Ambrose, has sister Matildy, and brother John, Nov. 1st, 1829.

Marr, James, son of John, March 25th, 1826.

Marr, Jane, is sister of Polly T. Harris, 1830.

Marr, John, Jr., 1825.

Marr, John, his "daughters Matilda and Jane, and their cousin Betsey Ames," Nov. 8th, 1830.

Marr, John, brother of Matilda and Ambrose R. Marr, 1829.

Marr, James, is son of John Marr, Aug. 1827.

Marr, John, "left with his family Nov. 22nd, 1830, for the Western country."

Marr, Sophia, "wife of John Novrell?, and widow of Ben Morgan deceased, and daughter of James Marr, died Oct. 31st, 1824."

Martin, Eziah, 1794.

Martin, Henry B., of Rockfish, son of Hudson Martin, died, Jan. 14th, 1828.

Martin, John M., Dec. 19th, 1824.

Martin, H. B.—"funeral sermon was preached Feb. 14th, 1828, by the Rev. Stevens of Staunton. His text was, "give an account of thy stewardship."

Martin, Hudson, "former merchant of Charlottesville, and another of the Spirit of 1776," died Nov. 23rd, 1830, on Rockfish.

Martin, John R., son of the late Isiah Martin, died Jan. 10th, 1829.

Martin, Pleasant, 1792.

Martin, Dr. Wellington, May 31st, 1828.

Martin, Dr. William, Aug. 1824.

Massie, Charles, of Albemarle County, died April 8th, 1830.

Massie, Maj. Thomas, Sept. 7th, 1828.

Massie, Dr. Thomas, and Dr. David R. Patteson, were returned as representatives for County of Nelson, April 25th, 1825. Robt. Rives Jr., was defeated.

McAlexander, Capt. James, had son David, 1793.

McAlexander, David, son of above.

McAlexander, Permela, daughter of Capt. Alexander McAlexander, married Dec. 20th, 1827, a Mr. Foster of Albemarle County.

McClain, James, 1791.

Meeks, "Betsey Meeks, John Meeks and Susan Meeks were here to get their teeth drawn, Sept. 18th, 1828."

Meeks, Lawrence, son of Richard Meeks, married Dec. 25th, 1828, a daughter of Sarah Hamilton. He is overseer for Carter B. Harris.

Meeks, Richard, overseer for Carter B. Harris, left for the West, Oct. 8th, 1827.

Meeks, Richard, "and his daughter, Susan," July 20th, 1828.

Meeks, Susan, daughter of Richard, 1828.

Meeks, Thomas, Jan. 25th, 1825.

Mitchell, Z., married Clarissa Jones at Will Thackers, Oct. 20th, 1824.

Megginson, "Mr. Joseph C. Megginson lost his wife, April 12th, 1830. She was the daughter of Capt. James Montgomery."

Mills, Jessie, and a daughter of Jessie Woods, married, Oct. 30th, 1829. "The infare lasted all night."

Montgomery, James — daughter married Nov. 15th, 1826, a Mr. Mikerson (Megginson). (See above.)

Montgomery, John S., April 25th, 1824.

Montgomery, daughter of Joseph Montgomery, married Oct. 23rd, 1828, Seaton Loving.

Montgomery, Joseph, 1791.

Montgomery, Thomas, son of James Montgomery, 1824.

Montgomery, Margaret, daughter of Col. James Montgomery, died June 25th, 1829.

Montgomery, Rachael, daughter of Col. James Montgomery, died June 24th, 1829.

Montgomery, William, son of Col. James Montgomery, died May 18th, 1831. He was born in 1796.

Maurfett (Moffett), James, of Augusta County, died July 1826.

Moseby, Daniel, 1797.

Moore, James, May 5th, 1821.

Moore, Wm., 1790.

Martin, Wm. C. J., nephew of Wm. Faber.

Morgan, Ben, married Sophia Marr, and left her a widow (see S. Marr).

Morrison, Capt. A. H., Feb. 17th, 1827.

Morrison, James, 1791.

Morrison, Thomas, 1791.

Morrison, James "arrived from Kentucky with Thomas Coleman, July 16th, 1828."

Morrison, Thomas, "stayed all night with Capt. T. Morrison's at 'Landcraft'," Nov. 19th, 1825.

Morrison, Joseph, of Waynesboro, Sept. 8th, 1827.

Morrison, Dr. Robt., 1794.

Morriss, Rise "started his house Nov. 20th, 1827, where the old corn house stood on the estate of James Brent, dec'd."

N

Nash, Daniel, April 28th, 1828.

Nevil, Lewis, 1793.

Nevil, Col. Z., April 6th, 1829. "Col. Zachariah Nevil, Capt. Henry Rives, Wm. Montgomery and Capt. C. B. Harris stopped by here ——"

Nevil, Zachariah, "returned to the next legislature from Nelson County," April 28th, 1829.

Nevil, Col. Zachariah, died April 8th, 1830.

Northam, Ase, from Connecticut, April 4th, 1824.

Norvol?, John, "was here today," Sept. 24th, 1826.

O

Owens, Levy, died "Spring of 1828."

P

Page, Joseph, 1794. Has son Edward.

Page, Edward, son of Joseph, 1794.

Page, Dillard, 1794.

Parrish, Samuel — daughter Lewandy, 1827 and 1831.

Parrish, Lewandy, married Feb. 3rd, 1831, Benjamin Hughes, son of John Hughes.

Patteson, Dr. David R., "here" (campaigning) April 5th, 1825. He was elected to the Legislature April 25th, 1825.

Paul, Parson, "preached at Mrs. Shields, April 1st, 1824.

Perkins, Wm., 1793.

Perry, George, 1791.

Perry, "Old Mrs. Perry died July 14th, 1828, on Rockfish, aged eighty-nine years." She was mother of Wm. Perry. Her funeral was preached Sept. 25th, 1828.

Perry, Wm.

Perry, Jane and Geo. W. Perry left James D. Brent's for Augusta, March 14th, 1828.

Perry, Geo. W.

Perry, Sally, died Oct. 20th, 1827, and was buried the next day at Capt. James Hughes' apple orchard. Her things were sold by Wm. Perry, Dec. 15th, 1827.

Perry, Wm., and son George, and daughters Polly and Betty, and Miss Ann S. Witt, Aug. 1st, 1827.

Perry, Betty.

Perry, Polly.

Perry, Jane — household goods moved to James D. Brent's, Nov. 2nd, 1827.

Peters, Eason, shoemaker, July 21st, 1828.

Phillips, Richard, Jan. 1st, 1827.

Phillips, Thomas, 1792.

Plesbbs?, Dr. John, March 21st, 1824.

Plunkett, Mrs. Margaret, consort of Willis Plunkett, and daughter of James Shields, died April 2nd, 1831.

Plunkett, Willis, 1831.

Powell, Thomas, 1805.

Purrow, Col. Charles, Regimental commander, 1826.

R

Reed, Samuel, sold land to James Brent dec'd, on Hat Creek before 1816.

Repeto, Peter, died Feb. 10th, 1827. He was born in April 1740.

Repeto, William, lived on Back Creek in Augusta County May 1824.

Repeto, Wm., and wife go to Sally Perry's (she is sick), Sept. 29th, 1827.

Randolph, Gov. Thomas M., son in law of Thomas Jefferson, died June 20th, 1828.

Rankin, Thomas, Aug. 10th, 1826.

Rawl, Parson, married Miss Aremstrong Sept. 3rd, 1827, at Dr. Kinkaid's.

Rives, R. — got 217 votes and H. B. Martin 207, and were returned to the Legislature from Nelson County, April 25th, 1825.

Rives, Robt., and Joseph Megginson returned to Virginia Assembly from Nelson County April 29th, 1828.

Roberts, Jacob, 1791.

Roberts, James — shop, 1795.

Roberts, Joseph C., Nov. 5th, 1827.

Roberts, Joseph, has son John, 1788.

Robertson, Thomas, 1791.

Reed, Samuel, 1792.

Roberts, John, son of Joseph, 1788.

Rodes, Widow Charles of Rockfish, died Feb. 11th, 1825, "nearly 100 years old."

Rodes, Woodson, grandson of Widow Charles Rodes, died Feb. 25th, 1825.

Rodes, David, 1794.

Roberts, Henry, son of widow Frances Roberts, Nov. 11th, 1824.

Roberts, James, March 1825.

Roberts, Matthew, son of widow Fanny Roberts, died Dec. 20th, 1826. He was the son-in-law of John S. Dawson of Nelson County.

Robertson, Thomas, of Rockfish, died June 2nd, 1828.

Rogers, Elizabeth Wood, wife of Edward Rogers, died July 22nd, 1827, "in child-bed." She was sister of John Wood, and daughter of Hannah Bridgewater.

Rose, Henry, son of Col. Patrick Rose, died Nov. 6th, 1826.

Rose, Col. Patrick (see above).

Rose, Capt. John N., April 23rd, 1828.

Royalty, Wm., of Amherst, "a traveller on James River, and from Port Republic to Harper's Ferry," Sept. 23rd, 1824.

Rudisil, Mr. John, April 27th, 1829.

S

Seay, Abraham, "an old resident of Tye River," died in December 1828.

Sheets, John, gunsmith of Staunton, 1827.

Shelton, Mrs., wife of Col. Joseph Shelton, was born March 12th, 1769.

Shelton, Maj. Joseph, 1795.

Shelton, Col. Joseph, 1824.

Shelton, Mr. Samuel, merchant; "Bought of 1804,"—

3¼ yds. of velvet	@ 10/6	—£ 1-14s 2d
3¼ yds. of corduroy	@ 10/	—£ –12s–6d
2 doz. buttons	@ 02/ —	- 4s-
silk	@ 1/9 —	- 1s-9d
1 pr. gloves	@ 4 —	- 4s- d

Shelton, Robt. P., son of Col. Joseph Shelton, Nov. 25th, 1826.

Shelton, Maj. Wm. H., died Aug. 21st, 1825, "at the dwelling place of the late Col. Samuel Cabell on the James River."

Shields, Alexander "got to his mother's home May 18th, 1824, and went back to Tennessee July 4th, 1824." His wife's name was Rebecca.

Shields, Betsey, daughter of James Shields, married Oct. 19th, 1826, James Marr, son of James Marr, dec'd, of Bedford County, and brother of John and Alexander Marr of Nelson County.

Shields, George, Samuel Shields and Wm. Smith and "families started to Kentucky Oct. 18th, 1825, with two wagons, and a riding carriage, negroes and all."

Shields, James, June 1825.

Shields, John James, married, Oct. 12th, 1826, a daughter of Ambrose Plunkett of Campbell County.

Shields, Samuel, went to Kentucky with his brother George, 1825.

Shields, Thankful, married Chas. Blunt; her daughter, Susannah, married Mr. Robert Hunter 11-10-1825.

Shields, Mrs. Margaret, has been sick for six years — 1828. She lost three slaves from sickness in 1828.

Shields, Nathan; Landon Haines Brent one of commissioners at the sale of his estate, which was dated Jan. 22nd, 1812.

Shields, Robt. 1797.

Shields, Maj. Robert, Sept. 22nd, 1825.

Shields, Robert, Nov. 18th, 1826.

Shields, Thankful, daughter of James Shields, married a Mr. Johnson of Bedford County, Nov. 6th, 1827.

Shields, Mary Ann, Feb. 26th, 1825; with Miss Thankful Shields.

Shields, William, "came to his mothers, Oct. 15th, 1824; he returned to Tennessee Oct. 31st, 1824.

Simson, David, and his son Walter, 1792.

Simson, Walter, son of David, 1792.

Shikles?, Ise?, Dec. 18th, 1824.

Small, William, 1794.

Smith, Henry, 1792.

Smith, John M. — his store, 1827.

Smith, Tilly, 1794.

Smith, Wm. F. — his shop, July 1824.

Smith, Wm. T. lives with Wm. Faber "below the rock spring" July 15th, 1827.

Snead, Capt. — has tavern at Warren, 1797.

Stern, Mr. — "a moving merchant," Jan. 16th, 1825.

Stratton, Capt. — "tanyard," Dec. 9th, 1824.

Strickland, Beal, "started to Missouri Sept. 29th, 1826, with his family, twenty-four in number, with Zachariah Lee in company."

Strickland, Joseph, 1790.

Stuart, Archibald, judge of Nelson Superior Court, Oct. 1st, 1827. Wm. B. Harris, sheriff.

Stuart, Robert, of Augusta, died March 1816.

Sutherland, G. W., Feb. 29th, 1824.

Thorpe, Adeline, 1827.

Thorpe, Wm., had blacksmith shop, 1827.

Thomason, Lucas P., "legislator from Amherst County, April 20th, 1829."

Thacker, Will — Z. Mitchell and Clarissa Jones married Oct. 20th, 1824, "at his house."

Tillman, Thomas, 1804.

Triall?, David, Aug. 1824.

Towles, William, 1792.

Towles, Joseph, 1795.

Trusler, Joseph, Feb. 12th, 1826.

Trusler, John, 1791.

Trusler, James, 1792.

W

Ware, Mrs., and her daughter Patsy Lowery, Nov. 13th, 1824.

Waire, Mrs. Thomas, baptized July 24th, 1825.

Wair or Ware, Robt., 1792.

Ware, Nancy, March 28th, 1826.

Warwick, Andrew, son in law of James Woods, died May 1828.

Williams, John, 1793.

Weaver, Joseph, 1792.

Whitehead, Floyd, and Landon H. Brent "got to Staunton Nov. 15th, 1825; we got to Pendleton Courthouse at 10 P. M. the next day. We left Franklin and got to Willfork (?) on the South Fork of the Potomac Nov. 17th, 1825. Back to Staunton the 18th." (Names of people they met later on.)

Whitehead, Maj. John, Dec. 11th, 1827.

Williams, George, married, Nov. 14th, 1826, Frances Kinkaid, by Rev. James Bogead.

Winston, Benjamin, June 1825.

Witt, Ann S., 1827 (See Wm. Perry).

Witt, Denitt, "The Rev. Wm. Duncan preached the funeral service at Denitt Witt's, over his daughter who died in Kentucky, the wife of Wm. Witt, their relative," Nov. 26th, 1824.

Witt, John W., July 1825.

Woodroof, D., "Cash paid," 1805.

Woods, James, and wife, Aug. 24th, 1828. He was son of widow Michael Woods.

Woods, Maj. J., Dec. 8th, 1825.

Woods, Dr. John N., son of Major James Woods, died, Nov. 6th, 1826. He was born in 1792.

Woods, Michael, son of Michael Woods, dec'd, died July 8th, 1826, in Lexington, Va.

Woods, Nelson, of Rockfish, died June 23rd, 1825.

Wood, Wm., overseer for Robt. Shields, 1824.

Wright, Geo. G., 1824.

V

Vaughan, Mr., commissioner of taxable property for Nelson County, May 5th, 1829.

Vaughan, William, "stayed all night with" at "Harewood," Nov. 2nd, 1825.

Y

Young, William, Aug. 1825.

Nov. 4th, 1828—"Kendall C. Brent went to Lovingston to vote for Andrew Jackson for President of the United States."

Nov. 5th, 1828—"Andrew Jackson 207 votes; John Adams 75 votes" (at Lovingston).

Dec. 29th, 1828, Monday—"Seven men stayed here on Sunday night with two lunatics for the Staunton hospital. . . . We sat up all night that night."

Tuesday, May 9th, 1826—Regimental Muster at Lovingston.

April 21st, 1827—"This is C. B. Harris's Muster day."

Oct. 27th, 1827—Battallion Muster at Maj. Alexander Fitzpatrick's on Rockfish.

May 8th, 1828—Regimental Muster at Lovingston.

April 25th, 1829—Regimental Muster at Lovingston. Col. Charles Purrow is commander-in-chief.

March 9th, 1828—"Great shock by earthquake about 10 P. M."

Friday Jan. 13th, 1826—"Had our house and greater part of our things burnt."

"People in Franklin Town (Pendleton County)—Wm. McCoy, John P. Tomelson, Jack Griner, James Kies, Geo. W. Amos, Henry Sughens, Thos. C. Goordon, Henry Poleson, Henry

Seenett on Black Thorne, Woolfunks on South Fork, and Jacob Hevener at line of South Fork." (See Floyd White-head.) 1825.

The Brent Family came to this neighborhood on Rockfish (Nelson County, Va.) in April 1787, which is 43 years past this 7th of April, 1830. Signed, Landon H. Brent.

"One bull hide weighed 37℔s after dressing, @ 30c per pd, 1/3 to tanner." 1824.

FROM LANDON NEWTON BRENT, Sr.

NOTES from the diary of Landon Newton Brent Sr. of "Wellington," Nelson County, Va. (1824-1909). THESE NAMES DO NOT APPEAR IN THE INDEX.

A

Akers, John, died March 24th, 1860, "from exposure from a fall in Tye River."

Allen, Robert, "Shot himself," November, 1896.

Anderson, Mrs. Mary, widow of Joseph K. Anderson, died Nov. 18th, 1875.

Anderson, Robert H., died in the Fall of 1902.

B

Brent, Florence, daughter of Jas. H. Brent and his wife Mildred Pierce, died Aug. 5th, 1865.

Brent, Jacob, died Dec. 3rd, 1881 (son of above).

Brent, Minnie, died July 14th, 1891, "On a visit to her brother Pierce, in Accomac County." She was 26 years old.

Brent, Otis, killed by a premature explosion of dynamite in the winter of 1902.

Bingley, horse, died Jan. 25th, 1870, "one of the last of the great stock of horses that has been in my family since 1755."

Bruts, "my old dog," died 1872. He was fifteen years old.

Brent, Fanny Hall, died Nov. 9th, 1872, age 5 years, 2 months and 14 days.

Brent, Ulla Bona, died 1855. (Not the Ulla Bona who married Patteson. Mrs. Patteson was originally named Adeline Thornhill Brent, but changed her name after the death of her elder sister.)

Brent, Metellus, married his first cousin, Susan Witt, Jan. 14th, 1874, "It displeased his father (Hugh) very much."

Brent, J. Claudius, son of Hugh, "went hunting and accidently shot himself in the mouth as he was getting over a rail fence," April 22nd, 1874. Fifteen and a half years old.

Bryant, Frankie, wife of Nathan Bryant, died July 4th, 1874. She was eighty years old.

[200]

Brent, Ulla Bona, married Dec. 16th, 1874, Henry C. Patteson.

Bryant, Nathan, died March 24th, 1875; 80 years old.

Brent, Mary Washington, married Dec. 20th, 1876, John Will Witt.

Bibb, John James, died Dec. 8th, 1878, "a man of social qualities and great mirth."

Bryant, Nelson, died Jan. 9th, 1879, 70 years plus.

Bridge, William, "on Back Creek in Augusta County," died March 23rd, 1879.

Brent, Hugh L., died June 25th, 1879, 59 years and 3 months old. He left one child(Metellus).

Harriett, "negro woman belonging to my father's estate," died 7-30-80.

Jenny, "my mother's cook," died 8-6-80.

Brown, Robt. L., died June 17th, 1880.

Brent, George William, married Nov. 26th, 1884, Jenny Harvey.

Bailey, W. W., died May 10th, 1883, "same night as his brother in law, Asa Witt."

Boyd, Mrs. Juliet A., died Sept. 17th, 1883.

Brent, Landon Newton Jr., married Dec. 23rd, 1885, Fanny Henderson Clarkson.

Brent, Missouri C., died June 26th, 1886 in her 58th year.

Brent, Kendall Carroll, "Came home with his family after spending eighteen years in Mexico," Aug. 31st, 1887.

Brent, Robt. Craig, "left home on his 18th birthday," Aug. 14th, 1887.

Brent, Jas. Pinckney, married Nov. 23rd, 1887, Willie A. Bowles.

Brent, daughter of Metellus B., died Feb. 8th, 1888, ten years old.

Bourne, Dr. Cyrus, died April 1886.

Brown, Mrs. (Judge) J. Thompson, died Sept. 11th, 1886, in her 39th year. She had eleven children.

Bryant, Nelson, married Mary E. Y. Hall, April 18th, 1889. She died April 5th, 1890, "in child-bed."

Bryant, Mrs. Nelson, Sr., died June 9th, 1890; 77 years old.

Bibb, Nat, died April 1894.

Bibb, Hill, died April 1894.

Bowling, Robt., died Dec. 1st, 1895, about 66 years old.

Brent, Mrs. L. N., "my dear wife fell dead, seemingly in good health, Monday morning May 24th, 1897, in her 69th year."

Boyd, Mrs. (Major), died Feb. 1897.

"Jin mule" died March 11th, 1898; 35 years old.

Brent, Geo. W. and family left my place April 5th, 1899.

Brent, James Haines, died Jan. 13th, 1902, 88 years and four months old: "the oldest Brent."

Brent, Mrs. James H., (Mildred Pierce), died the Fall of 1906.

Brent, Nicie Otelia, died May 1852 (dau. of H. L. Brent).

Brent, infant dau. of Hugh Littleton Brent, died 1854–two weeks old.

Brent, Wm. Kossouth, died 1861, aged five years. Son of H. L. B.

Brent, Sarah, wife of William Dold of Augusta County and Rockbridge County, died 1848.

C

Coleman, John C., died 1869, about 70 years old.

Coleman's mill burned Feb. 1871.

Clarkson, Nelson C., died Sept. 12th, 1872; 86 years old.

Cabell, Frederick Mortimer, died March 2nd, 1873; 70 odd years old.

Carter, Geo. Washington, died July 29th, 1873.

Calloway, Dr. Paul C., died May 25th, 1876; 65 years old.

Coleman, Dr. Hawes N., died July 21st, 1877; 52 years old; *Eccles. 9th chap., 10th verse.*

Camp, Albert, died Feb. 5th, 1879.

Camp, Andrew, died Feb. 18th, 1879.

Coffey, Mrs. Peter, died Jan. 1883; 91 years old.

Coffey, Reuben and wife, died Dec. 1883.

Coffey, Peter C., died April 6th, 1885.

Clark, E. F., died Jan. 1888; over 55 years old.

Coleman, John J., died Sept. 21st, 1888; over 55 years old; *St. Johns 11-14-23.*

Coleman, Mrs. John, died Aug. 1892.

Coles, Mrs. E. G. (nee Jane Knight), died April 1894. "She was an old schoolmate of mine."

Carter, Dr. E. V., died Nov. 9th, 1894; 66 years old.

Cabell, William M., died Nov. 1898.

Carter, "Pink" (nee Shields), wife of Shadrack Carter, died Feb. 15th, 1905.

Coleman, Walter, died May 14th, 1899; age 76 plus.

Cash, "Honest" Richard James, died April 1900; "he would have been 100 years old the coming June."

D

Dean, John, died May 1874.

Davis, Robt. C., died Oct. 21st, 1877; 52 years old.

Dinwiddie, Nathan, "last servant but one born before the death of my grandfather (James D. B.) died in the Fall of 1880."

Daniel, Sam, died Oct. 17th, 1882.

Dold, Samuel, of Lexington, died "Winter of 1883."

Davis, John F. ("Tony"), died April 23rd, 1885.

Dickie, William, died June 23rd, 1886; over 80 years old.

Dillard, Rev. James M., died Dec. 1893.

Dold, Sarah (Brent), wife of Wm. Dold of Augusta County, died 1848.

F

Fitzpatrick, Col. Alexander, died Nov. 1871.

Fortune, William, died Sept. 1872—"a man of considerable talent after leading a dissipated life."

Fitz-Giles, Samuel, "killed by Jesse Dillard, Feb. 1881."

Farrell, Thomas J., "moved today after having been with me over nine years," Jan. 26th, 1883. "Killed Logan steer today."

Fitzpatrick, Miss Betsie, died May 31st, 1884; 70 years old.

Foster, David, d. Oct. 29th, 1888—"fox-hunter, good shot, and lover of ardent spirits."

Fortune, Alexander, died "Fall of 1892."

Fortune, George, died January 1893.

Fitzpatrick, Judge T. P., "fell from his horse" and died Dec. 24th, 1897, age seventy-two.

G

Garman (Gorman?), Mrs. Mary, wife of Capt. G ——, died Nov 25th, 1875.

Garland, Maj. James, died Aug. 1885; 93 years old.

Garman (Gorman?), Capt. William P., "shot himself intentionally, as an aftermath of the Civil War's vicissitudes," Dec. 1885.

Goodwin, Wm. N., died Aug. 18th, 1886; 81 years old.

Giles, William, died Sept. 30th, 1889: "old citizen."

H

Heath, Harlow W., died Dec. 22nd, 1875; 68 years old.

Higginbotham, G. W., died Jan. 31st, 1883.

Hubbard, William, died Dec. 1884; over 50 years old.

Hill, Wm. A., died Dec. 2nd, 1887; in 65th year.

Harris, Wm. W., died Feb. 3rd, 1888, "a bachelor, and rich before the War."

Higginbotham, A. B., died Dec. 1st, 1888; 70 years old.

Hall, Mary E. Y., married April 18th, 1889, Nelson Bryant.

Hill, John H., died June 22nd, 1890; 83 years old.

Hight, James M., died Jan. 1893.

Hill, Marshall, died Jan. 1894.

Henry, Ann, died March 4th, 1900; 78 years old. "She and family were the first negroes to help me after mine were freed, and left me."

I

Ireland, James P., died March 12th, 1885, age 62 years.

J

Jordan, Capt. William, died April 3rd, 1871.

Jordan, Mrs., widow of Capt. William Jordan, died Sept. 17th, 1876. "I boarded with her thirty years ago."

Jones, Wyatt, died Sept. 25th, 1873.

Jones, Mrs. Sally, wife of George Jones, died Jan. 16th, 1876; 80 years and over.

Jones, Andrew, "well known negro," died Dec. 24th, 1880.

Jones, William G., died June 5th, 1882.

Jones, George, died May 26th, 1883; age 93 years.

Jones, C. I., died July 1891, "an old friend."

[204]

L

Liggon, Mrs. Elizabeth, wife of Dr. Littlebury Liggon, died Aug. 1873.

Loving, John H., died May 18th, 1876; 67 years old.

Lawhorn, John, died Dec. 1884; over 80 years old.

Loving, Mrs. Mary, died April 1885.

Loving, H. Caleb, died April 1886; over 50 years old.

Loving, Seaton, died Feb. 1887; 83 years old.

Loving, Nicholas, died in Bath County, Dec. 5th, 1887.

Loving, Dr. A. S., died July 15th, 1890.

Loving, Jimmy, died Feb. 1894; 92 years old.

Loving, Alexander, died June 1896; over 70 years old.

Loving, Orvil, died Aug. 1896; 93 years old.

Loving, W. G., died Aug. 1896; 43 years old.

M

Massie, Patrick C., died Sept. 22nd, 1877.

Morrison, Mrs. Harriett, died June 20th, 1878.

Mays, Armstead, died April 1885; 90 years old.

Mays, Jeff, died Jan. 3rd, 1888.

Massie, Mrs. William, died Oct. 23rd, 1889, in her 76th year.

Mitchell, John J., died March 1890.

Moyer, Mrs. Bill Camden, died Feb. 19th, 1892; 22 years old.

Massie, Hope, died Dec. 1892.

Massie, Paul, died Jan. 1894.

Mays, Mrs. Parmela, died Feb. 1894; 90 years old.

Mays, Dabney, died Aug. 1896; 71 years old.

Meeks, Billy, died March 1900.

P

Penn, Jas. T., died Aug. 24th, 1873.

Plunkett, Mrs. Willis, died April 29th, 1875; 70 years old.

Patteson, Ulla Bona (Brent), gave birth to a son between 3 and 4 A. M. Sat. Feb. 12th, 1876.

Ponton, Mrs. Martha, died Feb. 11th, 1879.

Pierce, Jacob D., died Aug. 5th, 1884.

Plunkett, Willis R., died Aug. 6th, 1883; 87 years old.

Perrow, Spottswood, died Oct. 24th, 1885; 73 years old. He was member of Congress.

Pamplin, A. G., died April 1886; over 70 years old.

Patteson, N. C., died June 26th 1886; 76 years old.

Puckett, John, died April 25th 1887; 100 years old.

Perry, Mrs. John, died Oct. 21st, 1890.

Pamplin, John Hunt, died June 1896, "a fine mind and a gambler".

R

Roberts, Wm. C., died Aug. 1871, "my old friend, and quite a social man and great fiddler."

S

Staples, Fidelia, died Feb. 3rd, 1869.

Stevens, Sam, died Feb. 26th, 1871; 80 years old.

Slaughter, Samuel P., died Aug. 2nd, 1885; 37 years old.

Smith, "Extra Billy," "noted in Virginia," died May 1887.

Stevens, Sam Cole, died Aug. 11th, 1887; 63 years old.

Staples, William, died Feb. 1894; 90 odd years old.

Stratton, Capt., died June 1896; 62 years old.

Shelton, Mrs., (dau. of Jas. H. Brent), died 1906.

T

Thacker, Wyatt, died 1869, age 83 years.

Tom, "blackman," died Feb. 18th, 1871; 88 years old.

Thornhill, John, died March 21st, 1875; age 68 years and 1 day.

Thompson, John, died June 28th, 1876; 82 years old.

Turner, Samuel, died Dec. 26th, 1878; 85 years old.

Thompson, W. B., died Oct. 27th, 1884.

Truslow, John, died April 1886; over 60 years old.

Taliaferro, Maj. Ben. B., died July 16th, 1888; 89 years old.

Thornhill, Adeline (Brent), died July 17th, 1889.

Trout, Philip, married Minnie Vaughan, Sept. 9th, 1890.

Tribble, Thomas, died June 1896; 81 years old.

Thacker, Charles, died 1898; 96 years old.

Trout, Geo. and Willie, d. 20 and 22 Oct. 1862, in Confederate Army.

Trout, Matilda C., aged 33 yrs., d. 20 Oct. 1871.

V

Vaughan, Minnie, married Philip Trout, Sept. 9th, 1890, "at my house."

Vaughan, Polly Cluff, died May 8th, 1875; 80 years old.

Vaughan, Capt. George, died Aug. 27th, 1877; 76 years old.

Vaughan, Dr. W. L., died March 23rd, 1882; he was 47 years old.

Vaughan, Corrinne, married J. E. Hoffman, Nov. 11th, 1897.

Vaughan, Fanny, died 1905.

Vaughan, Andrew J., d. 3 Nov. 1857.

W

Witt, Mrs. Bird, died Feb. 1870; 90 years old.

Willis, John, died Sept. 1871; over 100 years old.

Witt, Burgess, died March 9th, 1873; over 90 years old.

Witt, Mollie Washington (Brent) had a daughter born "a little after dark Jan. 1st, 1879: her name is Margaret."

Witt, Daniel, died Jan. 2nd, 1882; 52 years old.

Witt, Asa, died May 10th, 1883; 49 years old.

Whitehead, F. L. Sr., died April 19th, 1884.

Wills, Elisha, died Feb. 27th, 1886; over 50 years old.

Wills, Jefferson L., died Feb. 1887; 85 years old.

Watts, B. B., died Dec. 31st, 1887.

White, Ellison, died Jan. 15th, 1888.

Warwick, Ellen, died July 10th, 1888: "an old schoolmate"; 60 years old.

Word or Ward, Rev. Davis M., died April 1889.

Woods, Maj. William, died Jan. 4th, 1892; 87 years old; "the last link in the chain of old men who were acquainted and could tell me of my grandparents."

Wills, Willis P., died Aug. 1892; aged 83 years; "my friend and schoolteacher."

Wailes, B. M., died Jan. 1893.
White, William, died June 1896; 61 years old.
Writtenhouse (Rittenhouse) Mrs., died Feb. 1897.
Whitehead, Robt., died Nov. 28th, 1898.

ALLIED FAMILIES

THE CURD* FAMILY

[1] EDWARD CURD, immigrant ancestor, probably ancestor of all those named Curd* in America, was in Henrico County, Va. as early as 1704, where on October 2nd of that year he "Purchased of John Woodson for 30£ currency, six hundred acres of land on the north side of the James River, adjoining land formerly James Blairs' and being part of a greater tract granted John Woodson, Jr., by patent dated 23 Oct. 1690" (Valentine Papers). The following year 1705, he was assessed and paid taxes on this six hundred acres (Henrico Quit Rent Rolls, 1705, *Va. Historical Mag.*, Vol. 28, p. 210). Between 1716 and 1725 he received various land grants on the north side of James River in that part of Henrico County that was cut off in 1728 to form Goochland County. There was granted to him 31 Oct. 1716, 531 acres north side James River, west side north branch Beaver Dam Creek (*Book*, 10, p. 307), 2 Feb. 1724, 1,200 acres north side James River (*Book* 12, p. 130), 2 Feb. 1724, 341 acres north side James River on Beaver Dam Creek (*Book* 12, p. 131), 17 Aug. 1725, 400 acres on Beaver Dam Creek (*Book* 12, p. 238). In the next few years he deeded most of his Goochland County lands to his children. 6 June 1726, he deeds to his son John, for "love and affection," part of the 531 acre tract on Beaver Dam Creek (Henrico Court records), 7 Nov. 1726 he deeds to his daughter Mary McBride land lying on the north side of James River (Henrico Court records), 16 July 1733 he deeds 200 acres in Goochland County to each of his daughters, Mary Richardson and Elizabeth Williams (Goochland County Deeds), 20 Nov. 1733 he deeds 650 acres in Goochland County to his son Richard (Goochland County Deeds). In his will he gives 100 acres in Goochland County to his granddaughter, Jane McBride, and all of his remaining holdings in Goochland to his son Edward. All of his children, Edward excepted, eventually went to Goochland County to live. In the vestry book of the old St. John's Church at Richmond, we find the following records (*Kith and Kin*, p. 17,

---

*Richard Curd—headright of Mr. Henry Corbyn and Mr. Gerrard Fowke, 15 March 1658 . . . in Potomacke freshes between the two main branches, Extending towards Herne Island (Nugent, p. 388).

and records at Alexandria, Va.): "At a vestry held at Curl's Neck
Ch. for Henrico Parish ye 17th day June 1735. Present, Wm.
Randolph, Esq., Richard Randolph, Bowler Cocke, James Powell
Cocke, Gent. Vestrymen: Pursuant to the Directions of an Act
of Assembly directing the dividing of Henrico Parish, the Free-
holders and Householders present do unanimously elect Edward
Curd, John Williamson, James Cocke, John Povall, and Robt.
Moss, by which with the Vestrymen formerly of this Parish make
up the number of twelve who take Oaths and Declarations as
Vestrymen."* Oaths signed Edward Curd, first and others. 2 Sept.
1735, "Richard Randolph and Edward Curd, Gent. are appointed
to view the Chappell and report what reparation and addition are
thereunto wanting." 26 July 1743, "Beverly Randolph takes oath
as vestryman in place of Edward Curd, deceased: as chosen 2nd
Oct. 1742." Edward Curd died 1742. The Henrico County December Court 1742 appoints John Williamson, Thomas Watkins,
Daniel Price and James Young to appraise estate of Edward Curd,
deceased. Will dated 4 Feb. 1739/40, proved first Monday in
Dec. 1742, names the following: wife Elizabeth Curd, son Edward
Curd, son John Curd, son Richard Curd, Mary Mackbride and her
son Edward Mackbride, daughter-in-law (step-daughter) Mary
Punch, grandson John Curd, granddaughter Jane Mackbride,
daughter Mary Richardson, daughter Elizabeth Williams. Names
wife Elizabeth and son Edward Curd executors. Edward's will
leaves the home plantation and dwelling in Henrico to wife Elizabeth during her life. "Son, Edward to have half of everything
during Elizabeth's life, and at her death the whole of said Henrico estate." Son Edward is also given all lands "now possessed of"
in Goochland County, excepting 100 acres which goes to granddaughter Jane Mackbride.

The name of Edward's first wife, the mother of his children, is
not known; he m. (II) Elizabeth Branch, dau. of Thomas Branch
and Elizabeth Archer, widow first of Robert Goode whom she m.

---

*The Virginia Colonists were adherents of the church of England. The parish
vestry consisted of twelve of the most prominent and substantial men of the Parish
and divided with the court the responsibility for the public welfare of their respective communities.

in 1710 and who d. 1718, widow second of Page Punch, who d. 1726-27. Elizabeth died 30 Nov. 1766. In the *Goode Genealogy* (Virginia Cousins) Elizabeth Branch is erroneously referred to as a Curd (*William and Mary Quarterly*, Vol. 25, pp. 66-67). In the Henrico County Record Books, 1767-1774, we find the following: page 138, 24 May 1749, John Curd and Elizabeth his wife acknowledge to have received of the executors of Edward Curd deceased "our full share of the estate of the said deceased," Richard Curd witness. Page 139, 20 May 1749, John Richardson and Mary his wife make similar acknowledgment, Richard Curd and Isham Richardson witnesses. Page 139, 24 May 1749, Richard Curd and Sarah his wife make similar acknowledgment, John Curd witness. Page 140, 3 June 1749, Samuel Allen and Elizabeth his wife make similar acknowledgment, John Curd witness. All of the above were recorded 5 June 1769.

Children (CURD):

  I Edward, married and had issue.

+ 2 II John, m. Elizabeth Price, dau. of Daniel Price. He d. in Goochland County, 1752 and his widow m. (II) Sept. 3, 1758, Richard Oglesby.

  III Richard, m. Sarah Downer, dau. of John Downer. He d. in Goochland County, 1778.

  IV Mary, m. John McBride. Settled in Goochland County.

  V Mary, d. Charlotte County, Va., 1791; m. John Richardson.

  VI Elizabeth, m. (1) Richard (?) Williams; m. (II) Samuel Allen.

That Edward Curd had two daughters each named Mary and both living at the time of his death is shown by his will.

[2] JOHN[2] CURD (Edward[1]); d. Goochland County, Va., 1752; m. Elizabeth Price, dau. of Daniel Price, and his wife Mary, surname unknown, but perhaps Hughes. Division of his estate, 16 Jan. 1759 names wife Elizabeth and the following children. Elizabeth, John Curd's widow, m. (II) 3 Sept. 1758 Richard Oglesby.

Children (CURD):

I   John, m. in Lancaster County, Va. 7 April 1758, Lucy Brent(67), removed to Kentucky abt. 1780 (See her line).

II   William, m. (I) abt. 1763 Mary Watkins, prob. m. (II) Ann, surname unknown, removed to Buckingham County, Va., where he died about 1798.

III   Joseph, m. (I) 28 Sept. 1762, Mary Warren; m. (II) 6 Oct. 1772, Mary Truehart, removed to Buckingham County, Va., where he died abt. 1811-12.

IV   Mary, m. 18 March 1764, Edmund Curd, son of Richard Curd and Sarah Downer, d. in Goochland County.

V   Charles, received a grant of 800 acres of land in Jefferson County, Ky. in 1780 and a grant of 1,000 acres in Fayette County, Ky., 1784; not much is known of him; so far we have found no record of his marriage or children. He is supposed to have died in Fayette County, Ky., prior to 1788 (*Grant Book* 18, p. 67, grant to John Curd; Virginia Land Office Records).

VI   James, m. 20 Feb. 1766, Mary Graves, he lived and died in Goochland County, Va. Inventory dated 1792.

VII   Elizabeth, m. 2 Dec. 1764, John Bowles.

VIII   Ann, m. 24 Nov. 1771, Richard Sampson.

THE DOGGETT FAMILY

[1] BENJAMIN DOGGETT, "Minister," came to Lancaster County, Va. *circa* 1670, from England. He was the son of William Dogget, of Ipswich, "woolendraper." He was admitted at St. John's College, Cambridge, 27 Jan. 1654/5, received his B.A. 1659, and his M.A. 1662. That same year he was made Curate of Stoke in Suffolk.

Shortly after his arrival in Lancaster County, he was made minister of Christ Church and also St. Mary's White Chapel. From the tone of his will, Benjamin Doggett was very much opposed to the youthful marriages made in the colony, for he makes it very plain to his children that they will be disinherited—his sons, if they marry before 22, and his daughters before 18 years of age.

Benjamin Doggett was born *circa* 1635, in Ipwsich, England, and died in Lancaster County, Va., 1681/2. He married Jane ——, who survived him.

Children (Doggett):

+ 2   i   Benjamin, "eldest son," b. in England; d. in Lancaster County, Va., 1723; m. (i) ——; (ii), Mary Threlkeld, wid. of Christopher Threlkheld (w. 1711) of Northumberland County.

+ 3   ii   Richard, b. "in Virginia"; d. 1721, in Lancaster County; m. Elizabeth Bushrod.

+ 4   iii   William, b. "in Virginia"; d. 1710-16, "by unfortunate accident"; m. Elizabeth (George?).

   5   iv   Jane, "in England, 20 shillings and noe more, because she has been detained from me."

   6   v   Anne, "15,000 pounds of tobaccoe, 6 yg. cows, 6 breeding sowers . . . to be pd by my sons, provided she does not marry before reaching 18 years."

[2] BENJAMIN[2] DOGGETT (Benjamin[1]), was born in England, and died in Christ Church Parish, Lancaster County, 18 Sept. to 13 Nov. 1723. He married twice, but the name of his first wife

is not known; his second wife was Mary Threlkeld, widow of Christopher Threlkeld of Northumberland County, whom he married *circa* 1712, and she survived him. Benjamin Doggett was appointed constable 10 May 1710.

Children, 1st marriage (DOGGETT):

7   I   Benjamin, d. before his father; m. Mary ——, and had at least James, and probably Benjamin. Benj. Jr., appointed constable 1715, and paid 3 tithes 1717.

8   II   John, paid 2 tithes 13 Jan. 1713.

9   III   William.

10   IV   Richard, taxed 2 tithes 1717.

11   V   Elizabeth, wife of Philip Froud, by 1722.

12   VI   Hannah, m. 22 Feb. 1717/8, Thomas Yerby (see Brent, 41).

13   VII   Ann, m. George Reves before 1723.

14   VIII   Margaret.

15   IX   Jane.

Children, 2nd marriage (DOGGETT):

16   X   Thomas.

17   XI   Rueben, m. Hannah ——, and d. 1722; they had (DOGGETT):

    1 Reuben.

    2 Mary.

    3 Jeremiah.

    4 Sarah Light.

18   XII   Mary, prob. d. v. p.

19   XIII   Winnifred.

[3] RICHARD[2] DOGGETT (Benjamin[1]), was born in Virginia, and died 1721 in Lancaster County, Va. He married Elizabeth Bushrod; she married (II) by 8 March 1726, Charles Chilton, who died 1738.

[216]

Children (DOGGETT):

20 I George, d. 1758/9, in Culpeper County; m. Ann, dau. of Thomas Chattin (Chetwyn?), by 1725, and had (DOGGETT)—

    1 Chatwin.

    2 Thomas.

    3 Sarah Ann, m. —— Reynolds.

    4 Margaret, m. —— Scroggins.

21 II Bushrod, d. 1791 in Culpeper County, and had (DOGGETT)—

    1 Nancy, m. —— Brown.

22 III Ann.

[4] WILLIAM[2] DOGGETT (Benjamin[1]), was born in Virginia, and died in Christ Church Parish, Lancaster County, Va., 1710-1716. He states in his will "by unfortunate accident, being weak of body" (1710), so must have been injured in some manner; however, his will was not probated until 1716. He does not name all of his children, so I am assuming the ones he did name are the youngest. He married Elizabeth (George?), and she survived him.

Children (DOGGETT):

23 I Sarah.

24 II Hannah.

+ 25 III Elmore, d. 1772-81; m. (I) Lucy Hayden; (II) Mary Ann Hammond, 21 Jan. 1779.

26 IV Jane.

+ 27 V William, m. (I) ——; (II) Joanna Wale, dau. of John and Alice Wale.

28 VI Benjamin, b. 24 June 1717, posthumously.

[25] ELMORE[3] DOGGETT (William[2], Benjamin[1]), died in Lancaster County, Va., between 8 Feb. 1772 and 17 March 1781. He married (I), Lucy Hayden, who died *circa* 1775; m. (II), 21 Jan. 1779, Mary Ann Hammond. A Mary Ann Dogget (w. 1786),

leaves her estate to her daughter Betty Connolly Marsden, and John Marsden proved the will.

Children (DOGGETT):

29   I   John, m. Winnifred, dau. of John Carter; she m. (II) Thomas Mott. John Doggett d. 1780.

> Children (DOGGETT):
>
> 1 Mary Ann.
>
> 2 George.
>
> 3 Lucy, m. 30 May 1788, Ezekiel Hayden.
>
> 4 William.
>
> 5 John.

30   II   William, Jr.

31   III   Elmore.

32   IV   Elizabeth, m. 17 May 1771, Hillary Curtis.

33   V   George, died before his father, and had at least—
1 Elmour, who m. 30 March 1786, Eliz. Roberts.

[27] WILLIAM[3] DOGGETT (William[2], Benjamin[1]), was born *circa* 1705, in Lancaster County, Va., and died there between 27 Dec. 1764 and 16 April 1772. The name of his first wife is not known; m. (II) before 1749, Joanna Wale, dau. of John and Alice Wale.

Children, by 1st marriage (DOGGETT):

34   I   Coleman, d. 1782; m. *circa* 1755, Mary King (see Brent, 45), who m. (II) 2 Nov. 1782, John McTyre.

> Children (DOGGETT)—
>
> 1 John.
>
> 2 William.
>
> 3 Dennis.
>
> 4 Mary.
>
> 5 Prescilla.

   II   William.

   III   Mary Ann.

   IV   Lucy.

 v Betty, m. 24 July 1753, Josiah³ Carter (Henry², Thomas¹).

Children, 2nd marriage:

 vi Sarah, m. (1) James Cammell, Jr.; m. (11) 4 Oct. 1768, James Brent (see James Brent, 96).

 vii Mildred.

 viii Joanna.

 ix Ann.

 x Hannah.

THE EDMONDS FAMILY

[1] ELYAS EDMONDS, patented 890 acs. lying on N. side of Rappahannock River, in Corotoman Riv., on the Eastermost branch, on the North side thereof, 29 July 1650, for transportation of 18 persons: John Kendall, Nicho. Taylor, John Kesh (or Lesh), Duncom Grant, Rice Thoroughgood, Alice Dawes, Thomas Cuck, Ann Myler, Tho. Hobson, Kat. Geames, John Wakefield, Rich. Embrock, Eliza. Bassaye, Hellen Shore, Eliza. Stretton, Farrar Flinton, Jane his wife, Eliza. Flinton, Math. Harecastle, Hen. Nesfield (the above shows 20 persons, which at 50 acres per head, would mean that he received 1,000 acres).

On 10 Oct. 1652, he received 600 acs. in the same county (Lancaster) for the transportation of 12 persons . . . upon the head of another tract of land lying on the N. side of the Easterne branch of Corotoman Riv . . . —— Needham, —— Prine, —— Dillard, Henry Bray, Eliz. Philips, Thos. Payne, Fra. Morgan, three negroes, Eliz. Perry, Lawrence Dawby, from Abra. Moone (Nugent, p. 259).

Hayden states that Elias Edmonds' will is recorded in Lancaster Estate Book I, p. 207, dated 27 March 1654; there is no such record book listed in Lancaster County, nor can I find the will in other books extant there; and from excerpts of the following letter from Edwin Conway to Toby Smith, clerk, do not believe that Hayden is correct.

From my home at the head
of Corotomaon, March the 27th 1654
Hon'd Sir—

Service to you and your wife presented. These are to let you understand that I am by Elias Edmonds his last will and testament sole overseer of his estate and see that his children be not cheated nor defrauded of that estate their father left them yet John Meredith and Walter Heard not giving the Court intelligence thereof as I hear obtained an order for administration of this Estate nor I having not any notice thereof, saying that his (sic?) mother in Law Mrs. Edmonds made no will . . . Now I can prove but the Court is so remoat that I cannot

bring witnesses . . . that Mrs. Edmonds made an un-
capative will which I know in Law is authentick . . .
Meredith his pretence is that I am a Papist and ought
not to have the bringing up of the children . . .

This letter continues, and shows that Elias Edmonds left a
large estate, that his wife had since died, that the estate was being
wasted, and that the children were in a "desperate condition."
Mr. Conway was later appointed administrator of the estate, and
buys a maidservant for 1,600 pds. of tobaccoe, pays Mr. Forest
340 pds. of tobaccoe and buys stockings, shoes and bodices for
the children, without naming them.

From the above data, it would appear that Elias Edmonds
married, Frances, the mother-in-law (stepmother) of either Meredith or Heard, most probably Meredith; that she died soon after
her husband, Elias, and left minors. More research shows the following:

[1] ELIAS EDMONDS, immigrant to Virginia, before 1650, died
in Lancaster County, Va. before 1654. He married Frances, widow
of probably a Meredith or Heard; his wife was dead by March
1654; they left the following—

Children (EDMONDS):

2   I   Thomas, d. u. m., 1677, and left his estate to Elias
        Edmonds, son of William Edmonds.

+ 3   II William, d. between 26 Jan. 1697 and 12 Feb. 1700;
        m. (I) 1674, Lewys, relict of George Wale (I. 1674);
        (II) Jane (Brent) Reddock, 1688.

4   III Anne, "orphan of Elias Edmonds," m. 14 Sept. 1664,
        John Walker (L O B 1655-66, p. 298).

[3] WILLIAM[2] EDMONDS (Elias[1]), was born in Lancaster
County, Va. *circa* 1650, and died there 1700. He married (I)
Lewys, relict of George Wale (I. 1674), and she died *circa* 1688
(see WALE excursus). He married (II) Jane Brent, eldest daughter
of Hugh, the immigrant, and relict of John Reddock, *circa* 1688,

and she survived him, but from the records studied, was not the mother of his children.

Children (EDMONDS):

+   5   I   Elias, d. 1745, and left issue.

    6   II   William, "to take care of his sister, Lucy."

    7   III   Lucy.

[5] ELIAS³ EDMONDS (William², Elias¹), was born *circa* 1676 and died between 24 April and 14 Feb. 1745 (old style). He names his children and grandchildren, but no wife; she evidently died before he did. The Est. Div. of his son Robert names two generations, and for this reason is the source of the fourth and fifth generations of this family.

Children (EDMONDS):

+   8   I   William, d. 1741, Lancaster County, Va.; m. (I) ——; m. (II) Catherine ——, who m. (II) 21 Sept. 1754, Edward Rogers, widower, of Northumberland County.

    9   II   Robert, m. 10 June 1729, Ann Conway, dau. of Edwin Conway and Anne Ball, dau. of Col. Joseph Ball and his wife Elizabeth Romney. Robert Edmonds left no heirs. His widow, Ann, m. (II) 11 July 1752, Thomas Chinn.

+ 10 III   Elias, m. Winifred ——, and d. in Northumberland County, 1743; his wife died the following year.

  11 IV   Frances, m. 13 Oct. 1729, George Payne (Est. Div. 1775), and had (PAYNE)—

      1 Susanna, m. 6 Sept. 1750, Capt. Hugh Brent(64).

      2 William, m. 1759, Ann, relict of Wm. Edmonds Jr. (w. 1758).

      3 George.

      4 Ann, m. Moses Lunsford, 19 Feb. 1762.

      5 Frances, m. 20 Dec. 1756, Richard Stephens.

      6 Catherine.

      7 Margaret, m. 1 Dec. 1766, Benjamin Waddy.

      8 John.

      9 Richard.

12   v   Ann, m. 4 June 1737, Joseph Wharton, and had (WHARTON)—

      1 Thomas.

      2 Joseph.

      3 William.

      4 Lindsey.

      5 Rowell.

      6 Alice.

13   VI   Elizabeth, m. James[4] Pinckard (James[3], John[2], John[1]), and had (PINCKARD)—

      1 Robert.

      2 James.

      3 John.

      4 Charles.

      5 Richard.

14   VII   Sarah, m. (I) Thomas Sharpe (w. 1751); m. (II) 22 June 1753, John Bond; issue (SHARPE)—

      1 Elias Edmonds.

      2 Imogen or Thomasine.

      3 Betty.

      4 Sarah.

      5 Ann.

[8] WILLIAM[4] EDMONDS (Elias[3], William[2], Elias[1]), was born *circa* 1700 in Lancaster County, Va., and died there 1741; he married twice, but the name of his first wife is not known; he married (II) Catherine ——, who survived him and married Edward Rogers 21 Sept. 1754, each party to the marriage contract had several children.

Children, 1st marriage (EDMONDS)—

+ 15   I   Elias, d. 1784 in Faquier County, Va.; m. Elizabeth Miller, dau. of Simon Miller (w. 1769) of Faquier County.

16   II   Frances, m. 15 July 1740 (Rev.?) John Bell, in Lancaster County.

17   III   Joanna, m. 15 July 1749, Ephraim Hubbard, in Lancaster County, Va.

Children, 2nd marriage (EDMONDS):

+ 18   IV   William, d. 1816; m. 16 March 1764, Elizabeth Blackwell.

+ 19   V   John, d. 1798 in Faquier County, Va. He probably m. Helen Lancaster of Northumberland County, 8 April 1771.

[10] ELIAS⁴ EDMONDS (Elias³, William², Elias¹), was born *circa* 1700 in Lancaster County, Va., and died in Northumberland County, 1743; he married Winifred ——; she died March-May 1744, in Northumberland County. As one Peter Thomas is prominent in the settlement of her estate, it is possible that she was his daughter.

Children (EDMONDS):

+ 20   I   William, Jr., d. 10 Jan.—9 Oct. 1758, in Northumberland County; m. Ann ——, who m. (II) 1759, Wm. Payne, son of George Payne above.

21   II   Elias, m. (I) 28 July 1763, Frances Garner; m. (II) Frances or Lucy Denny, relict of John Denny, 7 Jan. 1776. This Elias Edmonds was a lieutenant, and later a colonel in the Rev. War. Cannot find his will. He had at least SARAH, who m. George Brent(110); she was b. 18 Feb. 1792.

22   III   Robert, m. 19 June 1762, Elizabeth Lee Taylor (L. M. B.), and left her shortly afterwards (Col. Gordon's "Bible").

[15] ELIAS⁵ EDMONDS (William⁴, Elias³, William², Elias¹), was born in Lancaster County, Va. *circa* 1720, and died in Faquier County, 30 Oct. 1782—28 June 1784. He married Elizabeth Miller, daughter of Simon Miller (w. 1769) of Faquier County, *circa* 1745. Elias Edmonds was one of His Majesties Justices of Prince William County 1755. He died in Leeds Parish, Faquier County. He leases his lands in the Northern Neck to Rev. John Bell 10 April 1747, and he was then living in Prince William County.

Children (EDMONDS):

    I   Elias, m. Helen Edmonds, his cousin, 5 Nov. 1792.

    II   Ann, m. Ephraim Hubbard, 27 Dec. 1774, in Faquier County.

    III   Judith, m. Richard Buckner, 27 Feb. 1772, in Faquier County.

    IV   Elizabeth, m. Peter Bruin, 27 Feb. 1781.

[18] WILLIAM[5] EDMONDS (William[4], Elias[3], William[2], Elias[1]), was born in Lancaster County, Va., and died in Faquier County, 1813-1816. He married 16 March 1764, Elizabeth Blackwell, dau. of William Blackwell and Elizabeth Crump, sister of George Crump. William Edmonds is appointed colonel of the Faquier militia, 24 March 1778 (*Faquier Minute Book*, 1775-1783).

Children (EDMONDS):

    I   William, m. and had Mrs. G. W. Foote.

    II   Elias, dead by 1813, leaving four children.

    III   John, m. and had a son.

    IV   Sally, m. and had a son.

    V   James, m. and had six children.

    VI   Frances, m. Robt. Green, her 1st cousin, 15 Aug. 1787.

    VII   Polly, m. Wm. Horner, 19 Oct. 1790.

    VIII   Betsy, m. James Westwood Wallace, 6 Aug. 1794.

    IX   Lucy, m. Robert Green, of "The Marsh."

    X   Kitty, m. George Payne.

    XI   Judith, m. (I) —— Carter; (II) Moore Fauntleroy.

[19] JOHN[5] EDMONDS (William[4], Elias[3], William[2], Elias[1]), was born in Lancaster County, Va., and died in Faquier County, 1 Sept—24 Dec. 1798. He did not name his wife in his will, but the Northumberland County bonds show that a John Edmonds m. (I) 1756, Jane Moorehead; (II) 8 April 1771, Helen Lancaster.

Children (EDMONDS):

    I   William.

    II   John, m. 5 June 1793, Naomi Hicks (F. M. B.).

    III   George, m. 10 March 1797, Mary Sophia Rust (F. M. B.).

    IV   Elias.

    V   Peggy.

    VI   Nancy.

    VII   Helen, m. 5 Nov. 1792, Elias Edmonds, Jr., with her father's consent.

[20] WILLIAM[5] EDMONDS (Elias[4], Elias[3], William[2], Elias[1]), was born in Northumberland County, Va., and died there, 10 Jan.—9 Oct. 1758. Kenner Cralle, one of the guardians to his minor children, gives to Sarah, dau. of Elias Edmonds, "a trunk of his first wife's" who was probably Sarah Ann Edmonds, whom he m. 18 Jan. 1753 (Hayden). William Edmonds names his wife Ann —— in his will; she m. (II) William Payne, son of George (Est. Div. 1775).

Children (EDMONDS):

    I   Elias, m. 22 March 1788, Susannah Stephens, and had (EDMONDS)—

        1   Ralph.

        2   Frances, m. 4 April 1808, Richard M. Glasscock.

        3   Janella P., m. 27 Nov. 1817, Benjamin Waddey.

        4   Susanna, m. 1 Jan. 1817, Addison Hall.

        5   Elias.

        6   John W. A.

        7   Phillip.

        8   William.

        9   Robert.

        10   Elizabeth.

        11   Margaret M.

THE FLEET* FAMILY

[1] WILLIAM FLEET, of Essex, England, married Katherine, daughter of Lady Mildmay (dau. of Robert Atwaters, Esq., of Royston, Essex), and her husband Robert Honeywood, of Henwood, Kent, who were married Feb. 1543; she was born 1527, and outlived her husband, who died 1576. William Fleet died 1584-86. He had at least—

[2] WILLIAM FLEET, who married Deborah Scott, daughter of Charles Scott and his wife Jane Wyatt, daughter of Sir Thomas Wyatt of Allington Castle, and granddaughter of Sir Reginald Scott of Scott's Hall, Kent. This William Fleet, Gent., was an incorporator of the 3rd Virginia Charter, 1612. He had at least—

[3] HENRY FLEET, and others that follow. Henry Fleet first settled in Maryland, and was one of the prominent associates of Gov. Calvert in establishing that province . . . Capt. Henry Fleete, Gent., of St. Georges Hundred, Maryland, his brothers Reinold Fleete, planter, of St. Georges, Edward Fleete, planter, of St. Mary's Hundred, John Fleete, planter, of St. George's Hundred, were all members of the first Maryland Assembly, 1637-1638. Henry Fleet came to Virginia as early as 1623 as he was one of the 26 men who, under Henry Spelman, in that year, went to trade with the Anacostan Indians on the Potomac, and was captured and taken to their dwelling place at a spot near the present Washington Monument. During four years of captivity he became thoroughly acquainted with the language and customs of the Indians, and thus was subsequently of great usefulness to the colonists as an interpreter. Ransomed in 1627, he went to England, and with merchants in London, engaged in the India trade. Lord Baltimore on 18 June 1644, commissioned him with the power of

*The source of most of the material comprising the first three generations of this family was from Hayden's, the *Va. Mag.*, and the *Encyc. Britannica*. Some additions and corrections have been added from the original records beginning with the third generation.

a Captain General to visit with the Susquehannan Indians and make a treaty of peace.

The earliest mention of Henry Fleete in the Virginia Land Office records is in a patent to one Thomas Graves, Ancient Planter. This Graves was granted a patent of 200 acres on the East side of the Shoare of the bay of Chesepeicke butting Southly on land of Capt. Henry Fleete, extending Northly along the water side, and Westly on the bay . . . 14 March 1628. Before 1634, Henry Fleete had patented land in Northampton County (Accomack), as he had sold same to one Jonathan Gylls, who on 20 Sept. 1634, willed this land to his daughter. The total land granted Capt. Henry Fleete before 1660 was over 6,000 acres.

In 1642, the Virginia Assembly gave Henry Fleete the privilege for 14 years of making discoveries westward and southward, with all profits thereof, extending the privilege in 1653 for fourteen years more. In 1645/6, Virginia employed him against the Indians at 15,000 pounds of tobacco. He wrote a "Brief Journal of a Voyage made in the Bark Virginia, to Virginia and other parts of the Continent of America."

Henry Fleete was born 1595/1600, and died *circa* 1661, at Fleete's Bay in Northumberland County, Va. He married Sarah ——, who outlived him, and later married Col. John Walker. He had—

[4] HENRY FLEETE, born in either St. George's Hundred, Maryland, or Northampton (Accomack) County, Va. He married Elizabeth,* daughter of Jane Wildey, widow, whose will was probated in Northumberland County, 10 April 1701. He died 1728-33. He was one of His Majesties Justices for Lancaster County, 1695, and High Sheriff, 1718-19.

Children (FLEET):
    1 Henry, d. 1735, unmarried.

---

*Thomas Hunt was granted one acre in James Cittie (Jamestown), 1 Aug. 1655 . . . ½ acre of the Sd land formerly granted unto MRS. ELIZABETH FLEETE, which by her death accrued to her children, and now by Thomas Lyne, guardian, assigned unto Thomas Wilkenson, to whom Sd. Hunt is successor, and the other half acre granted by order of the Quarter Court . . . (Nugent, p. 313).

II William, m. Ann Jones, dau. of Wm. Jones, Jr.; 1 Nov. 1718, and left issue; Geo. Wale, Sec.

III Elizabeth, m. Harry Currell, and had at least,

1 Harry Currell.

2 Ann Currell.

IV Judith, m. 28 June 1723, Wm. Hobson, of Northumberland County, born 28 April 1700, son of Thomas and Sarah Hobson; they had, at least—

1 Sarah, b. 29 May 1725.

2 Judith, b. 1727.

3 John, b. 13 April 1730.

4 Mary Ann.

5 Betty.

V Mary, "third daughter," m. 17 Oct. 1723, Presly Cox of Westmoreland County, and had at least—

1 Mary Ann.

2 Fleet Cox.

VI Ann, m. Leonard Howson of Northumberland County, 10 Nov. 1722, and had at least—

1 Elizabeth Howson.

VII Sarah, m. William Brent(12); she died before 1717; had—

1 Major Richard Brent, d. s. p.

2 Elizabeth, m. Samuel Hinton, by 1735 (see this line under Wm. Brent, 12).

THE LAWSON FAMILY

EPAPPHRODITUS LAWSON, witnessed deed of John Davis, Planter, of Kisekeiake, to Thomas Curtis, 20 July 1633.

ALICE LAWSON, headright of Capt. Wm. Peirce, one of the Councell of State, 22 June 1635 . . . in Lawnes Creek.

EPPA LAWSON renewed patent of Martha Tomlin wid., in his name, 14 July 1635 . . . 250 acres S. E. side of Nanzemund River.

EPPA LAWSON pattented 200 acres at the head of the back river, on the east side of Scones dam, 25 Nov. 1635 . . . due by deed of sale from John Davis [Note: Robt. Davis (PAYNE), m. Elizabeth, dau. of Eppa Lawson, by 1666].

HUGH LAWSON, headright of —— Safferton, Elizabeth Citty County, 17 Oct. 1636.

EPPA LAWSON pat. 200 acs. in Warwickquicke (Isle of Wight County), 23 Dec. 1636 . . . upon Nanzamund Riv. for transportation of four persons.

CHRISTOPHER LAWSON, 250 acs. in James Citty County, 23 May 1637, for transportation of five persons . . . beginning at a little Indian field over against land of John Dansey . . . also 400 acs. in James Citty County, 1 May 1638, at head of Rolphes Creeke for transportation of eight people.

EPPA LAWSON, 50 acs. in Isle of Wight County, 20 Nov. 1637, at the mouth of Warwicksquike River, *alias* Newtown Haven, assigned by Ellis Dunridge . . . also 200 acs. same county, 1 Nov. 1637, E. N. W. upon Nansamund Riv., for transportation of four persons.

EPPA LAWSON, 250 acs. in Upper Norfolk County (Nansemond), 15 March 1638 . . . on North side of Chuckatuck River, due for transportation of five persons.

EPPA LAWSON, 250 acs. from Martha Tomlyn, 29 May 1638.

EPPA LAWSON assigns 150 acs. in Upper Norfolk County

(Nansemond) to Mareene Delanmundayes, he having received it from Wm. Dawson, 16 Oct. 1638.

EPPA LAWSON, 1,400 acs. in Upper Norfolk County, 15 Sept. 1642 . . . upon Newtowne Haven River, running N. W. by a bay side called Mount Lawson, adjoining Moore Fantleroy . . . 450 acs. by assignment from Bartholomew Hoskins, Admnr. of John Bridges, of two pattents, 300 acs. by two former pattents, and 650 acs. for the transportation of 13 persons, viz: EPPA LAWSON ("his own transportation"?), WILLIAM LAWSON, LETTICE LAWSON, ROWLAND LAWSON, and others . . . EPPA LAWSON lived near Richard Bennett (Upper Norfolk County), 1643.

EPPA LAWSON received 450 acres 9 Jan. 1643, for trans. of 9 persons . . . he assigned 400 acs. to John Hill 2 April 1644.

APHA (EPPA) LAWSON assigned land in Upper Norfolk County, to John Hill, 1 April 1644 for transportation of four persons, his own personal adventure, Mr. William Hill, twice, and Robt. Tows . . . Eppa Lawson assigned 200 acs. in Elizabeth Citty County to Thomas Stephens through Sam'l Groose and John Davis, 6 Jan. 1647. This ends the data on EPPA LAWSON in Isle of Wight and Upper Norfolk Counties. Now we find him going to the Northern Neck or *Chickakoon Country* . . .

MR. EPAPPHRODITUS LAWSON, 700 acres in Rappahannock River, 3 Sept. 1649 . . . lying about 12 miles upon the N. side, beginning on the Edward side of the mouth of Slaughters Creek which parts this from the land of John Carter . . . for transportation of 14 persons into the colony . . . MR. EPPA LAWSON, 2,000 acres in Rappahannock River on the S. side beginning on the lowermost point of a great Island, running S. S. W. crossing Lawsons Creeke, 22 May 1650, for transportation of 40 persons . . . 1,000 acres lying about 10 miles up on the N. side of the Rappahannock River adjoining lands of John Slaughter, 22 May 1650, for trans. of 20 persons . . . 900 acs. in Rappa. Riv. on S. side beginning above land of Mr. John Cox, for trans. of 18 persons.

EPPA LAWSON assigned 900 acs. to his brother, Mr. Row-

LAND LAWSON on the Eastward side of the mouth of Cherry Point
Creek, and adjoining land of Richard Jones and ROWLAND LAW-
SON, 400 acs., for trans. of 8 persons, 20 June 1651.

RICHARD LAWSON, 1,400 acres . . . in Rappahannock
River . . . 1,000 acres granted to EPPA LAWSON and assigned
to Richard Lawson and 400 acres assigned to him by Rowland
Lawson to whom it was granted 6 Oct. 1654 (Nugent, p. 318).

ROWLAND LAWSON, 400 acs. upon S. side of Rappa. Riv.,
6 Oct. 1654, for trans. of 8 persons (*Ibid.*, p. 297).

GEORGE LAWSON, headright of Gervase Dodson, Gent., 4
June 1655, Lancaster County (*Ibid* p. 308).

RICHARD LAWSON, 640 acs. on S. side of Occapsason Creek,
27 Feb. 1656, for trans. of 13 persons (*Ibid* p. 341).

THOMAS LAWSON, headright of Miles Dixon, to Northumberland County, 4 March 1656 (*Ibid* p. 344).

WILLIAM CLAPHAM, JR., 500 acs. Lancaster County, 31
March 1657 . . . on N. side of Rappa. Riv. neere the head of a
creek which divides the land of Major Carter from the land formerly belonging to Mr. Eppa Lawson, now sd. Clapham's (Wm.
Clapham, Jr., m. widow of Eppa Lawson). Vincent Stanford, 600
acs., 1 June 1657 . . . land that was divident, of Eppa Lawson,
dec'd, now in the possession of Wm. Clapham, Jr. (this further
proves the marriage of the widow of Eppa Lawson to Clapham).

ELIZABETH LAWSON, 1,400 acres in Gloucester County, 20
Feb. 1662, granted to RICHARD LAWSON, 6 Oct. 1656, and
given to sd Elizabeth, his wife by will (*Ibid* p. 423).

ROBERT LAWSON, headright of John Hughlett, Northumberland County, 3 June 1663 (*Ibid* p. 461).

In the above records we find that Alice Lawson was a headright of Capt. Wm. Peirce, 1635, also that Christopher Lawson was
granted 250 acres for the transportation of 5 persons into James
Cittie County, 1637. *Hotten** shows that Christopher Lawson and
uxor eius (his wife) Lawson were living in Virginia 16 Feb. 1623;

*Hotten, pps. 174 and 232.

[232]

also that in the musters of the inhabitants in Virginia 1723/4, that at Capt. Roger Smith's Plantation, James Cittie County, "Over ye Water," are listed among others, Christopher Lawson and Alice his wife. It has long been the belief of genealogists that many of the immigrants to Virginia actually arrived many years before they were recorded in the records of the Land Office. This is one case in proof of this belief.

In the records searched, I have found nothing to connect Christopher and Alice Lawson with members of this family which follow.

[1] ROWLAND LAWSON, married *circa* 1640, Lettice Wale, daughter of George Wale (I. 1674). He died 1661 (*W. & M. Quarterly*, Oct. 1933).

Children (LAWSON):

    i   Epapphroditus, d. 1652; m. Elizabeth (Medastard?), who m. (II) Wm. Clapham, Jr., 1653.

        Issue (LAWSON)—

        1 Elizabeth, —— m. Robt. Davis, who had his name changed to PAYNE, 1666.

+ 2   ii   Rowland, b. 1644; d. 1704/5; m. Ann ——.

    iii Richard, d. 1658 in Rappahannock County, Va., and made a noncupative will, leaving his estate to his wife, Elizabeth, and Elizabeth, dau. of Eppa Lawson.

    iv Elizabeth.

+ 3   v   John, m. Mary Kilby or Kirby; she m. (II) Geo. Harwood, who d. 1704, Lancaster County.

    vi Henry.

   vii Letitia.

  viii Joanna, m. Lancelot Sockwell, who d. 1668.

[2] ROWLAND[2] LAWSON (Rowland[1]), was born 1644, and died 1704/5 in Lancaster County. He married Ann ——. John Chaplin (w. 1682) of Lancaster County, left all of his estate to Rowland Lawson; John Lawson to have a heifer etc. John Lawson was a witness to the will.

Children (LAWSON):
+ 4   I   Henry, m. Mary Sallard, relict of John Kelley.
+ 5   II   Rowland, m. Jane ——.

[3] JOHN[2] LAWSON (Rowland[1]), married Mary Kilby or Kirby, who married (II) George Harwood who died 1704, leaving her a widow, for the second time.

Children, from Geo. Harwood's will (LAWSON):
+ 6   I   Eppa, "eldest son," died 1722; m. Eliz. Dymer.
      II   John,* had at least Elizabeth (named in Katherine Lawson's will, 1721).
      III   Katherine, d. u. m. 1721/2; names in her will her two brothers, and several of their children.

[4] HENRY[3] LAWSON (Rowland[2], Rowland[1]), died in Lancaster County, *circa* 1725. He married by 1709, Mary Kelly, the relict of John Kelly, and daughter of Simon Sallard and his wife, Elizabeth Taylor, daughter of John Taylor, "Ancient Planter." In the Lancaster records, the children of Elizabeth Sallard (after her marriage with Thomas Baker) are "called Baker."

Children (LAWSON):
      I   Rowland.
      II   Sarah, m. by 1732, Wm. Hathaway, who was b. 1695; d. 1772.
+ 7   III   Henry, m. Winifred ——, and d. 1752.
      IV   Ann, d. 1761, unmarried.
      V   Mary.
      VI   Elizabeth, m. 31 May 1727, Robert Biscoe of Lancaster County, and had at least (BISCOE)—
          1 John.
          2 Sarah.
      VII   Judith, m. 9 March 1730, Francis Timberlake, and had at least Sarah Lawson Timberlake, b. 21 April

---

*A John Lawson and wife Mary, had a daughter Joanna who married 30 July 1741, Adcock Hobson. (Carter Family, p. 135).

[234]

1739; m. 26 Dec. 1754, Capt. John Hathaway* (1732-1786), and had at least Judith Hathaway (1756-1846), who m. 1772, Rev. James Kemper, who moved to the now site of Cincinnati, and built the first "block house" there; also Lawson Hathaway who m. Miss Sullivan, and Elizabeth Hathaway, b. 25 Jan. 1762; d. 3 Jan. 1835; m. 3 Dec. 1788, Richard Nutt of Northumberland County.

[5] ROWLAND[3] LAWSON (Rowland[2], Rowland[1]), died in Lancaster County, Va., 1716. He m. Jane ——, whose will was probated 1738, in which she mentions son, Thomas Lawson and daughter, Joanna Steptoe; the other children were probably dead when her will was written. Their ages from their father's will.

Children (LAWSON):

    I   Rowland, under 18 years of age.

   II Thomas, under 18 years of age; m. Margaret —— and d. 1747, leaving a son Thomas.

  III John, under 18 years of age.

  IV Anthony, under 18 years of age; he and John are "two youngest sons."

    V Sarah, under 21 years of age.

  VI Joanna, under 16 years of age; m. 10 June 1727, John Steptoe, Jr., with consent of Jane Lawson, and John Steptoe; had at least a son John Steptoe.

 VII Elizabeth.

[6] EPAPPHRODITUS[3] LAWSON (John[2], Rowland[1]), died in Lancaster County, 1722. He married Elizabeth Dymer, daughter of Nicholas (w. 1697) and his wife Elizabeth. His children not named in his will; those below given to him are from his sister

---

*William Hathaway, (1636-1692), of near Stratford, England, came to Va. *circa* 1660, and bought "Error" from Wm. Downing, 1666. He had a son William (1666-1725), who had a son William(1695-1772), who m. Sarah[4] Lawson (Henry[3], Rowland[2], Rowland[1]). Capt. John Hathaway was a son of this last William, and moved to Faquier Co. 1760. He was captain of Faquier Co. militia during the Revolution and associate Justice of the Court of Common Pleas. (Wm. A. Brent's notes).

Catherine's will. He gives to his sister Catherine Lawson, 800 pounds of tobaccoe per year for looking after his children . . . loving brother John Lawson "my best suit of Wearing clothes" . . . to his kinsman Fortunatus Sydnor "my riding horse and saddle," and he is the Exor of the estate, and should he die before my children receive their estates (my sons at nineteen years of age and my daughter at sixteen), his loving friends Mr. Hugh Brent and Mr. William Martin are to be the trustees of his estate.

Children, probably others (LAWSON):

+ 8   I   Eppa.

     II   Judith.

     III   —— (youngest son)*.

[7] HENRY[4] LAWSON (Henry[3], Rowland[2], Rowland[1]), was born in Lancaster County, Va., *circa* 1710, and died there by 19 June 1752. He married Winifred ——, who survived him. She was to have all of his estate during her widowhood or natural life, and after her death or marriage, it was to be equally divided between his children, none of whom are named.

Children (LAWSON):

+ 9   I   Henry, m. 21 Oct. 1768, Esther Chinn.

+ 10   II   William, m. Betty (Sydnor?).

     III   Ann.

     IV   Elizabeth, d. u. m. 1778.

     V   Mary, m. 17 Dec. 1771, John Riveer, and had at least (RIVEER)—

       1 Ann.

[8] EPPA[4] LAWSON (Eppa[3], John[2], Rowland[1]), was born in Lancaster County, Va., *circa* 1705, and died there about 1 April 1745. His wife survived him but is not named in his will. His children were all minors.

---

*Nicholas Lawson, will written 2-6-1749/50; probated 4-13-1750, Lanc. Co., names wife Winifred, eldest dau. Catherine, daus. Betty, Judith & Sarah. (L.W. B. 10, p. 277).

Children (LAWSON):

+ 11   I   Eppa, m. before 1765, Mary Brent of Northumberland County, Va.

      II   Elizabeth, m. 1 Aug. 1748, Ezekiel Gilbert.

     III   John, "after his schooling at sixteen, to learn a trade for four years"; he m. (I) before 1774, Ann ——; (II) 20 Jan. 1794, Mary Tunstall Digges (L. M. B.). His will is among the loose papers of Lancaster County, but not probated. It is recorded in Faquier County under date of 22 Jan. 1798. It was written 19 April 1794. He left no issue.

     IV   Ann Steptoe, d. u. m. Nov. 1774, in Faquier County, Va.

[9] HENRY[5] LAWSON (Henry[4], Henry[3], Rowland[2], Rowland[1]), was born in Lancaster County, Va., and died there *circa* 1802. He married 21 Oct. 1768, Esther Chinn, daughter of Thomas Chinn and his wife Sarah Mitchell. Thomas Chinn was the son of Rawleigh Chinn and Esther Ball, daughter of Joseph Ball, and half-sister of Mary Ball, the mother of George Washington. There was a Henry Lawson, captain in the Rev. War.

Children (LAWSON):

      I   Winifred, m. 30 Aug. 1804, John McNamara.

      II   Sally, m. Theodoric Bland.

     III   Susan, m. John McNamara, widower.

     IV   Fanny, m. 15 July 1807, Timothy McNamara, "mariner."

+ 12   v   Henry Chinn, m. 18 Jan. 1796, Margaret Steptoe Lee.

     VI   William, m. —— Glasscock, and had at least (GLASSCOCK)—

         I   Melissa, m. 15 April 1841, James H. Digges.

    VII   Thomas, went south and nothing known of him.

[10] WILLIAM[5] LAWSON (Henry[4], Henry[3], Rowland[2], Rowland[1]), was born in Lancaster County, Va., and died there before 19 April 1790. He married Betty (Sydnor?) *circa* 1775. All of his children were minors 1789.

Children (LAWSON):

    I   Elizabeth Sydnor Lawson.

   II Ann.

  III Anthony, m. 19 July 1802, Ann Shelton (L. M. B.).

  IV (unborn child).

[11] EPPA[5] LAWSON (Eppa[4], Eppa[3], John[2], Rowland[1]), was born in Lancaster County, Va., and died there Jan.-June 1778. He married before 1765, Mary Brent, daughter of William Brent and Elizabeth Pinckard, relict of Charles Lee. Mary (Brent) Lawson died 1787. The first two children listed below are named in the father's will; the others from the will of Ann Steptoe Lawson. He was a soldier in the Rev. War from Lancaster County, or possibly it was his son.

Children (LAWSON):

    I   Epapphroditus.

   II Elizabeth, m. (I) 22 Dec. 1774, John Hunt; (II) 25 May 1780, James Brent; (III) 7 Sept. 1795, Thomas James; she left issue by all three husbands.

  III Ann Steptoe Lawson.

  IV Mary Lawson.

[12] HENRY[6] CHINN LAWSON (Henry[5], Henry[4], Henry[3], Rowland[2], Rowland[1]), was born in Lancaster County, Va., and probably died there. He married 18 Jan. 1796, Margaret Steptoe Lee, daughter of Thomas Lee (w. 1809) of Lancaster County.

Children (LAWSON):

    I   Elizabeth C. (Betsy), m. 25 Oct. 1815, Peter Beane, Jr., of Lancaster County.

   II Thomas L., m. 28 Nov. 1821, Judith N. Brent, dau. of Capt. Hugh Brent and his wife, Alice Martin. He died by 21 June 1841, leaving minors—

        1 Elizabeth C. Lawson.

        2 Marian L. Lawson.

III   Margaret L., m. 9 July 1822, William Gibson.

IV   Henry B., m. 23 Jan. 1826, Sally McNamara.

V   Pauline, m. 13 Nov. 1826, Spencer George.

VI   Rowland, d. young.

VII Osborne, d. at sea.

VIII Octavius, m. 2 March 1840, Judith Brown of North-umberland County.

IX   Mordecai, m. 1 March 1841, Hannah Basye of North-umberland County.

X   Charles N., m. (I) 26 Dec. 1843, Sarah E. Brent(340), and left issue; m. (II) 1855, Catherine A. Brent (345: see Brent line), and left issue by this marriage.

THE NUTT FAMILY

From the Virginia Land Office records as abstracted in *Cavaliers and Pioneers*, by Mrs. Nell Nugent, appear the following records of the earliest immigrants by the name of Nutt:

WILLIAM NUTT, headright of Bridges Freeman . . . 1 June 1635 . . . upon Wly side of Chichahominy Riv . . . adjoining the place commonly called Jurying Point (James Cittie County) . . . again 11 Aug. 1637.

WILLIAM NUTT and his wife, RICHARD NUTT (his son?), h'rights of Gervase Dodson, Gent., 1 Feb. 1650 . . . in Northumberland County . . . upon Potomeck Riv. . . . Mr. Gervase Dodson's transportation is also included.

MR. WILLIAM NUTT, 683 acres Northumberland County, on N. side of Great Wicocomoco Riv., 4 July 1655, S. S. W. upon sd Riv from Lamdens Cr. to Island Cr., Wly upon same and land of William Thomas, E. N. E. upon Thomas Garret, the land of Henry Smith, orphant, and towards land Richard Span bought of Edward Cole . . . 350 acres granted to Robert Lamden, who assigned to sd Nutt . . . 333 acres for trans. of 7 persons: Wm Goward, Jno. Holloway, Geo. Pickeringe, Math. Wilcocks, Jn. Smith, Sarah Roberts, WM. NUTT (his own transportation?). This patent renewed 4 Feb. 1662.

JAMES NUTT, h'right of Patrick Miller on S. side of Rappa. Riv. 20 Aug. 1655, adjoining land of Capt. Brocas, dec'd, and Geo. Wading.

THOMAS NUTT, h'right of John Renny, Accomack County, 10 Jan. 1662.

JONATHAN NUTT, h'right of Robt. Talifero and Lawrence Smith, 26 March 1666 . . . in the freshes on the S. side and about 4 miles above Waire creek.

PHILIP NUTT, made has will 1660/1, Northumberland County, and leaves all of his estate to Richard Flynt. This is the only mention made of him in the records; nor is he mentioned in the land office grants. Richard Flynt married Mary, dau. of John Sharpe.

[1] Capt. WILLIAM NUTT, immigrant to James Cittie County, Va., 1635, living in Northumberland County, by 1650. He was a Gentleman Justice and High Sheriffe in 1656, and died intestate 1668. Elizabeth, his relict m. (II), Rev. John Farnefold (w. 1702), of Fairfield Parish.

Children:

+ 2   I   Richard, m. Ann Downing.

   3   II   Elizabeth, m. ——— Tarpley.

[2] RICHARD[2] NUTT (William[1]), was probably born in England and came to Virginia with his parents in 1650. He married Ann, daughter of William Downing, Jr., as per deed he made to Samuel Blackwell, 20 July 1712. He was of Wiccomicco Parish, Northumberland County. His will was proven 22 March 1715/6, by Ann, his relict and Joseph his son (N. O. B. 6, p. 153). She probably married 1718, Geo. Harrison of Westmoreland County.

Children:

+ 4   I   Joseph, d. 1766; m. Judith ———.

   5   II   William, d. 1712; m. Hannah ——— whose inventory
             is dated 1748; they had at least:
             1 Frances, a minor 1712.

   6   III Benjamin, d. u. m. 1728.

+ 7   IV   Farnifold, d. intestate 1772.

+ 8   V   John, d. 1768; m. (I) Sarah ———; (II) March 1759,
             Winifred Christopher.

+ 9   VI   Richard, b. 17 Jan. 1694; d. 1746; m. (I) Elizabeth
             Smith; (II) Alice Ruth Hackney(?).

[4] JOSEPH[3] NUTT (Richard[2], William[1]), died in Wiccomicco Parish, Northumberland County, Va., April-July 1766. His wife was Judith ——. He names granddaughters, Frances who intermarried with John Humphries, and Elizabeth Hudnall.

Children:

+ 10   I   Moseley, d. 1801; m. 11 May 1767, Sarah Garlington.

+ 11   II   Richard, m. (I) Elizabeth Rawlings;* (II) Miss. Yerby, after birth of Carmen.

   12   III   Winefred, m. Joseph Hurst.

   13   IV   Ann, m. John White.

[7] FARNEFOLD[3] NUTT (Richard[2], William[1]), died intestate 1772; cannot find the name of his wife.

Children, from St. Stephen's Parish Register:

     I   Richard, b. 1725; m. Alce or Ales ——.

     II   John, b. 1728; d. 1768; had Sally who m. Jas. Brent (133).

     III   Mosley, born 1729.

     IV   Farnefold, born 1731; died 1762; m. Mary ——, and had John, b. 1749, and Thomas, b. 1753.

+ 14   V   William, born 1733, of whom later.

[8] JOHN[3] NUTT (Richard[2], William[1]), died in the Parish of Wicomico, Northumberland County, Va., between Nov. 1767 and Feb. 1768. He m. (I) Sarah ——; (II) March 1759, Winifred Christopher. In his will he names, besides his children, granddaughters, Betty and Margaret Short:

Children:

+ 15   I   Col. William, of whom later.

   16   II   Susannah, m. Thomas Clarke.

---

*This data taken from a chart compiled by S. P. Nutt, 1885. I cannot find anything concerning either of the above marriages. The Northumberland Co. Marriage Bonds show that Richard Nutt, widower, married Nancy (Kelly) Roebuck, widow, 2 March 1791. Nancy Kelly m. William Roebuck 17 Aug. 1787.

17   III   Winifred, m. Wm. Everett.

18   IV   Lucy.

[9] RICHARD[3] NUTT (Richard[2], William[1]), died in Wicomico Parish, Northumberland County, Va., by 14 April 1746. He married Elizabeth Smith, sister of Edwin, William, James, John and Lazarua Smith of Northumberland County, and she survived him. James Nutt, son of his son Benjamin, 1 May 1773, claims land Wm. Hackney (w. 1729) gave to his grandmother Alice Ruth; Wm. Hackney, in his will gives land to Alice Ruth, without mentioning relationship, or her surname. Elizabeth Smith died by 1753. It might be possible that Richard Nutt m. (1) Alice Ruth Hackney, and that she was the mother of all of his children except Richard, as the latter is the only *cousin* named in the Smith wills.

Children:

+ 19   I   Benjamin, d. intestate 1767; m. Winifred ——.

20   II   Richard, d. intestate 1777, and had at least—
         1 Judith.

21   III   Agatha

22   IV   Mary

[10] MOSELEY[4] NUTT (Joseph[3], Richard[2], William[1]), died March-April 1801, in Northumberland County, Va. He married 11 May 1767, Sarah Garlington, daughter of Christopher Garlington and Elizabeth Conway. He took the oath as Vestryman of Wicomico Parish, 10 Aug. 1784. (It is possible that this Moseley or Mosley, and Richard that follow might be the sons of Farnefold (7) instead of Joseph; the records are not very clear.)

Children:

23   I   William

24   II   Walter, m. 2 Feb. 1809, Eliz. Sharp Lunsford.

25   III   Judith, m. 22 Dec. 1796, Jesse Chilton.

[11] RICHARD[4] NUTT (Joseph[3], Richard[2], William[1]), was born in Northumberland County, Va. *circa* 1750 and died while on a visit to the springs in Augusta County, Va., 12 Sept. 1811, "at an old age." He married (I) Elizabeth Rawlings; (II) 2 March 1791, Nancy (Kelley) Roebuck, relict of William Roebuck. He is appointed 2nd lieutenant of Capt. William Nutt's Company of Militia 8 Sept. 1777.

Children, 1st marriage:

+ 26   I   Leroy, m. 18 March 1802, Alcy Conway, relict of Severn Galle.

+ 27   II   Rushworth, m. (I) in Va. ——; (II) Eliz. Ker.

28   III   Collin, d. s. p. 1814.

29   IV   Emily, m. 25 June 1799, Onesiphoras Harvey, and had issue.

30   V   Carmen, m. (I) 1 Aug. 1808, John Pullin; (II) 24 Dec. 1816, John Carter of Wicomico. He d. 1821; had three sons.

Children, 2nd marriage:

+ 31   VI   Delia, m. (I) 7 Jan. 1805, Thomas Yerby of Lancaster County; (II) 30 Sept. 1819, John Waddy of Wicco. Church.

32   VII   Richard

+ 33   VIII   Austin, sold his mill in Northumberland County, Va. 1817, and moved to Mississippi Terr., where he m. a Miss Dixon of Jefferson County.

34   IX   Nancy Y., m. 16 May 1815, John Kirk, and had a son William and a daughter.

35   X   John, d. s. p. 1820.

[14] WILLIAM[4] NUTT (Farnefold[3], Richard[2], William[1]), was born 1733 as listed in St. Stephen's Parish Register. Cannot find his will. His marriages are mixed with that of Col. Wm. Nutt (15), but he must have m. (I), Jan. 1760, Susannah Christopher, and she died by 1762. S. P. Nutt's chart states that "William Nutt was cousin of Richard Nutt (11)."

Children:

+ 36   I   Richard, b. 8 Jan. 1762; d. 20 Apr. 1852; m. 3 Dec. 1788, Elizabeth Hathaway, who was b. 25 Jan. 1762; d. 3 Jan. 1835.

  37   II   Rudolph, "went West."

+ 38   III   James, m. —— Deakins.

[15] Col. WILLIAM⁴ NUTT (John³, Richard², William¹), of "Monday's Point" Northumberland County, Va., died 1792; his marriages are badly mixed with that of his cousin William above, as a Wm. Nutt married six times between 1760-1785, viz— William Nutt m. Jan. 1760, Susannah Christopher; 1761, Judith Gibbons; 16 Jan. 1769, Mary Downing; 5 Aug. 1772 Martha Williams; 27 Oct. 1781, Jane Swann Brent. Col. William Nutt did marry 5 March 1785, Sarah Edwards, and she was at least his last wife, and survived him and died 1827-40. A William Nutt was appointed Lt. in John Heath's Co. of Militia 15 Feb. 1765; Maj. 14 Oct. 1882; one of his Majesties Justices 10 Dec. 1781; church-warden Wicomico Parish 1777.

Children:

  39   I   Elizabeth, m. John Downing, and had at least Dymer and Judith Downing.

  40   II   Henry L.

  41   III   William D., m. 6 Dec. 1798, Eliz. Chinn.

  42   IV   Mary, m. 3 March 1796, Kendall Lee.

Children, by Sarah Edwards:

  43   V   Thomas Edwards, m. 22 May 1812, Mary K. Beach-am, wid.

  44   VI   Sarah

  45   VII   Elizabeth F., m. 8 Dec. 1807, Wm. J. McClanahan, with the consent of Wm. Davenport as to Elizabeth.

  46   VIII   Robert, m. (I) 27 June 1813, Ann Lee Carr; (II) 23 Jan. ——, Charlotte McAdam Taylor; (III) 8 June 1829, Elizabeth R. Atwell, dau. of Thomas T. Atwell.

[19] BENJAMIN⁴ NUTT (Richard³, Richard², William¹), died intestate in Northumberland County, 1767. He married Winifred ——, and had, at least—

Children:

    1 James

[26] Dr. LEROY[5] NUTT (Richard[4], Joseph[3], Richard[2], William[1]), was born in Northumberland County, and died 13 Sept. 1811 "at the Springs" in August County, Va. He moved from Northumberland County to Culpeper County, about 1800. Married 18 March 1802, Alcy Conway, relict of Severn Galle. She married 1820, Wm. Lovel of "Nose Neck," who died 1822.

Children:

47   I Leroy D., of Nuttsville, Culpeper County, Va., m. and had—
      1 Moncure Leroy, m. Ann —— of Frankfort, Kentucky, and left two daughters. He d. 1870, Shreveport, Louisiana.

48   II Dr. Conway Rawlins, m. Adaline Blake of Va.; moved to Onega, La., and then to Houston and Galveston, Texas, where he married the second time. He left two daus. by first marriage and numerous children by second marriage.

49   III Moncure, m. and left two daughters.

50   IV Olivia, no issue.

[27] Dr. RUSHWORTH[5] NUTT (Richard[4], Joseph[3], Richard[2], William[1]), was born in Northumberland County, Va. 1781 and died in Mississippi 1837. He married (I) in Virginia but had no issue; (II) Elizabeth Ker, daughter of Hon. David and Mary Ker, professor at Chapel Hill, N. C., and later County Down, Ireland. Dr. Nutt is described by his grandson as a Planter, Geologist, Scientist and Traveller.

Children:

51   I Rittenhouse, b. 1810; d. 1862; m. Ellen Rowan, of Natchez, Miss., and had—
      1 Rushworth, m. —— Yerby.

      2 Austin, m. —— Manning of New Orleans.

      3 Rittenhouse.

      4 Ellen, m. —— Whitaker, M. D.

52   II Mary Lyle, b. 1813; m. (I) —— Mason, of Natchez; (II) a Dr. Lyle.

53   III Elizabeth, d. s. p.

+ 54   IV Haller, b. 1816; d. 1864; m. Julia Augusta Williams, of Natchez.

     v David, d. s. p.

     VI Sarah, m. Dr. C. B. New of Jefferson County, Miss.; she d. 1853, and all of her children(!)

     VII Rushworth, d. s. p.

     VIII Elizabeth, b. 1826; m. —— Bachelor, and had (BACHELOR)—

      1 James.

      2 Mary.

      3 Ann.

      4 Edward.

      5 Sarah.

      6 Maria.

     IX Margaret, m. (I) —— Clark; (II) Dr. C. B. New, her brother-in-law. She had—(CLARK)—

      1 Charles.

      2 Margaret, m. E. N. Cabeniss, of Clinton, Miss.

[31] DELIA[5] NUTT (Richard[4], Joseph[3], Richard[2], William[1]), was born in Northumberland County, Va., and in all probability died there. She married (I) 7 Jan. 1805, Thomas Yerby, of Lancaster County, Va.; he died 1814. She married (II) 20 Sept. 1819, John Waddy of Wiccomoco Church, Northumberland County.

Children, first marriage, (YERBY):

     1 William, went to Mississippi, then to Lake Village, Arkansas. He had—

    1 (daughter) who m. —— Seizes, of Jackson, Miss.

    2 (daughter), who m. R. Nutt.

II Henry.

III Mary, m. 10 April 1828, Hiram Stonham.

Children, second marriage, (WADDY):

    IV Ann.

[33] AUSTIN[5] NUTT (Richard[4], Joseph[3], Richard[2], William[1]), was born in Northumberland County, Va. The Orders show that he sold his mill in 1817, so probably left for Mississippi Terr. about that time. He and his brother Rushworth of the State of Mississippi and county of Jefferson, appoint John H. Fallin, Sr., agent and atty. to collect or adjust any property belonging to them in Northumberland County, Va., *circa* 1830. (N. D. B. 26, p. 438). He married a Miss Dixon in Miss. Terr.

Children:

    I Ann, m. Capt. —— Denman, and had two daughters.

    II Virginia, m. Capt. —— McLean, U. S. A., and had—

        1 Ann McLean.

[36] RICHARD[5] NUTT (William[4], Farnefold[3], Richard[2], William[1]), was born at "Monday's Point," Northumberland County, Va., 8 Jan. 1762, and died 20 April 1852, in Virginia. He moved to St. Louis, Mo. 1835, probably to live near relatives there, as there is one branch of this family living in that state. He married 3 Dec. 1788, Elizabeth Hathaway, of Lancaster County, Va., daughter of John Hathaway and his wife Elizabeth Lawson Timberlake. She was born 25 Jan. 1762, and died 3 Jan. 1835.

Children:

    I Alice, b. 23 Dec. 1789; m. Col. John C. Herndon, and had sixteen children.

    II Sarah, b. 23 April 1792; d. 31 Dec. 1864; m. Amos Johnson, who d. March 1853. They had—(JOHNSON)

1 Richard W., m. Ann M. Wheatley of Culpeper County, left issue.

2 Juliette P., m. Lafayette Brent (310: see his line).

III James, b. 9 Jan. 1794; d. in Ky., and left issue.

IV Catherine, b. 2 Feb. 1796; d. u m. 13 July 1824.

V John, b. 16 Aug. 1798; d. 11 Sept. 1844; m. Jane F. Rogers, and had—

1 Kate E.

2 George Whitfield Nutt, of Manassas, Va.

VI William, b. 13 Oct. 1800; was M. D.; d. Lincoln, Neb.

VII Judith Lawson, b. 22 July 1803; d. 2 April 1849; m. —— Ferguson, widower; no issue.

VIII Collin, b. 7 July 1805; d. in Missouri with a family; m. Mildred Barnett, dau. of Achilles Barnett of Madison County, Va.

IX Joseph Allen, b. 17 Dec. 1809; d. 6 Feb. 1810.

[38] JAMES[5] NUTT (William[4], Farnefold[3], Richard[2], William[1]), was born in Northumberland County, Va. He married a Miss Deakins. While much of this data was gleaned from letters between his son William D. Nutt, and S. P. Nutt, a cousin, most of the data coming from the latter, very little is shown of this line. I have tried to contact the Mississippi branch but have not been successful.

Children:

I Major William D., b. 1805 in Fairfax County, Va.; was in Treasury dept. of the Confederate Gov.; m. Pamelia Andrew, and had a daughter Alice Elizabeth, who m. Peter Wise, of Alexandria, Va.

II Elizabeth, b. 7 Sept. 1805; m. Wm. L. Deakins of Washington, D. C.; he d. 1884.

[54] HALLER[6] NUTT (Rushworth[5], Richard[4], Joseph[3], Richard[2], William[1]), was born in Mississippi Terr. 1816, and died there 1864. He married Julia Augusta Williams of Natchez, Miss., *circa*

[249]

1838. He was a large landholder and cotton planter and left considerable estate, much of which was destroyed during the Civil War.

Children:

I   Carrie Routh, b. 1840; d. 1867; m. C. S. Forsyth, of Chicago, and had Carrie Nutt, b. 1867.

II   Mary Ella, b. 1841.

III   Frances Smith, b. 1846; d. 1848.

IV   Haller, b. 1848.

V   John Ker, b. 1850; m. Mary Worthington of Washington County, Miss.

VI   Austin Williams, b. 1853; d. 1860.

VII   Sergeant Prentiss, b. 1855; m. 1896, Lily Barrett of Newport, Rhode Island.

VIII   Julia Williams, b. 1857.

IX   Calvin Routh, b. 1859.

X   Frances Elizabeth, 1861.

XI   Rushworth, b. 1863; d. 1863.

THE WALE FAMILY

[1] GEORGE WHALLE patented 500 acs. on S. side of the Petomeck Riv., at the mouth of Matchotique Riv., & c., 18 May 1655, for the transportation of 10 persons into the Collony (Lancaster County, Va.). On 29 Nov. 1658, Mr. George Wale pattents 300 acs. neere the Glade above Wiccocommoccoe Indian Towne, adjoining S. side of land of John Cossens and Thomas Steed and parallel to tract assigned sd Wale by Gervas Dodson, for transportation of six persons . . . Mr. George Wale, 1400 acs. in Lancaster County, 10 Oct. 1662 . . . 600 acs. on S. side of Corotoman Cr. being the next creek Nly. to Haddawaies Cr., south easterly upon land surveyed for Tobias Horton, by some called Mr. Wetherlies land, and S. Wly. upon the land of John Taylour, dec'd. . . . 300 acs. near the glade above Wiccomicco Indian Towne . . . 500 acs. assigned to sd Wale by sd Dodson . . . 300 acs. near the head of a Creek by some called Chesticon and by others Corratoman . . . 1100 acs. granted to sd Dodson by patents dated 29 Nov. 1658 (Nugent).

In all probability, George Wale settled first in Maryland, viz: "An Inventory of the Estate of belonging to Mr. Geo. Wale, dec'd, in the province of Maryland being this day exhibited to this Court by William Edmonds who married the relict and Admx. of the sd Geo. Wale and it appearing that the same was in the province of Maryland sold in Tobaccoe by the Sd Wm. Edmonds and Mr. Thomas Haynie, Guardian to George Wale, eldest son of the sd George Wale, dec'd . . ."

George Wale died intestate 1674; his brother, Edward, who was one of the headrights of Col. Edmund Scarborough of Accomack County, 1664, proved his inventory.

George Wale was descended from Sir Thomas Wale, who was made a Knight of the Order of the Garter in the first creation by Edward III, 1340. He married Lewys ——, who after his death married William Edmonds. She died 1688.

George Wale was one of His Majesties Justices, with Capt.

[251]

Henry Fleet and Mr. Thomas Haines. He was a member of the 1687 militia, "appointed for Horse Service."

Children (Wale):

+ 2   I   George, "eldest son," d. 1720, intestate; m. (I), Mary Jones, dau. of Robert Jones and Martha Llewellyn (Boddie notes); m. (II) Thomasine ——, who m. (II), 1721, John Bond.

3   II   dau. ——, m. by 1685, William Morris, who d. 1728.
Issue (from his will; probably others—MORRIS):
1 William, "eldest son."
2 Elizabeth, m 1726, Hugh Brent (II).

4   III   Elizabeth, m. Thomas Martin, widower, who d. 1711/2; (he had Thomas, Ann and Margaret by a prior marriage).
Issue (MARTIN):
1 Catherine, m. Wm. Dare 1707; he was Cl. Cur. of Lancaster County, and d. March 1742.
2 Thomasine.

5   IV   Benjamin, m. Ann Mahollom, wid., who had a son John Mahollom. No issue.

+ 6   V   John, m. Elizabeth Sallard, dau. of Simon Sallard and Elizabeth Taylor, dau. of John Taylor, "Ancient Planter." Elizabeth m. (II) John Brown, who left Va. very much in debt to his neighbors, especially Rich. Doggett "for the care of a child," 1709. John Wale d. 1699.

7   VI   Lettice, named in the second filing of the inventory of George Wale, 1688, as Lettice Lawson, relict; Lettice m. Rowland Lawson (w. 1661).
Issue (Bulkley notes—LAWSON):
1 Epapphroditus, m. Elizabeth ——.
2 Rowland, b. 1644; m. Ann ——.
3 Richard.
4 Elizabeth.
5 John, m. Mary Kilby or Kirby, and had Eppa, who m. Eliz. Dymer.
6 Henry, not 21 in 1668.
7 Letitia.
8 Joanna, m. Lancelott Sockwell.

[2] GEORGE[2] WALE (George[1]), was born in either the Province of Maryland or Lancaster County, Va., *circa* 1650, and died in Lancaster County, 1720, intestate. He m. (I) Mary Jones, daughter of Robert and Martha (Llewellyn) Jones; (II) Thomasine ——, who m. (II) 1721, John Bond. He was named in more suits during his lifetime than any one man in Lancaster: he was plaintiff in twenty suits, and defendant in fourteen, which might imply that he held some office in connexion with the inspection of Tobacco, but the Orders do not show this. He was under-sheriff 9 April 1712. He was probably church warden of St. Mary's White Chapels Parish with Richard Flint 1717, as they are sued for 32,000 pound of tobacco by James Ball and Rawleigh Chinn, late Church Wardens. George Wale was one of His Majesties Justicies for Lancaster County, 1678. Children (Wale):

+ 8   I   John, died 1749, in Lancaster County, m. by 1705, Alice, relict of Samuel Wright (I. 1706). She survived him.

[6] JOHN[2] (George[1]), was born in Lancaster County, and died there by 1700. He m. before 1690, Elizabeth, dau. of Simon Sallard and his wife Elizabeth Taylor, dau. of John Taylor, "Ancient Planter." Elizabeth m. (II) John Brown, and died 1714-1715, naming in her will Joseph Cropper, Eliz. Wood, William Wale, cousin John Angell, dau. Mary Lawson, and George Flower . . . the remainder of her estate to William Waugh, and my granddaughter Elizabeth Wale to be equally divided, and they are to be the Exors . . .

Children (Wale):

   9   I   John.

   10   II   Mary, m. —— Lawson.

+ 11   III   William, m. ——.

[8] JOHN[3] (George[2], George[1]), died in Lancaster County by 1749; he m. by 1705, Alice, relict of Samuel Wright (I. 1706). He is appointed surveyor of the Highways from Capt. Swan's to the Main Road in Christ Church parish, 14 June 1721, again in 1722.

John Bond and Thomazina, his wife, agt. John Wale, for her dower of 70 acs. of land in poss. of the deft. in Christ Church Parish, formerly belonging to her dec'd husband, George Wale. Hugh Brent, and William Dymer to lay off sd land; granted against John Wale (LOB., 1723, p. 116).

Children, from Est Div. (Wale):

12   I   Elizabeth George.

13   II   Ann, m. 15 Nov. 1754, Thomas Hunton.

14   III   Joanna, m. William Doggett, widower.

15   IV   Judith Tucker.

16   v   Letitia, b. 17 Aug. 1711; d. 26 April 1776; m. (I) 9 Aug. 1734, William Brent (12); m. (II) 1744, William Griggs.

[11] WILLIAM[3] (John[2], George[1]), was probably born in Lancaster County, *circa* 1698. There is nothing to prove his birth, death or marriage in the records searched. He appears in the will of Elizabeth Brown, relict of John Wale, in 1714, and a William Wale of Wicocomoco Parish in Lancaster County, is fined 50 pounds of tobacco 9 Dec. 1737, for not having attended church for one month. He is used here as the only Wale extant who can fill in this gap, except Thomas, who is named in the will of Thomas Martin (1727), as his cousin.

Children (Wale):

+ 17   I   George, m. Sarah ——, and died 1767.

+ 18   II   Thomas, m. Margaret Stamps, *circa* 1757.

[17] GEORGE[4] (William[3], John[2], George[1]), was born *circa* 1730 and died 1767, in Lancaster County, Va. He m. *circa* 1755, Sarah ——, who survived him. His children at his death were minors.

Children (Wale):

19   I   George.

20   II   John, listed in the 1783 census as having "1 black soul."

21 III Lawson, m. 15 May 1783, Winnifred Spriggs; he d. 1785, leaving child, unnamed in his will.

22 IV William*, d. 1777, "in the 5th Va. Regiment."

23 V Caty.

24 VI Mary Ann.

25 VII Joanna, m. (I) 17 Dec. 1772, Geo. Brent (102); (II) James Lewis, and d. in Loudon County, Va. 1827.

26 VIII Sarah, m. 2 June 1776, Zachariah Barr and "bound for Kentucky, 1788."

[18] THOMAS⁴ (William³, John², George¹), was probably b. in Lancaster County, Va., and died in Culpeper County; m. by 1757, Margaret Stamps, dau. of Timothy Stamps of Lancaster County.

Children (from H. K. Bower's data—Wale):

27 I Lawson, d. *circa* 1832; m. 1791, Lucy Thornton of Culpeper County, whose mother was a Miss Davis. Issue—

1 Hannah, d. v. p. 9 years old.

2 Thomas, d. v. p.

3 George, m. widow Petty, and lived at Stevensburg, Va., and had

I William.

II Henry Jackson.

III Laura Montraville.

4 John Thornton Davis, m. Susan Shackleford, and moved to Woodbury, Tenn.; they had—

I John.

---

*At a Court held for the sd county of Lancaster on the 17th day of April 1777, this last will of William Wale was presented in Court and being proved to be the Hand Writing of the said Wale and the Hand Writing of three of the Witnesses to the said Will, viz, of Elmor Doggett Junr., Thomas West and Isaac Currell, who are now in the Army at the Northard being also proved in Court was admitted to Record.

Test: Thomas B. Griffin Cl Cur.

This will was proven again 17 April 1797 by the oath of Edward Blackmore, "a witness thereof, who also proved that he saw all of the other witnesses subscribe their names thereto, and that all of them are deceased except Thomas West, who is suggested to be dead."

Test: Henry Rowles, C. L. C.

  ii Patrick Henry.

  iii George.

5 Martin Buford, d. u. m.

6 Judith Kirk, b. 27 Feb. 1804; m. 1 April 1825, Samuel Flinn, and left issue.

7 Juliet, m. Washington Kennedy, of Madison County, Va., and went to Tenn.

8 Lucy, m. (1) —— Bates; (ii) —— James, and went to Tenn. (or prob. m. them there).

9 Matilda, m. —— Hare, of Tenn.

10 Ann Lawson, m. Gabriel Hume, and moved to Tenn.

INDEX

ABNEY, 152.

ACHERSONE (Ochersone), Mary, 22.

ADAMS, Rebecca, 107; Sarah F., 116.

ADKINS, Jos., 144.

AKERS, Brent, 164; Joseph, 164; R. D., 164.

ALDERSON, Fanny E., 136; Geo. D., 136; Georgia, 136; Joseph, 136; Mabel, 136.

ALEXANDER, Capt. Morgan, 179; Charlton, 144; Col. ——, 145.

ALLEN, Benjamin, 15; Edward C., 125; Eliz., 213; Emaline, 125; Fanny, 116, 117; Julia Brent, 125; Richard, 116; Samuel, 213; Wm. H., 125.

ALLERTON, Willoughby, 43.

AMBLER, Cary, 156.

AMRINE, Ira, 139.

ANDERSON, Ella, 164; Frank, 127; John, 58; Kimbrough, 125.

ANDREW, Pamelia, 249.

ANDROS, John, 24.

ARCHER, Elizabeth, 212.

ARMSTRONG, Margaret, 143.

ARNOLD, Eliz. Susan, 142.

ARUNDEL, Sir John, 15.

ASH, Frances, 89; Margaret, 89.

ASHBY, John, 121; Mary, 142; Mary Jane, 121.

ASKINS, Susan, 116.

ATKINS, 97; Mark, 38.

ATWATERS, Robt., 227.

ATWELL, Eliz., 245; Hugh, 59; Thomas, 245.

BACA, Charlotte, 156.

BACHELOR, Ann, 247; Edward, 247; James, 241; Maria, 247; Mary, 247; Sarah, 247.

BAILEY (Bayley), Catherine, 90; Charles, 90; Hugh, 90; Jesse, 90; John, 66, 90; Judith Brent, 90; Molly, 90; Sally, 90; Wm. Pierce, 102.

BAKER, Emily (Streit), 140; Fanny E., 140; Geo. W., 140; Harriett E., 140; Thomas, 234.

BALDOCK, James, 123; John, 121; Rebecca, 123.

BALL, Anne, 222; David, 157; Eliz., 136; Esther, 89, 237; George, 67, 88; Geo. Summerfield, 157; Hannah Catherine, 157; Hannah Gaskins, 157; Harriett, 157; Hilkiah, 157; James, 253; Joseph, 237; Col. Joseph, 222; Judith, 67; Mary, 237.

BALLARD, Annie, 131.

BANNERMAN, Katherine, 67; Mark, 67.

"BARFORD", 60.

BARKER, Russell, 161.

BARNETT, Achilles, 249; Mildred, 249.

BARR, Zachariah, 255.

BARRETT, Lily, 250.

BASAYE (Basye), Eliz., 220; Hannah, 239.

BATES, 256; A. K., 173; J. Schuyler, 164; Kenton, 164; Margaret, 164; Robt., 164.

Battle Abbey, The Roll of, 18.

BAUCAS, Odo, 11.

BAYLIS, Carr W., 79.

BAYLOR, Lucy, 80.

BAXTER, Eliz., 59, 79; Margaret, 78; Philip, 79.

BEACHAM, Mary K., 245.

BEALE, Charlotte, 69; Lucy, 143.

BEALERT, Molly, 94.

BEANE (Bean), Gertrude, 158; Peter, 238.

BEAUCHAMP, Ida, 13.

BECHTEL, Archer E., 162; Eliz. Ann, 162; Milford A., 162; Orpha M., 162; Roy V., 162.

BEHETHLAND, The Family, 63; Mary, 63; Capt. Robt., 63.

BELL, David, 103; Howell, 156; John, 223, 224; Judith (Cary), 103.

DE BELOIS, Henry, 12.

BENNETT, Richard, 231.

BENTON, Hugh Brent, 132.

BERNARD, The Family, 152; Behethland, 64; John, 152; Mary Byron, 152; Capt. Thomas, 63; Major Allen, 152.

BERRY, Ann, 143; Col. John S., 156; John Washington, 143; Mary Frances, 143; Mary Washington, 143; Peter, 143.

[257]

JAMES, Bartley, 108; David, 153; John, 73; Nancy, 153, 154; Thomas, 40, 89, 107, 108, 238; Wm., 148.
JAMISON, Alpheus, 168; Bulah, 163; Catherine K., 167; Catherine N., 168; Cecil B., 167; Cecilia, 167; Cornelia A., 167; Cordelia, 163; Edwin, 163; Eliz., 167; Eliz. Ann, 168; Ella N., 167; Estelle, 163; Estella C., 167; Eugene, 167; Fanny C., 168; Glenna, 167; Herschel, 167; James, 162; J. Edmonds, 168; James Eric, 167; Jessie F., 167; John K., 167; John S., 167; Leonora, 167; Mabel E., 168; Madison L., 167; Margaret E., 162; Martha, 163; Martha J., 168; Mary, 162; Michael, 163; Michael V., 163; Ora E., 168; Paul, 168; Robt. L., 168; Samuel S., 167; Sarah A., 168; Sarah Ellen, 165; Wm., 168; Wm. A., 167; Wm. B., 168; Wm. O. 167.
JENNINGS, Margaret, 124; Theron F., 163.
JOHNSON, Amos, 155, 248; Benj. C., 112; Juliet, 155, 249; Richard W., 249.
JONES, Ann, 229; Clarissa B., 171; Jane, 111; Mary, 38, 253; Mary Ann, 149; Richard, 232; Robert, 38, 253; Wm., 229; Rev. Walter, 64.
JORDAN, Harriett, 155; John, 178.
JOYES, Annie, 118; Patrick, 118.
JUNKIN, Ella, 148.

KAMP, Edna, 160.
KAY, John, 121; Mary, 121; Polly, 121; Robt., 121.
KEENE, Maj. Alderson, 119; Newton, 64.
KEITH, Alexander D., 132; Susan Tarlton, 132.
KELLY (Kelley), Ann,103; James Y., 94; John, 73, 234; Mary K., 234; Nancy, 242.
KEMPER, James, 235.
KENDALL, John, 220.
KENNEDY, Washington, 256.
KENNER, Brererton, 63, 64, 81; Judith, 63, 81; Rodham, 49.
KENT, 76; Jane, 76, 94; Judith, 76, 94.

KER, David, 246; Eliz., 246; Mary, 246.
KESH, John, 220.
KILBY, Mary, 234, 252.
KING, Henry C., 120; John, 52, 73, 77; Judyth, Judith, 52, 73, 76, 96; Lettice, 77; Mary, 52, 77, 218; Will, 30; William, 50, 52, 77.
KIRBY, Charles, 30; Mary, 234.
KIRK, Anthony, 52, 63, 83, 99; Catherine, 83, 99; Christopher, 30; Geo., 77; James, 83, 99, 110; John, 244; Judith, 83; Mary, 83; Sarah, 83; Thomas, 83.
KIRKPATRICK, Capt., 180.
KYLE, Donald B., 161; James P., 161; Mildred, 161; Wm. S., 161.

LADNAR, Elizabeth, 67; Hugh, 67; Susannah, 67.
LALLER, Henry, 139.
LAMDEN, Robert, 240.
LANE, Ann, 132; Rebecca, 101.
LANCASTER, Helen, 225.
LANGHORNE, Eliz., 101; Elizabeth (Trotter), 103, 145; John, 103; John Trotter, 103; Maurice, 103; Sarah (Bell), 103.
LATIMER, Joan, 13; Sir Robert, 13.
LAWRENCE, John, 91.
LAWSON, The Family, 230.
LAWSON, Alice, 230, 233; Ann, 233, 234, 236, 237, 238; Ann Steptoe, 82, 237, 238; Anthony, 71, 235, 238; Augusta, 160; Capt., 96; Catherine, 38, 236; Catherine B., 160; Maj. Chas. N., 158, 159; Chas. N., 239; Christopher, 230, 232, 233; Earnest J., 160; Edward E., 159; Elizabeth, 88, 232, 233, 234, 235, 236, 237, 238, 252; Eliz. Sydnor, 238; Eliz. C., 111; Elliott W., 158; Emma C., 160; Eppa (Epapphroditus), 20, 37, 38, 65, 88, 107, 230, 231, 232, 233, 235, 237, 238, 252; Fanny, 237; Francis W., 160; George, 232; Hathaway, 160; Henry, 88, 158, 233, 234, 236, 237, 252; Henry B., 239; Henry C., 158; Henry Chinn, 238; Capt. Henry, 110; Hilda, 160; Hugh, 230; James O., 158; Jane, 235; Joanna, 233, 234, 252; John, 233, 234, 235, 236, 237, 252; Judith,